Corporate Communication

u

Corporate Communication

A Guide to Theory and Practice
Second Edition

Joep Cornelissen

Los Angeles • London • New Delhi • Singapore

First edition published 2004

SAGE Publications Ltd
1 Oliver's Yard
55 City Road
London EC1Y 1SP

SAGE Publications Inc.
2455 Teller Road
Thousand Oaks, California 91320

SAGE Publications India Pvt Ltd
B 1/I 1 Mohan Cooperative Industrial Area
Mathura Road
New Delhi 110 044

SAGE Publications Asia-Pacific Pte Ltd
33 Pekin Street #02-01
Far East Square
Singapore 048763

Library of Congress Control Number: 2007939295

British Library Cataloguing in Publication data

A catalogue record for this book is available from the British Library

ISBN 978-1-84787-245-6
ISBN 978-1-84787-246-3 (pbk)

Typeset by C&M Digitals (P) Ltd., Chennai, India
Printed in Great Britain by The Cromwell Press, Trowbridge, Wiltshire
Printed on paper from sustainable resources

Contents

List of Figures, Tables and Case Studies

Figures

Tables

Case Studies

Preface to the Second Edition

Since the first edition of *Corporate Communications* was published in late 2004, there have been a number of high-profile scandals and reputation management disasters in the corporate world, including WorldCom, Enron, and Martha Stewart Living. In addition, large companies such as Wal-Mart have had a rough time in communication and reputation terms.

For many years, Wal-Mart was seen as a company that had grown from very humble beginnings and had excelled in a very effective market expansion and low-cost growth strategy. However, the company recently has received much more criticism than previously for its strategy and for the way in which it engages with, and cares for, important stakeholder groups such as employees and members of the local communities in which the company operates. The State of Maryland, for example, passed the so-called "Wal-Mart Healthcare Bill" early in 2006, introducing a law that would fine large companies, and particularly Wal-Mart, for not picking up their fair share of employee healthcare coverage. Wal-Mart's plan to open a store in New York City has also continued to draw organized opposition from a broad coalition of labor, small business, local government and community groups. The company has been repeatedly censured by the Environmental Protection Agency in the US over waste water run-offs from its stores, and the company is facing activism and opposition from many stakeholder groups including disgruntled former employees. Opposition to Wal-Mart appears to run deep, and Wal-Mart executives and communication professionals have now realized that its poor reputation could eventually pose a threat to its growth in the US and elsewhere.

The central message coming from this and other examples is clear: executives and practitioners within organizations need to be empowered with a way of thinking and with tools that can help them navigate the current corporate landscape in which reputations have become more fragile and stakeholders have become more demanding. The basic ideas underlying the book therefore remain as relevant as when this book was first published, because it seeks, above all else, to equip the reader with an understanding of the concepts and tools of corporate communication.

Purpose of the book

This book is about corporate communication. Its chief aim is to provide a comprehensive and up-to-date treatment of the subject of corporate communication – the criticality of the function, strategies and activities involved, and how it can be managed and organized effectively. The book incorporates current thinking and developments on these topics from both the academic and practitioner worlds, combining a comprehensive theoretical foundation with numerous practical insights to assist managers in their day-to-day affairs and in their strategic and tactical communication decisions. Illustrative examples and case studies are based on companies in the United States, the United Kingdom, continental Europe, and elsewhere.

Specifically, the book provides insights into the nature of corporate communication, the issues that define this area of practice, the strategies and activities that fall within its remit, and the ways in which it can be managed and organized in companies. It addresses three important questions:

1. What is corporate communication, and how can it be defined?
2. What strategies and activities are central to this area of practice?
3. What is the organizational location, status and role of this practice?

In addressing these questions, the book will deliver a number of benefits. The reader will learn about the following:

- the nature of corporate communication; its historical emergence and its role in contemporary companies;
- the critical role of the corporate communication function in building and maintaining relationships with the stakeholders of a company;
- the key issues – corporate social responsibility, reputation management, corporate branding, corporate identity, integrated communication – that dominate this profession, and how to deal with them;
- different approaches to developing corporate communication strategies and to implementing communication programs;
- different approaches to measuring and monitoring the impact of communication upon the images that stakeholders have of a company's reputation;
- different ways of organizing communication practitioners within a company and of maximizing their performance.

Approach of the book

For the second edition of the book, as for the first one, the aim was to satisfy three key criteria by which any management text can be judged:

- *Depth*: the material in the book needed to be presented in a comprehensive and thorough manner, and needed to be well grounded in the academic and practitioner literature and knowledge base on corporate communication.
- *Breadth*: the book had to cover all the topics that define the field of corporate communication and that practising managers and students of corporate communication management find important or of interest.
- *Relevance*: the book had to be well grounded in practice and easily related to past and present communication activities, events and case studies.

Although a number of books have been written on corporate communication in recent years, no book has really maximized these three dimensions to the best possible extent. Accordingly, this book sets out to fill that gap by accomplishing three things.

First, instead of being solely based on practitioner anecdotes (that rashly lead into sound-bite steps to communication success) or simple frameworks, the book provides a more informed and evidence-based account of the practice of corporate communication by including insights from academic research.

Second, all the contemporary and important themes and topics within the remit of corporate communication, including 'corporate social responsibility' and 'stakeholder management', are discussed in detail. Particular attention is paid to the central topics of the structuring of the communication function within organizations, the development of communication strategy and programs, and the roles and sensemaking of communication professionals – these have received little attention in other books.

Third, the book not only presents the latest academic thinking and research on the subject, but also features toolkits, management briefs, and case studies to illustrate the concepts and themes of the book and to meet the 'double hurdle' of rigour and relevance.

For the second edition, all the case studies and topics have been updated. Also, whole new sections on specialist disciplines within corporate communication such as media and investor relations, issues management, change communication and internal communication have been added. Based on feedback from lecturers and students, the book also spells out in greater detail some of the key concepts and contemporary developments in corporate communication with more figures and tables throughout the text.

In short, by combining theory and research with practitioner accounts on corporate communication, the second edition of the book provides a comprehensive, realistic and up-to-date overview of the state and playing field of this area of practice within organizations. Important issues in managing and organizing corporate communication are discussed, providing practising managers with appropriate concepts, theories and tools to enable them to make better management and communication decisions. Readers will gain a greater appreciation and a better in-depth understanding of the range of topics covered in corporate communication management as well as a means to organize their thoughts on those topics.

Readership of the book

A wide range of people can benefit from reading this book, including the following groups:

- Students at the graduate level enrolled on a business, management, marketing, corporate communication, public relations, or business communication course interested in increasing their understanding of the theory and practice of corporate communication.
- Managers and analysts with a professional interest in the area of corporate communication (and with responsibility for a slice of the corporate communications cake), concerned with making informed decisions that will maximize their day-to-day performance.
- Senior executives looking for an understanding of corporate communication and what it can do for their business.
- Academics researching and reading in the areas of corporate communication, public relations, marketing and strategic management looking for a resource guide that contains the themes and development of corporate communication in a single volume.

Organization of the book

As mentioned, the aim of this book is to present a major retrospective and prospective overview of the theory and practice of corporate communication. The distinction made between the 'theory' and 'practice' of corporate communications is intentional and implies that the book aims to draw out and integrate theoretical and intellectual accounts of the development of corporate communication with more hands-on, practice-based insights and skills from the profession. In the book, I also take the view that corporate communication is a field of management within organizations, and that not only our understanding of it but also the development of the field (as both a discipline and practice) is best served by a management spectre. This means that alternative perspectives on corporate communication such as the critical, rhetorical and mass communication accounts that consider the role and effect of communication at the macro level, that is, at the level of society, are included in the book's ruminations on the field, yet are considered of secondary importance in view of the core management perspective and theme of the book.

In framing, addressing and synthesizing corporate communication as an area of management, the book starts with the existing academic and practitioner works and their respective accounts of the current status and role of this area of practice. However, in addressing issues about the future shape and development of the field of corporate communication (again as a discipline and practice), the book will be more aspirational and adventurous. In organizing the chapters in to five parts, the book not only includes current descriptions of corporate communication from both the theory and practice ends, but also addresses professional challenges for the future.

Part 1, *Historical Background*, provides a theoretical characterization of the historical, conceptual and practical roots of the field of corporate communication, and defines the role and use of corporate communication in contemporary organizations.

Part 2, *Conceptual Foundations*, includes two chapters on the key concepts of stakeholder, corporate identity and corporate reputation as well as communication models that provide the theoretical background to the practice of corporate communication.

Part 3, *Corporate Communication in Practice*, includes three chapters that focus on the development of corporate communication strategy and planning communication programs and campaigns, the organization and management of communication within companies, and the roles, skills, competencies and professional development of communication practitioners.

Part 4, *Specialist Areas in Corporate Communication* covers important specialist areas within the remit of corporate communication: media relations, internal communication and change communication, and issues and crisis management.

The Appendix consolidates many of the book's strands in a full-length case study of Toyota that connects with the main themes of the entire book.

Joep Cornelissen
Leeds, October 2007.

Acknowledgements

In writing this book, I have had a lot of help and encouragement from colleagues and friends. Andrew Lock, Phil Harris, Danny Moss and Hanne Gardner were influential in shaping my early steps in the corporate communication field. I have also benefited from the wisdom of my colleagues and graduate students at the various institutions with which I have been associated: the Manchester Metropolitan University, the Amsterdam School of Communication Research and Leeds University Business School. I would also like to thank my reviewers Gary Radford, Antonie Van Nistelrooij, Gary Lunt, Kim Johnston, Ralph Tench, Beverley Hill and Nigel Jackson. At Sage, Delia Alfonso has been an enthusiastic supporter from start to finish, providing invaluable editorial guidance and pulling me through the writing process. Finally, as always, I would like to thank Mirjam for her support.

About the author

Dr Joep Cornelissen is Professor in Corporate Communication at Leeds University Business School, and previously taught at the Amsterdam School of Communications Research, the University of Amsterdam. He currently teaches corporate communication on MA and MBA programmes at Leeds. He is a regular contributor to leading international journals such as the *Academy of Management Review, Organization Studies, Journal of Advertising Research, British Journal of Management, Journal of Management Studies, Psychology & Marketing* and the *Public Relations Review*. He is a prominent keynote speaker on issues relating to corporate communication and has been a consultant to organizations such as Novartis, KPN (Dutch Telecom) and the National Health Service.

Part 1

HISTORICAL BACKGROUND

Communication management – any type of communication activity undertaken by an organization to inform, persuade or otherwise relate to individuals and groups in its outside environment – is not new. Whenever people have depended on one another to complete tasks or meet their needs, they have formed organizations. The act of organizing, at first in clans, families and feudal structures, already required people to communicate with other workers, as well as with (prospective) buyers. The modernization of society, first through farming and trade, and later through industrialization, created ever more complex organizations with more complicated communication needs. Industrial organizations in particular needed a more *organized* form of handling communication with governments, customers and the general public, which required them to invest in public relations, marketing and advertising campaigns.

In Part 1, we explore the historical development of communication management within organizations, describe why corporate communication emerged and demonstrate the importance of corporate communication to organizations. The basic characteristics of corporate communication are described vis-à-vis related concepts such as marketing communication and public relations.

After reading Part 1, the reader should be familiar with the basic characteristics of corporate communication, its historical emergence and its relevance to contemporary organizations.

1

Introduction to Corporate Communication

CHAPTER OVERVIEW

This introductory chapter provides a definition of corporate communication and lays out the themes for the remainder of the book. The chapter starts with a brief discussion of the importance of corporate communication followed by an introduction to key concepts such as corporate identity, corporate image and stakeholders.

1.1 Introduction

There is a widespread belief in the management world that in today's society the future of any company critically depends on how it is viewed by key stakeholders such as shareholders and investors, customers and consumers, employees, and members of the community in which the company operates. Public activism, globalization and recent accounting scandals have further strengthened this belief and have put much greater emphasis on the work of communication practitioners. This book is about the activities that are carried out by these communication practitioners; how these practitioners strategically manage and execute communication programmes to build and nurture relationships with stakeholders.

1.2 The relevance of understanding corporate communication

CEOs and senior executives of many large organizations and multinationals consider protecting their company's reputation to be 'critical' and as one of their most important strategic objectives.[1] This objective of building, maintaining and protecting the company's reputation is the core task of corporate communication practitioners.

Despite the importance attributed to a company's reputation, in many companies the role and contribution of corporate communication is still far from being fully understood. In these companies, communication practitioners feel undervalued, their strategic input into decision-making is compromised and senior managers and CEOs feel powerless because they simply do not understand the events that are taking place in the company's environment and how these events can affect the company's operations and profits. There is therefore a lot to gain when both communication practitioners and senior managers are able to recognize and diagnose communication-related management problems and understand appropriate strategies and the courses of action for dealing with these. Such an understanding is not only essential to the effective functioning of corporate communication, but it is also empowering. It allows communication practitioners and managers to understand and take charge of events that fall within the remit of corporate communication; to determine which events are outside their control, and to identify opportunities for communicating and engaging with stakeholders of the organization.

The primary goal of this book, therefore, is to give readers a sense of how corporate communication is used and managed *strategically* as a way of guiding and channelling how organizations communicate with their stakeholders. The book combines reflections and insights from academic research and professional practice in order to provide a comprehensive overview of strategies and tactics in corporate communication. In doing so, the book aims to provide an armoury of valuable concepts, insights and tools to communication practitioners and senior managers to be used in their day-to-day practice.

In this introductory chapter, I will start by describing corporate communication and will introduce the strategic management perspective that underlies the rest of the book. This perspective suggests a particular way of looking at corporate communication and indicates a number of management areas and concerns that will be covered in the remaining chapters. As the book progresses, each of these areas will be explained in detail and the strategic management perspective as a whole will become clearer. Good things will thus come to those who wait, and read.

1.3 Defining corporate communication

Perhaps the best way to define corporate communication is to look at the way in which the function has developed in companies. Until the 1970s, practitioners had used the term 'public relations' to describe communication with stakeholders. This 'public relations' function, which was tactical in most companies, largely consisted of communication with the press. When other stakeholders, internal and external to the company, started to demand more information from the company, practitioners subsequently started to look at communication as being more than just 'public relations'. This is when the roots of the new corporate communication function started to take hold. This new function came to incorporate a whole range of specialized disciplines including corporate design, corporate advertising, internal communication to employees, issues and crisis management, media relations, investor relations, change communication and public affairs.[2] An important characteristic of the new function is that it focuses on the organization as a whole and on the important task of how an organization presents itself to all its key stakeholders, both internal and external.

This broad focus is also reflected in the word 'corporate' in corporate communication. The word of course refers to the business setting in which corporate communication emerged as a separate function (alongside other functions such as human resources and finance). There is also an important second sense with which the word is being used. 'Corporate' originally stems from the Latin words for 'body' (corpus) and for 'forming into a body' (corporare) which emphasize a unified way of looking at 'internal' and 'external' communication disciplines. That is, instead of looking at specialized disciplines or stakeholder groups separately, the corporate communication function starts from the perspective of the 'bodily' organization as a whole when communicating with internal and external stakeholders.[3]

In other words, corporate communication can be characterized as a management function that is responsible for overseeing and coordinating the work done by communication practitioners in different specialist disciplines such as media relations, public affairs and internal communication. Van Riel defines corporate communication as 'an instrument of management by means of which all consciously used forms of internal and external communication are harmonized as effectively and efficiently as possible', with the overall objective of creating 'a favorable basis for relationships with groups upon which the company is dependent'.[4] Defined in this way, corporate communication obviously involves a whole range of 'managerial' activities such as planning, coordinating and counselling the CEO and senior managers in the organization as well as 'tactical' skills involved in producing and disseminating messages to relevant stakeholder groups.

Overall, if a definition of corporate communication is required, these characteristics can provide a basis for one:

> Corporate communication is a management function that offers a framework for the effective coordination of all internal and external communication with the overall purpose of establishing and maintaining favourable reputations with stakeholder groups upon which the organization is dependent.

One consequence of these characteristics of corporate communication is that it is likely to be *complex in nature*. This is especially so in organizations with a wide geographical, range, such as multinational firms, or with a wide range of products or services, where the coordination of communication often appears to be a balancing act between corporate headquarters and the various divisions and business units involved. However, there are other significant challenges in developing effective corporate communication strategies and programmes. Corporate communication demands an *integrated approach* to managing communication. Unlike a specialist frame of reference, corporate communication transcends the specialties of individual communication practitioners (e.g., branding, media relations, investor relations, public affairs, internal communication, etc.) and crosses these specialist boundaries to harness the *strategic interests of the organization at large*. A good example of a company that has achieved such integration in its communication is Orange (see Case Study 1.1). When the Orange brand was launched, marketing and communication specialists from the company worked closely with consultants from corporate identity and advertising agencies. Together, they developed the brand and streamlined the release of communication messages to customers in the market, to the employees of the newly branded company and to the general public.

CASE STUDY 1.1

THE LAUNCH OF ORANGE: AN EXAMPLE OF CORPORATE COMMUNICATION

The story of Orange is one of the most exciting corporate brand-building successes in recent years with the company's market value having gone from nothing in 1994 to £28 billion ($46.6 billion, €39.7 billion) in 2000. Apart from great deal-making, shrewd distribution-building, service innovations and technological developments, the lion's share of this achievement can be attributed to the power of the Orange corporate brand and the integrated approach towards communication that enabled the company to reach the corporate objectives that it had set at its launch.

The enormity of the task facing Orange at its launch is perhaps difficult to grasp and appreciate today, given the current popularity of mobile phones. In 1994, the mobile phone market in the UK was a confusing place for customers. Digital networks had just been introduced, but few people yet understood the benefits. On top of this, Orange also faced an uphill task in differentiating itself in this market as the last entrant in a field of four. Cellnet and Vodafone, two of its competitors, had already ten years of market dominance at that time; with full national coverage for their mobile phones and millions of captive subscribers on their analogue networks. Both Cellnet and Vodafone had also successfully developed low-user tariffs as part of a pre-emptive strategy to block entry into the consumer market and had continuously strengthened their dominance of the business market through the development of their digital (GSM) networks.

Orange faced a daunting task in 1994 to reach the ambitious corporate objective that it had set 'to become the first choice in mobile communications'. Before the Orange name was launched in 1994, the company's trading name was Microtel. Executives of Hutchison group, Microtel's mother corporation, met at that time to discuss strategies of overcoming, or minimizing, the huge disadvantage of being last in the market. They soon realized that effective communication would be an integral part of this and crucial in achieving the company's ambitious aim of market leadership. In May 1993, a team of senior managers and communications specialists from Microtel, corporate identity specialists Wolff Olins and advertising agency WCRS was set up and was charged with developing a clear and strong communication strategy and positioning. This team quickly realized that the new corporate brand could not be built on a 'low cost' strategy, emphasizing price benefits, as this would have pitched the brand directly against one of Cellnet and Vodafone's greatest strengths, namely exceptionally low entry costs. Instead, there was room to develop a fully rounded corporate brand identity built upon the market high ground, which had been left conspicuously unoccupied by the competition and would be a better alternative for capturing market share.

The team brainstormed names and propositions and finally arrived at the word Orange as best representing their ideas, with its connotations of hope, fun and freedom. Market research at the time indicated that people found the name Orange distinctive and friendly, extrovert, modern and powerful. The name Orange, along with the term 'wire-free' (as one of the communicable values), was subsequently registered as a trademark. Advertising and the design of a logo followed and were all based on the positioning for Orange as formulated by the team:

> There will come a time when all people will have their own personal number that goes with them wherever they are so that there are no barriers to communication; a wire-free future in which you call people, not places, and where everyone will benefit from the advances of technology. The Future is Bright. The Future is Orange.

The team also realized that given the doubts which surrounded Orange as a late entrant at its launch, the most important task for media was to imbue the brand with as much confidence as possible. A multi-media schedule was therefore adopted; a dominating presence for the Orange brand with advertising posters heralding each new campaign theme, TV adverts communicating core brand benefits and public relations and press providing detailed messages in the information-led environment of newspapers. Since its launch, the communication strategy chosen has delivered on its corporate targets. Although Orange has not become the market leader in the UK, a position still firmly in the hands of Vodafone, it quickly gained market share and a market capitalization that enabled it to expand into other international markets. In 1996, barely two years after its launch, Orange Plc underwent its first public offering with shares being listed on the London and Nasdaq markets on the 2nd of April 1996. With a valuation of £2.4 billion, Orange Plc became the youngest company to enter the FTSE-100.

(Continued)

(Continued)

In October 1999, Orange was acquired by Mannesmann AG, which itself was bought in February 2000 by Vodafone, a deal approved by the European Commission subject to an undertaking from Vodafone to divest Orange Plc. In August 2000, France Télécom acquired Orange Plc from Vodafone. Despite the changes in ownership, Orange has continued to concentrate on its brand-led communication strategy, rather than on hard-hitting competitive strategies including price cuts and distribution growths, as this strategy has propelled the company to the corporate success and position that it now enjoys.

In 2006, France Télécom announced its intention to make Orange its flagship commercial brand and has extended the brand beyond mobile telecommunications to internet, fixed line and TV offers. In 2007, Millward Brown and the *Financial Times* listed Orange at number 67 in the worldwide BRANDZ Ranking with an estimated brand value of $9,922,000.

Questions for reflection

1. Reflect upon the process by which the Orange brand was developed. Why do you think Orange did adopt an integrated approach towards developing the Orange brand and communication rather than a more specialist approach based on advertising or marketing communication?
2. Consider the corporate image of Orange in relation to the following three stakeholder groups; (a) the company's employees; (b) customers and consumers; and (c) investors and shareholders. To what extent do you feel Orange has succeeded in creating a strong and distinctive image with each of these three groups?

A variety of concepts and terms are used in relation to corporate communication. Here, the chapter briefly introduces these concepts but they will be discussed in more detail in the remainder of the book. Table 1.1 lists the key concepts that readers will come across in this and other books on corporate communication and that form so to speak the vocabulary of the corporate communication practitioner. Table 1.1 briefly defines the concepts, and also shows how these relate to a specific organization – in this case, British Airways.

Not all of these concepts are always used in corporate communication books. Moreover, it may or may not be that mission, objectives, strategies, and so on are written down precisely or indeed formally laid down within an organization. As will be shown in Chapter 4, a mission or corporate identity, for instance, might sometimes more sensibly be conceived as that which is implicit or can be deduced about an organization from what it is doing and communicating. However, as a general guideline the following concepts are often used in combination with one another.

Table 1.1   Key concepts in corporate communication

Concept	Definition	Example: British Airways*
Mission	Overriding purpose in line with the values or expectations of stakeholders	'British Airways is aiming to set new industry standards in customer service and innovation, deliver the best financial performance and evolve from being an airline to a world travel business with the flexibility to stretch its brand into new business areas'
Vision	Desired future state: the aspiration of the organization	'To become the undisputed leader in world travel by ensuring that BA is the customer's first choice through the delivery of an unbeatable travel experience'
Corporate objectives and goals	(Precise) statement of aims or purpose	'To be a good neighbour, concerned for the community and the environment', 'to provide overall superior service and good value for money in every market segment in which we compete', 'to excel in anticipating and quickly responding to customer needs and competitor activity'
Strategies	The ways or means in which the corporate objectives are to be achieved and put into effect	'Continuing emphasis on consistent quality of customer service and the delivery to the marketplace of value for money through customer-oriented initiatives (on-line booking service, strategic alliances) and to arrange all the elements of our service so that they collectively generate a particular experience'... 'building trust with our shareholders, employees, customers, neighbours and with our critics, through commitment to good practice and societal reporting'
Corporate identity	The profile and values communicated by an organization	'The world's favourite airline' (this corporate identity with its associated brand values of service, quality, innovation, cosmopolitanism and British-ness is carried through in positioning, design, livery, and communications)
Corporate image	The immediate set of associations of an individual in response to one or more signals or messages from or about a particular organization at a single point in time	'Very recently I got a ticket booked to London, and when reporting at the airport I was shown the door by BA staff. I was flatly told that the said flight in which I was to travel was already full so my ticket was not valid any further and the airline would try to arrange for a seat in some other flight. You can just imagine how embarrassed I felt at that moment of time. To add fuel to the fire, the concerned official of BA had not even a single word of apology to say' (customer of BA).
Corporate reputation	An individual's collective representation of past images of an organization (induced through either communication or past experiences) established over time	'Through the Executive Club programme, British Airways has developed a reputation as an innovator in developing direct relationships with its customers and in tailoring its services to enhance these relationships' (long-standing supplier of BA).

(Continued)

Table1.1   (Continued)

Concept	Definition	Example: British Airways*
Stakeholder	Any group or individual who can affect or is affected by the achievement of the organization's objectives	'Employees, consumers, investors and shareholders, community, aviation business and suppliers, government, trade unions, NGOs, and society at large'
Public	People who mobilize themselves against the organization on the basis of some common issue or concern to them	'Local residents of Heathrow Airport appealed in November 2002 against the Government and British Airways concerning the issue of night flights at Heathrow airport. The UK Government denied that night flights violated local residents' human rights. British Airways intervened in support of the UK Government claiming that there is a need to continue the present night flights regime'
Market	A defined group for whom a product is or may be in demand (and for whom an organization creates and maintains products and service offerings)	'The market for British Airways flights consists of passengers who search for superior service over and beyond the basic transportation involved'
Issue	An unsettled matter (which is ready for a decision) or a point of conflict between an organization and one or more publics	'Night flights at Heathrow Airport: noise and inconvenience for local residents and community'
Communication	The tactics and media that are used to communicate with internal and external groups	'Newsletters, promotion packages, consultation forums, advertising campaigns, corporate design and code of conduct, free publicity/public relations.....'
Integration	The act of coordinating all communication so that the corporate identity is effectively and consistently communicated to internal and external groups	'British Airways aims to communicate its brand values of service, quality, innovation, cosmopolitanism and British-ness through all its communications in a consistent and effective manner'

* Extracted from British Airways annual reports and the web.

A *mission* is a general expression of the overriding purpose of the organization, which, ideally, is in line with the values and expectations of major stakeholders and concerned with the scope and boundaries of the organization. It is often referred to with the simple question 'What business are we in?'. A *vision* is the desired future state of the organization. It is an aspirational view of the general direction that the organization wants to go in, as formulated by senior management, and that requires the energies and commitment of members of the organization. *Objectives and goals* are the more precise (short-term) statements of direction in line with the formulated vision and that are to be achieved by strategic initiatives or *strategies*. Strategies involve actions and communications that are linked to objectives; and are often specified in terms of specific organizational functions (e.g. finance, operations, human resources, etc.). Operations strategies for streamlining operations and human resource strategies for staff support and development initiatives are common to every organization as well as, increasingly, full-scale corporate communication strategies.

Key to having a corporate communication strategy is the notion of a *corporate identity*: the basic profile that an organization wants to project to all its important stakeholder groups and how it aims to be known by these various groups in terms of the *corporate images* and *reputations* that they have of the organization. To ensure that different stakeholders indeed conceive of an organization in a favourable and broadly consistent manner, and also in line with the projected corporate identity, organizations need to go to great lengths to *integrate* all their *communication* from brochures to websites in tone, themes, visuals and logos.

The *stakeholder* concept takes centre stage within corporate communication management at the expense of considering the organizational environment simply in terms of markets and publics. Organizations increasingly are recognizing the need for an 'inclusive' and 'balanced' stakeholder management approach that involves actively communicating with and being involved with *all* stakeholder groups upon which the organization depends and not just shareholders or customers. Such awareness stems from high-profile cases where undue attention to certain stakeholder groups has led to crises and severe damage for the organizations concerned.

All these concepts will be discussed in detail in the remainder of the book, but it is worthwhile to emphasize already how some of them hang together. The essence of what matters in Table 1.1 is that corporate communication is geared towards establishing favourable corporate images and reputations with all of an organization's stakeholder groups, so that these groups act in a way that is conducive to the success of the organization. In other words, because of favourable images and reputations customers and prospects will purchase products and services, members of the community will appreciate the organization in its environment, investors will grant financial resources, and so on. It is the spectre of a damaged reputation – of having to make costly reversals in policies or practices as a result of stakeholder pressure, or, worse, as a consequence of self-inflicted wounds – that lies behind the urgency with which integrated stakeholder management now needs to be treated.

This definition and these concepts furthermore point to a number of topics that define this strategic management perspective upon corporate communication. Each of these topics is discussed in more detail in the remaining chapters of this book. The first main topic involves the process of developing a communication strategy and communication programmes in line with the overall corporate strategy of an organization and with an account of the important stakeholders and issues that are of concern to that organization. Another important topic involves the question of how communication practitioners and their work can best be organized and coordinated. Viewing corporate communication as a management function also involves the question of which professional competencies and skills are required of different communication practitioners. Each of these topics is covered in detail in the remaining chapters of the book by combining knowledge from academic theory ('principles') with insights from best practice cases from organizations in the United States, the United Kingdom, continental Europe and Asia. My goal in the remaining chapters of this book is to explain those principles and to indicate how communication practitioners can use those principles to become more effective and skilful in their jobs.

1.4 Chapter summary

All organizations, of all sizes, sectors and operating in very different societies, must find ways to successfully establish and nurture relationships with their stakeholders upon which they are economically and socially dependent. The management function that has emerged to deal with this task is corporate communication and this chapter has made a start by outlining its importance and key characteristics. Chapter 2 describes in more detail how and why corporate communication historically has emerged and how it has grown into the management function that it is today.

KEY TERMS

Corporate communication	Market
Corporate identity	Mission
Corporate image	Public
Corporate reputation	Stakeholder
Integration	Theory-practice
Issue	Vision

Notes

1 See, for example, AON's global risk management survey, 24 April 2007. (http://www.aon.com/nl/nl/about/perscentrum/persberichten_nederland/archief2007/Global_RM_Survey_07_Key_Findings.pdf).

2 Argenti, P.A. (1996), 'Corporate communication as a discipline: toward a definition', *Management Communication Quarterly*, 10 (1): 73–97.

3 See, for example, Christensen, L.T., Morsing, M. and Cheney, G. (2008), *Corporate Communications: Convention, Complexity and Critique*. London: Sage.

4 Van Riel, C.B.M. (1995), *Principles of Corporate Communication*. London: Prentice Hall, p. 26.

2

Corporate Communication in Historical Perspective

CHAPTER OVERVIEW

This chapter describes the historical development of communication within organizations and the emergence of corporate communication. It starts with a brief discussion of the historical development of separate communication disciplines such as marketing communication and public relations and moves on to explain why organizations have increasingly drawn these disciplines together under the umbrella of corporate communication.

2.1 Introduction

The evolution of communication disciplines and techniques that are used by organizations to promote, publicize or generally inform relevant individuals and groups within society about their affairs began at least 150 years ago. From the Industrial Revolution until the 1930s, an era predominantly characterized by mass production and consumption, the type of communications that were employed by organizations largely consisted of publicity, promotions and selling activities to buoyant markets. The move towards less stable, more competitive markets, which coincided with greater government interference in many markets and harsher economic circumstances, led from the 1930s onwards to a constant redefining of the scope and practices of communication in many organizations in the Western world. Since then, communication practitioners have had to rethink their discipline and have had to develop new practices and areas of expertise in response to changing circumstances in markets and societies at large.

This chapter is about the changing definition, scope and practices of communication management in organizations, and about the societal and market dynamics that challenged and triggered its evolution. The central point is that the nature of communication management as we now know it, in terms of the way in which it is practised in contemporary organizations, is steeped in historical circumstances and developments. Disentangling these historical forces provides a first step towards contextualizing and understanding corporate communication. To do this, a brief sketch will be provided of the historical evolution of two individual communication disciplines: marketing and public relations. The chapter will describe the historical development of both disciplines and will then move on to discuss why organizations have increasingly started to see these disciplines not in isolation but as part of an integrated effort to communicate with stakeholders. This integrated effort is directed and coordinated by the management function of corporate communication.

2.2 Historical background

Communication management – any type of communication activity undertaken by an organization to inform, persuade or otherwise relate to individuals and groups in its outside environment – is not new. Whenever people have depended on one another to complete tasks or meet their needs, they have formed organizations. The act of organizing, at first in clans, families and feudal structures, already required people to communicate with other workers, as well as (prospective) buyers. The modernization of society, first through farming and trade, and later through industrialization, created ever more complex organizations with more complicated communication needs.

The large industrial corporations that emerged during the Industrial Revolution in the nineteenth century in the United Kingdom, in the United States and later on in the rest of the Western world required, in contrast to what had gone before, professional communication officers and a more *organized* form of handling publicity and promotions. These large and complex industrial firms sought the continued support of government, customers and the general public, which required them to invest in public relations and advertising campaigns.[1]

In those early years and right up until the 1900s, industrial corporations hired publicists, press agents, promoters and propagandists for their communication campaigns. These individuals often played on the gullibility of the general public in its longing to be entertained, whether they were being deceived or not, and many advertisements and press releases in those days were in fact exaggerated to the point where they were outright lies. While such tactics can perhaps now be denounced from an ethical standpoint, this 'publicity-seeking' approach to the general public was taken at that time simply because organizations and their press agents could get away with it. At the turn of the nineteenth century, industrial magnates and large organizations in the Western world were answerable to no one and were largely immune to pressure from government or public opinion. This situation is aptly illustrated by a comment made at the time by William Henry Vanderbilt, head of the New York Central Railroad, when asked about the public rampage and uproar that his company's railroad extensions would cause. 'The public be damned,' he simply responded.

The age of unchecked industrial growth soon ended, however, and industrial organizations in the Western world faced new challenges to their established ways of doing business. The twentieth century began with a cry from 'muckrakers'; investigative journalists who exposed scandals associated with power, capitalism and government corruption and raised public awareness of the unethical and sometimes harmful practices of business. To respond to these 'muckrakers', many large organizations hired writers and former journalists to be spokespeople for the organization and to disseminate general information to these 'muckraking' groups and the public at large so as to gain public approval for their decisions and behaviour.[2] At the same time, while demand still outweighed production, the growth of many markets stabilized and even declined, which led organizations to hire advertising agents to promote their products with existing and prospective customers in an effort to consolidate their overall sales.

In the following decade (1920–1930) economic reform in the US and the UK and intensified public scepticism towards big business made it clear to organizations that these writers, publicists and advertising agents were needed on a more continuous basis, and should not just be hired 'on and off' as press agents had been in the past. These practitioners were therefore brought *'in-house'* and communication activities to both the general public and the markets served by the organization became more systematic and skilled.[3] This development effectively brought the first professional expertise to the area of communication within organizations and planted the seeds for the two professional disciplines that defined for the majority of the twentieth century how communication would be approached by organizations: marketing and public relations.

Both marketing and public relations emerged as separate 'external' communication disciplines when industrial organizations realized that in order to prosper they needed to concern themselves with issues of public concern (i.e. public relations) as well as with ways of effectively bringing products to markets (i.e. marketing). Both the marketing and public relations disciplines have since those early days gone through considerable professional development, yet largely in their own separate ways. Since the 1980s, however, organizations have increasingly started to bring these two disciplines together again under the umbrella of a new management function that we now know as corporate communication. This trend towards 'integrating' marketing and public relations was noted by many in the field, including Philip Kotler, one of the most influential marketing figures of modern times. Kotler commented in the early 1990s, 'there is a genuine need to develop a new paradigm in which these two subcultures [marketing and public relations] work most effectively in the best interest of the organization and the publics it serves'.[4]

In 1978, Kotler, together with William Mindak, had already highlighted the different ways of looking at the relationship between marketing and public relations. In their article, they had emphasized that the view of marketing and

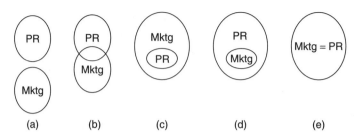

Figure 2.1   Models for the relationship between marketing and public relations

public relations as distinct disciplines had characterized much of the twentieth century, but they predicted that a view of an integrated paradigm would dominate the 1980s and beyond as 'new patterns of operation and interrelation can be expected to appear in these [marketing and public relations] functions'.[5] Figure 2.1 outlines the different models that Kotler and Mindak described to characterize the relationship between marketing and public relations, including the integrated paradigm (model (e)) where marketing and public relations have merged into a single external communication function.

2.3 Marketing and public relations as distinct disciplines

Until the 1980s, marketing and public relations were considered rather distinct in their objectives and activities with each discipline going through its own trajectory of professional development.[6] Central to this traditional view (model (a) in Figure 2.1) was the simple point that marketing deals with markets, while public relations deals with all the publics (excluding customers and consumers) of an organization. Markets, from this perspective, are created by the identification of a segment of the population for which a product or service is or could be in demand, and involves product or service-related communication. Publics, on the other hand, are seen as *actively* creating and mobilizing themselves whenever companies make decisions that affect a group of people adversely. These publics are also seen to concern themselves with more general news related to the entire organization, rather than specific product-related information. Kotler and Mindak articulated this traditional position (model (a)) by saying that 'marketing exists to sense, serve, and satisfy customer needs at a profit', while 'public relations exists to produce goodwill with the company's various publics so that these publics do not interfere in the firm's profit-making ability'.[7]

   This split in publics versus markets was also emphasized by many academics who argued that the process of communication with publics is rather different from how organizations communicate with customers and consumers in a market. Communication towards the market, the argument went, involves a 'one-way' communication process with an organization simply trying to persuade a prospect or customer in order to boost sales. This was seen to be distinct from a 'two-way' process of dialogue that organizations may engage in whenever they communicate with publics.[8]

2.4 Marketing and public relations as distinct but complementary disciplines

Over time, however, cracks appeared in this view of marketing and public relations as two disciplines that are completely distinct in their objectives and tactics. Rather than seeing them as separate, marketing and public relations were actually seen to share some common ground (model (b) in Figure 2.1). In the 1980s, for instance, concern over the rising costs and decreasing impact of mass media advertising encouraged many companies to examine different means of promoting customer loyalty and of building brand awareness to increase sales. Companies started to make greater use of 'marketing public relations': the publicizing of news and events related to the launching and promotion of products or services. 'Marketing public relations' (MPR) involves the use of public relations techniques for marketing purposes which was found to be a cost-effective tool for generating awareness and brand favourability and to imbue communication about the organization's brands with credibility[9] (see Case Study 2.1 for a recent example). Companies such as Starbucks and the Body Shop have consistently used public relations techniques such as free publicity, features in general interest magazines and grass roots campaigning to attract attention and to establish a brand experience that is backed up by each of the Starbuck and the Body Shop stores.

CASE STUDY 2.1

THE USE OF MARKETING PUBLIC RELATIONS TO PROMOTE *THE PASSION OF THE CHRIST*

The movie, *The Passion of The Christ*, released in 2004, tells the story of the last 12 hours in the life of Jesus Christ. Directed and produced by Mel Gibson, the film tells in Aramaic (believed to have been Jesus' native language), Latin and Hebrew the moment of Christ's arrest, trial and crucifixion. Because of the subject, the graphic violence in the film and the fact that the moviegoing public had to watch the movie with subtitles, Gibson reportedly had difficulty finding a company to distribute the movie. Newmarket and Icon Films eventually agreed to distribute the movie in the United States and around the world.

(Continued)

(Continued)

To promote the film, Gibson did not rely on traditional advertising but instead used public relations (pre-screenings and publicity in the media) and grassroots marketing techniques. Gibson recognized that creating controversy was the key to building awareness of the film. He therefore invited prominent Christian and Jewish church leaders known for their political and social conservatism to watch the movie. An early version of the movie script was also leaked by an employee of the production company to a joint committee of the Secretariat for Ecumenical and Inter-Religious Affairs of the United States Conference of Catholic Bishops and the Department of Inter-religious Affairs of the Anti-defamation League. This committee concluded that the 'main storyline presented Jesus as having been relentlessly pursued by an evil cabal of Jews headed by the high priest Caiphas who finally blackmailed a weak-kneed Pilate into putting Jesus to death. This is precisely the storyline that fueled centuries of anti-semitism within Christian societies.' When the movie was released, although some Jews were supportive of Gibson and the movie, the overwhelming reaction from within the Jewish community was negative. Jewish religious groups expressed concern that the film blames the death of Jesus on the Jews as a group which, they claimed, could fuel anti-semitism.

Through the pre-screening of the movie to church leaders and the leaking of the script Gibson had created an enormous amount of media coverage focused on how incensed certain people were about the film and its message. This controversy in turn created so much buzz and word-of-mouth around the movie that not only the core audience of Christian moviegoers wanted to see the movie but also general moviegoers.

A further step that Gibson took to raise awareness and to further increase the controversy surrounding his movie was to claim that the late Pope John Paul II had seen the movie at a private viewing of the film shortly before its release. He claimed that the Pope had allegedly remarked to his good friend, Monsignor Stanislaw Dziwisz: 'It was as it was.' Dziwisz later denied that this ever happened, but it was widely reported by CNN and other news organizations that the Pope had said those words.

Finally, Gibson also undertook a grassroots marketing effort with local church groups, who promoted the film with their constituents through free tickets and discounted ticket prices. In this way, he ensured that the core audience would not only watch the movie but would also spread favourable word-of-mouth about it to others.

In the end, many moviegoers went to see *The Passion of The Christ* and the movie went on to gross $611,899,420 worldwide ($370,782,930 in the US alone), making it the eleventh highest-grossing film of all time.

'Marketing public relations' (MPR), because it is focused on the marketing of a company's products and services, is distinct from the 'corporate' activities within public relations. These corporate activities, often labelled as 'corporate public relations' (CPR), involve communication with investors, communities, employees,

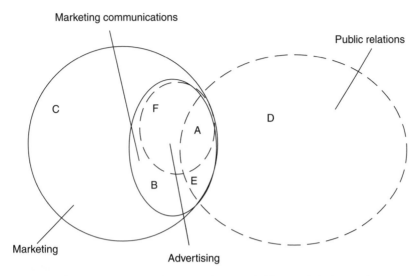

Figure 2.2   Marketing and public relations activities and their overlap

Key:
A = corporate advertising (advertising by a firm where the company, rather than its
    products or services, is emphasized).
B = direct marketing (direct communication via post, telephone or e-mail to customers
    and prospects) and sales promotions (tactics to engage the customer including
    discounting, coupons, guarantees, free gifts, competitions, vouchers, demonstrations
    and bonus commission).
C = distribution and logistics, pricing and development of products.
D = 'corporate' public relations (public relations activities towards 'corporate'
    stakeholders, which excludes customers and prospects in a market); includes issues
    management, community relations, investor relations, media relations, internal
    communication and public affairs.
E = 'marketing' public relations (the use of what are traditionally seen as public relations
    tools within marketing programs); includes product publicity and sponsorship.
F = mass media advertising (advertising aimed at increasing awareness, favour or sales
    of a company's products or services).

the media and government. Figure 2.2 displays a number of core activities of
both the public relations and marketing disciplines, and outlines a set of activities (including specific tools and techniques) that are shared, indicating the overlap between the two functions.[10] Figure 2.2 also displays the difference between
'marketing public relations' (MPR) and 'corporate public relations' (CPR).

Starting on the left of the figure, marketing of course involves a range of
activities such as distribution, logistics, pricing and new product development
(area 'C' in Figure 2.2) besides marketing communications. Marketing communications, in the middle of the figure, involves corporate advertising ('A') and
mass media advertising ('F'), direct marketing and sales promotions ('B'), and
product publicity and sponsorship ('E'). Two of these activities; corporate
advertising ('A') and product publicity and sponsorship ('E') overlap with public relations. Corporate advertising involves the use of radio, TV, cinema, poster

or internet advertising to create or maintain a favourable image of the company and its management. Although it is a form of advertising, it deals with the 'corporate' image of the company, and is as such distinct from mass media advertising ('F') which is focused on the company's products or services to increase awareness or sales. Product publicity and sponsorship involve activities that aim to promote and market the company's products and services. Both sets of activities draw upon techniques and expertise from public relations. Publicity in particular is often achieved through coverage in the news media. Sponsorship of a cause or event may also serve both marketing and corporate objectives. It can be tied into promotional programs around products and services but can also be used to improve the company's image as a whole.

Besides the direct sharing of activities such as sponsorship, there are also a number of ways in which marketing and public relations activities can complement one another. For example, there is evidence that a company's image, created through public relations programs, can positively reflect upon the product brands of a company, thereby increasing the awareness of the product brand as well as adding an additional attribute that enhances consumers' favourable impression of the brand.[11] Another complementary relationship that exists is the guardian role of public relations as a 'watchdog' or 'corrective' for marketing in bringing other strategic viewpoints to bear besides the need to boost sales with customers.[12] In other words, public relations can emphasize a broader perspective than simply a focus on customers and sales.

2.5 Integrating marketing and public relations

This overlap and complementarity between marketing and public relations have suggested to organizations that it is useful to align both disciplines more closely or at least manage them in a more integrated manner. Not surprisingly, a lot of discussion and debate during the 1980s and 1990s took place on the importance of 'integration' and what such integration could look like within organizations. Back in 1978, Kotler and Mindak articulated three models of integration (models 'c', 'd' and 'e' in Figure 2.1). Each of these models articulates a different view of the most effective form of integration.

Model 'c' involves a view of marketing as the dominant function which subsumes public relations. In this model, public relations becomes essentially part of a wider marketing function for satisfying customers. An example of this perspective involves the notion of Integrated Marketing Communications (IMC) which is defined as

> a concept of marketing communication planning that recognises the 'added value' of a comprehensive plan that evaluates the strategic role of a variety of disciplines (advertising, direct marketing, sales promotions and public relations) and combines these disciplines to provide clarity, consistency and maximum communication impact.[13]

Within IMC, public relations is reduced to activities of product publicity and sponsorship, ignoring its wider remit in communicating to employees, investors, communities, the media and government.

Model 'd' suggests the alternative view that 'marketing should be put under public relations to make sure that the goodwill of all key publics is maintained'.[14] In this model, marketing's role of satisfying customers is seen as only part of a wider public relations effort to satisfy the multiple publics and stakeholders of an organization. An example of this perspective involves the notion of 'strategic public relations' which assumes that all 'communication programs should be integrated or coordinated by a public relations department' including 'integrated marketing communication, advertising and marketing public relations' which should 'be coordinated through the broader public relations function'.[15]

Model 'e', finally, favours a view of marketing and public relations as merged into one and the same 'external communication' function. In the view of Kotler and Mindak; 'the two functions might be easily merged under a Vice President of Marketing and Public Relations' who 'is in charge of planning and managing the external affairs of the company'.[16] Despite Kotler and Mindak's preference for this model, it is not a form of integration that is much practised within organizations. Instead of merging the two disciplines into one and the same department, organizations want to keep them separate but actively coordinate public relations and marketing communication programs. In hindsight, then, most organizations appear to practise model 'b' to coordinate marketing communications and public relations.

2.6 Drivers for integrated communication

In short, marketing and public relations disciplines are not merged or reduced within organizations to one and the same function. This may not be feasible in practice given the important differences in activities and audiences addressed by each (see Figure 2.1). However, both disciplines, while existing separately, are balanced against each other and managed together from within the overarching management framework of corporate communication. This management framework suggests a holistic way of viewing and practising communication management that cuts across the marketing and public relations disciplines (and activities such as advertising and media relations within them). According to Gronstedt, a communication consultant, corporate communication 'inserts the various communication disciplines into a holistic perspective, drawing from the concepts, methodologies, crafts, experiences, and artistries of marketing communication and public relations'.[17]

The importance of 'integrating' marketing communications and public relations in this way has resulted from a variety of factors or 'drivers' as these can be more aptly called. Generally, these 'drivers' can be grouped into three main categories: those drivers that are market- and environment-based, those that

Table 2.1   Drivers for integration

Market- and environment-based drivers
Stakeholder roles – needs and overlap
Audience fragmentation
Greater amounts of message clutter

Communication-based drivers
Increased message effectiveness through consistency and reinforcement of core messages
Complementarity of media and media cost inflation
Media multiplication requires control of communication channels

Organizational drivers
Improved efficiency (increasing profits)
Increased accountability
Provision of strategic direction and purpose through consolidation
Organizational positioning

---

arise from the communication mix and communication technologies, and those that are driven by opportunities, changes and needs from within the organization itself. All these drivers are set out in Table 2.1.

Market and environment-based drivers

The environment in which organizations operate has changed considerably over the past two decades. Not only has the environment become more complex for many organizations, but also greater public scepticism, government interference and increased competition in many markets have created a situation where organizations need to *meet the demands of multiple and diverse stakeholder groups*; while at the same time expressing a coherent image of themselves. Back in 1994, Robert Heath, a communication scholar, formulated this challenge as follows:

> Some companies and other organizations are well known for their ability to conduct a truly integrated communication campaign designed to get the message across even though it is tailored to various stakeholders. Not only is the matter one of providing a coherent and consistent message that fosters an understanding of the company as its management and employees want it to be understood, but it also means that key audiences are addressed in terms of the stake each of them holds with regard to the organization.[18]

The demands of different stakeholders such as customers, investors, employees and NGO and activist groups have forced organizations to put considerable effort into integrating all their marketing and public relations efforts. This integration is also important when one considers the multiple stakeholder roles that any one individual may have, and the potential pitfalls that may occur when conflicting messages are sent out.[19] Case Study 2.2 on Barclays Bark illustrates this problem, and emphasizes the importance of coordinating all marketing and public relations messages that can originate in very different departments and divisions within an organization.

CASE STUDY 2.2

BARCLAYS BANK (UK): THE IMPORTANCE OF COORDINATING MARKETING COMMUNICATION AND PUBLIC RELATIONS

Early in 2003, Barclays, a UK-based financial services group, engaged primarily in retail banking, investment banking and investment management, appointed a new advertising agency Bartle Bogle Hegarty (BBH). BBH was hired to spearhead a 'more humane' campaign, after the bank was lambasted for its 'Big Bank' adverts in 2000 that featured the slogan 'a big world needs a big bank'. Barclays had spent £15 million (approx. $24.6 million) on its 'Big' campaign, which featured celebrities such as Sir Anthony Hopkins and Tim Roth. The adverts were slick and had received good pre-publicity, but they turned into a communications disaster when they coincided with the news that Barclays was closing about 170 branches in the UK, many in rural areas.

One of the earlier adverts featured Welsh-born Sir Anthony Hopkins talking from the comfort of a palatial home about the importance of chasing 'big' ideas and ambitions. The adverts provoked a national debate in the UK when a junior government minister Chris Mullin said that Barclays customers should revolt and 'vote with their feet'. Barclays' image crisis worsened when it was revealed that the new Chief Executive, Matthew Barrett, had been paid £1.3 million ($ US 2.1 million) for just three months' work. Competitor NatWest has since capitalized on the fall-out from the Big Bank campaign. It has been running adverts, which triumph the fact that it has abolished branch closures.

Local communities that had lost their branch were particularly angry with the closures. The situation was further aggravated by the arrogance with which Barclays announced and justified the decision. Matthew Barrett had explained the branch closures by saying, 'We are an economic enterprise, not a government agency, and therefore have obligations to conduct our business in a way that provides a decent return to the owners of the business. We will continue to take value-maximising decisions without sentimentality or excuses.' Barclays was admitting openly that their main focus was on shareholder returns and larger customers across their investment and retail businesses.

Perhaps the most amusing story of the many that emerged during that period was of the fact that the village where Anthony Hopkins was born was one of the victims of the branch closures. He was seen as a traitor to his heritage, and the local Welsh Assembly Member wrote to him as part of her campaign about the closures. Hopkins was moved to write back to her, complaining about being used as a scapegoat when in fact he was just an actor and felt that he needed to set the record straight by pointing out that he did not run Barclays Bank.

In an attempt to respond to the image crisis, Barclays has since extended opening hours at 84 per cent of its branches and recruited an extra 2,000 staff

(Continued)

(Continued)

to service the extra hours. Together with new adverts in 2003 that were 'more humane and more tangible and based on actual products rather than the brand', Barclays had hoped that the damage from the Big Bank campaign would finally start to heal.

However, the incident was all over the news again in 2003 when Matthew Barrett made a blunder by saying to a Treasury Select Committee that he did not borrow on credit cards because they were too expensive and that he has advised his four children not to pile up debts on their credit cards. The press jumped on his comments, saying that he would be dogged by what he said for the rest of his life. Journalists also said that he had 'done a Ratner' in memory of the famous blunder committed by jeweller Gerald Ratner back in 1991 when he admitted selling 'crap' jewellery products in his high street shops.

According to some analysts, the press jumped on the comment because the general public and by proxy the media had been waiting to land one on Matt Barrett and Barclays for three and a half years. The media openly linked Barrett's comments with what they saw as the other blunder of closing branches while launching an advertising campaign extolling the virtues of being a 'big' bank.

Questions for reflection

1. What was the exact cause or event that led to this communication crisis for Barclays?
2. What could Barclays have done to avoid this crisis? And what, would you suggest, does the bank need to do now to repair the damage done to its reputation?

Stakeholder groups have also become more fragmented and less homogeneous than before. Customers, for example, have become much more individual in their consumption. Similarly, when organizations want to communicate to the news media, they have to communicate with a much wider range of news organizations than before. As well as distinctions between print, television and the internet, there are also qualitative differences between news organizations such as Fox News, CNN, the *New York Times*, the *Financial Times*, the *Guardian* and tabloid newspapers.

This greater *fragmentation* of stakeholder groups means that when organizations want to communicate with any one stakeholder group, they have to use more channels and different media to reach them. In addition, media and communication experts have estimated that on average a person is hit by 13,000 commercial messages in their lifetime. Integrated communication strategies are more likely to break through this *clutter* and make the company name or product brand heard and remembered than ill-coordinated attempts would.

Communication-based drivers

In today's environment it is more difficult for an organization to be heard and stand out from its rivals. Through *consistent messages* an organization is more likely to be known and looked favourably upon by key stakeholder groups. Organizations have increasingly put considerable effort into protecting their corporate image by rigorously aligning and controlling all communication campaigns and all other contact points with stakeholders.

Organizations also realized that *messages in various media can complement one another*, leading to a greater communication impact than any one single message can achieve. Because of the increasing costs of traditional mass media advertising and the opportunities afforded by the internet, many organizations have therefore re-examined their *media presence and how to control it*. As a result of these two developments, organizations now tend to look at media in a much broader sense and across the disciplines of marketing and public relations. Organizations have also become more creative in looking beyond corporate and product advertising to other media for communicating with stakeholders[20]. Many organizations today use a whole range of media including corporate blogs and internet communication including websites, banners, and sponsored on-line communities.

Organizational drivers

One of the main organizational drivers for integration has been the need to *become more efficient*. By using management time more productively and by driving down the cost base (for example, as research and communication materials are more widely shared and used for more than one communication campaign), organizations have been able to substantially improve the productivity of their communication practitioners.

The 1980s saw a powerful restructuring trend where every function was examined on its *accountability*. This led many organizations to restructure communication disciplines such as media relations, advertising, sales promotions and product publicity. This restructuring of communication, basically consisting of bringing various communication disciplines together into more integrated departments or into specific working practices, also proved productive in that it offered further organizational and managerial benefits. First of all, the consolidation of communication disciplines into one or a few departments enabled organizations to *provide strategic direction* to all of their communication with different stakeholder groups and to guide communication efforts from the strategic interests of the organization as a whole. In other words, organizations recognized that fragmentation and spreading out of communication responsibilities across the organization were counterproductive. Fragmentation is likely

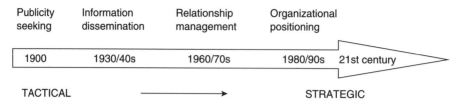

Figure 2.3   The shift from a tactical to strategic orientation
to communication

to lead to a situation where 'each department sub-optimizes its own performance, instead of working for the organization as a whole'.[21] Many organizations have therefore developed innovative procedures (e.g., communication
guidelines, house style manuals) and have implemented coordination mechanisms (e.g., council meetings, networking platforms) to overcome fragmentation and coordinate their communication on an organization-wide basis.

A further driver for integration at the organizational level was the realization
that communication had to be used more strategically to position the organization in the minds of important stakeholder groups of the organization. Since the
early 1990s, organizations have started to become concerned with ideas such as
'corporate identity', 'corporate reputation' and 'corporate branding' which
emphasize the importance of linking communication to the organization's corporate strategy and the importance of positioning the organization in the minds
of important stakeholders groups. Figure 2.3 displays this move from a tactical
orientation in communication to an orientation that emphasizes the strategic
role of communication in 'positioning' the organization. Case Study 2.3 describes
this shift from a tactical to strategic view of communication within British
Petroleum (BP). Obviously, when organizations adopt a strategic perspective on
communication and aim to build a distinctive reputation for their organization,
the activities of marketing and public relations practitioners need to be actively
coordinated so that messages to different stakeholders communicate the same
corporate values and image for the organization.

CASE STUDY 2.3

FROM A TACTICAL TO STRATEGIC APPROACH TO COMMUNICATION IN BP

British Petroleum is one of the world's largest petroleum and petrochemicals
groups, with business operations around the world for the exploration
and production of crude oil and natural gas; refining, marketing, supply and
transportation of gas and oils; and the manufacturing and marketing of
petrochemicals.

Early steps in communication

The name British Petroleum or BP did not feature in any communication for the oil company until the 1920s and 1930s. Until that time, the company had traded under its original name (the Anglo-Persian Oil Company) but then decided to label its gasoline pumps around Britain with the BP name. When Anglo-Persian at that time also entered other European markets, it again decided to brand itself with the BP name. Early communication consisted mainly of adverts and publicity campaigns to help people see the potential in reaching the countryside by car. Adverts in those days consisted of stylish images that often communicated very little directly about the company's products but reflected broad ideals such as patriotism or a fascination with the countryside. The overall purpose, it seems, was to simply publicize the BP name and link the brand to some higher ideals – an approach known as *publicity-seeking*.

The following years saw the use of lobbying and mediation tactics to ease the company's relationships with the Iranian government and with all allied and occupying forces during the Second World War. After the war, BP again had to lobby governments and disseminate information to the general public when nationalist voices throughout the Middle East angrily questioned Western companies' right to profit from Middle Eastern resources (*information dissemination*). Among the nationalists, Iran's prime minister spoke vehemently against Anglo-Persian's presence in Iran. Despite the company's best efforts in disseminating information about its intentions and operations to the people in Iran, Iran's prime minister convinced the Iranian Parliament in 1951 to nationalize oil operations within the country's borders. The Iranian part of the company was shut and the company then went on to trade in full under its BP name.

It was not until 1957, however, that the entire company was called BP. Originally the BP mark was designed as the letters 'B' and 'P' with wings on their edges and set into the outline of a shield. For many years, the actual colors inside this shield could be almost anything: red, blue, black, green, yellow or white. In the 1930s, the company realized that it needed to use a consistent house style and green and yellow became the norm. The shield would serve the company for 80 years in all and until 2000, with a few subtle changes along the way.

An era of relationship management

After a period of diversification (including a move into the nutrition business) in the 1970s and 1980s, BP rationalized its operations in the 1990s and started to focus again on its core activities in petroleum and chemicals. In 1989, the company launched a campaign to introduce a stronger corporate identity, featuring a restyled BP shield and an emphasis on the colour green. And in a complementary program BP started to re-image its global network

(Continued)

(Continued)

of service stations in a new design and livery. The idea of all this was to have a stronger and more consistent image in the marketplace and to build long-term relationships with customers, employees, governments and anyone affected by the company's business operations.

At the same time, to equip itself for the challenges of the 1990s and beyond, the company introduced a program called Project 1990 which involved major changes in its organization and ways of working to improve efficiency and flexibility. The key turning point for this came with the 1992 recession. 'We suffered a downturn like many companies in '92', said one BP executive, 'and it became a crisis for us. Our '92 financials were dramatically bad and that triggered a sea change in how BP viewed its operations. We took a lot of steps to refocus and became a much flatter organization. Browne [at the time the CEO of BP] was crucial in this organization.'

One of the outcomes of this organizational change at BP was a greater emphasis on partnering with stakeholders and on strategic business alliances (*relationship management*). BP became organized around small business units that were free to acquire what they needed from the best sources. This decentralization of business operations went hand in hand with group-wide consultation meetings that gathered feedback from environmental NGOs and experts on health, safety and the environment as an input for BP's overall strategy and its communication. These meetings presented the company with a report card on its environmental performance and its relationships with key stakeholders, from which they took specific recommendations and guidance.

The move to organizational positioning

One outcome of these meetings, a point taken in the company's strategy ever since, is that BP could be the first of the pack, taking an overall proactive stance on climate change and demonstrating a long-term strategic awareness that competitive advantage comes from proactively creating policy rather than attempting to slow the course of change. In May 1997, BP's CEO, John Browne, announced to the world both BP's decision to accept that climate change is occurring and its intention to reduce its contributions to the process. This action attracted attention from then US President Clinton, environmentalists, and the business press, and raised expectations regarding the actions of its direct competitors. Browne's speech was a breakthrough, as BP was the first multinational corporation other than insurance companies, to join the emerging consensus on climate change, and committed itself to reducing greenhouse emissions from all of its own business operations. 'It transformed the global climate issue because there was no one in the corporate world who, in such a public way, came out and said, this is a problem and we have a responsibility to do something about it', according to Eileen Claussen, President of the Pew Center on Global Climate Change.

The Environmental Defence Fund (EDF) called BP's action an 'historic acceptance of responsibility for the overriding environmental problem of our time'. The executive director of the EDF, Fred Krupp, said that it 'puts real pressure on the other oil companies to act like responsible adults, and I think it puts substantial pressure on the Clinton White House to advance a meaningful reduction target'. In a second address in Berlin, late September 1997, Browne re-emphasized BP's commitment to reducing the greenhouse effect and reflected upon the widespread support that existed for this strategy within his own organization: 'I've been struck since I first spoke on this subject ... by the degree of support there is within our company for a constructive approach – an approach which doesn't start with a denial of the problem, but rather with a determination to treat this as another challenge which we can help to resolve.'

A few years later, in 2000, BP unveiled a new global brand with a new mark, a sunburst of green, yellow and white symbolizing energy in all its forms. In a press release announcing the company's new brand, BP articulated its newfound aspirations: 'better people, better products, big picture, beyond petroleum'. The letters BP were to be interpreted as 'Beyond Petroleum' emphasizing the company's wider perspective on other sources of energy besides crude oil and its thought leadership on addressing the greenhouse effect. Together with the new brand symbolism, BP has positioned itself as a company that in a responsible and sustainable way aims to meet the world's current and future energy needs (*organizational positioning*).

Under this new banner, BP has taken more steps towards addressing climate change. The company installed solar panels at its service stations, brought solar power to remote villages in the Philippines, helped bring hydrogen-fuelled buses to London and introduced new, cleaner types of motor fuel. BP also annually publishes an environmental and social report (audited by third parties to ensure that views of stakeholders truly have an impact upon BP's operations) and has set up interactive policy-making and environmental forums in relation to sensitive projects (e.g. operations in China). With each and every one of these steps, BP aims to position itself in a market that is demanding more responsible behaviour of the company. As John Mogford, BP's Global Head of Safety and Operations, remarked: 'The industry is going to change, and we need to be positioned to take advantage of this and not be on the outside.'

Nonetheless, the new organizational positioning has also had its critics. In 2002, *Fortune* magazine criticized the company's re-branding on the basis that the company's revenues are still firmly rooted in traditional oil and gas extraction, exploration and chemical production. Very little of its revenues come from developing and commercializing alternative forms of energy, which has led a number of environmental groups to accuse the company of spin and 'greenwashing'. Investigations by the US authorities into the explosion in 2005 at a refinery in Texas which killed 15 people and injured 70 has led to a criticism of the company as being too much focused on climate change, alternative fuels and cost-cutting at the expense of health and safety investments.

(Continued)

(Continued)

Questions for reflection

1. Can you describe in your own words the development of BP's corporate brand and communication over time?
2. What, in your view, explains the different uses of the brand name and communication over time?

2.7 Corporate communication as a framework for managing communication

This chapter began with a description of the historical context of communication in organizations and reviewed different perspectives on the relationship between two main disciplines of communication: marketing and public relations. These different perspectives on the relationship between marketing and public relations each present different views of how communication in organizations is given shape and managed. The historical developments which led to a view of these two disciplines first as distinct then as complementary, and finally as one that sees them as integrated, provides a stepping stone for understanding the emergence of corporate communication. Corporate communication is a management framework to guide and coordinate marketing communication and public relations. Figure 2.4 displays this integrated framework of corporate communication.

Within this framework, coordination and decision-making take place between practitioners from various public relations and marketing communication disciplines. The public relations disciplines are displayed towards the left in Figure 2.4, whereas marketing communication disciplines are aligned towards the right. While each of these disciplines may be used separately and on their own for public relations or marketing purposes, organizations increasingly view and manage them together from a holistic organizational or corporate perspective with the company's reputation in mind. Many organizations have therefore promoted corporate communication practitioners to higher positions in the organization's hierarchical structure. In some organizations senior communication practitioners are even members of their organization's management team (or support this management team in a direct reporting or advisory capacity). Marks & Spencer and Sony are two examples of companies that have recently promoted their most senior communication director to a seat on the executive board. These higher positions in the organization's hierarchy enable corporate communication practitioners to

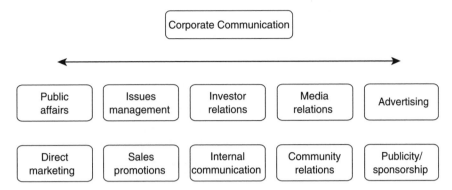

Figure 2.4   Corporate communication as an integrated framework for managing communication

coordinate communication from a strategic level in the organization in order to build, maintain and protect the company's reputation with its stakeholders. Corporate communication practitioners in companies as ABN-AMRO, BNP, Air France, Philips and Renault, for example, approach communication in such an integrated way and 'have bridged the traditional gaps between public relations and marketing communication'. These practitioners work 'from the position that the total communication effort must serve the corporate strategy, the importance of which is paramount' and they therefore 'found it natural to link the two disciplines'.[22]

2.8 Chapter summary

This chapter has discussed the historical development of communication in organizations, and the emergence of corporate communication, in particular. This discussion provides a context for understanding why corporate communication emerged and how it is useful for today's organizations. The chapter also described the variety of factors or 'drivers' that triggered the emergence of corporate communication and continue to drive its widespread use within companies around the globe. Corporate communication has brought a number of changes to how communication is managed for the benefit of the entire organization. The rest of the book expands on these changes regarding how communication is organized, staffed, coordinated, planned, programmed and executed. The next two chapters begin this journey by providing an overview of key theoretical concepts and communication models within corporate communication.

KEY TERMS

Accountability	Marketing public relations
Advertising	Markets
Audience fragmentation	Publicity
Communication clutter	Public relations
Corporate communication	Publics
Corporate public relations	Sales promotions
Direct marketing	Sponsorship
Marketing	Stakeholders

Notes

1 Marchand, R. (1998), *Creating the Corporate Soul: The Rise of Public Relations and Corporate Imagery*. Berkeley, CA: University of California Press.

2 Grunig, J.E. and Hunt, T. (1984) *Managing Public Relations*. New York: Holt, Rinehart & Winston.

3 See, for instance, Ewen, S. (1996), *PR! A Social History of Spin*. New York: Basic Books; Marchand, (1998); Grunig and Hunt, (1984); Cutlip, S.M., Center, A.H. and Broom, G.H. (2000), *Effective Public Relations*; 7th edn. London: Prentice-Hall.

4 Kotler (1989) cited in Grunig, J.E. and Grunig, L.A. (1991), 'Conceptual differences in public relations and marketing: the case of health-care organizations', *Public Relations Review*, 17 (3): 257–278, quote on p. 261.

5 Kotler, P. and Mindak, W. (1978), 'Marketing and public relations, should they be partners or rivals?', *Journal of Marketing*, 42 (10): 13–20, quote on p. 20.

6 See, for example, Ehling, W.P., White, J. and Grunig, J.E. (1992), 'Public relations and marketing practices', in Grunig, J.E. (ed.), *Excellence in Public Relations and Communication Management*. Hillsdale, NJ: Lawrence Erlbaum Associates, pp. 357–383; Ehling, W.P. (1989), 'Public relations management and marketing management: different paradigms and different missions', paper presented at the meeting of the Public Relations Colloquium, San Diego.

7 Kotler and Mindak (1978), p. 17.

8 Ehling et al. (1992).

9 See, for example, Harris, T.L. (1991), *The Marketer's Guide to Public Relations: How Today's Top Companies Are Using the New PR to Gain a Competitive Edge*. New York: John Wiley & Sons; Harris, T.L. (1997), 'Integrated marketing public relations', in Caywood, C. (ed.), *The Handbook of Strategic Public Relations and Integrated Communications*. New York: McGraw-Hill, pp. 90–105; Ries, A. and Ries, L. (2002), *The Fall of Advertising and the Rise of PR*. New York: HarperCollins.

10 Based on Hutton, J.G. (1996), 'Integrated marketing communications and the evolution of marketing thought', *Journal of Business Research*, 37: 155–162.

11 See, for example, Brown, T.J. and Dacin, A. (1997), 'The company and the product: corporate associations and consumer product responses', *Journal of Marketing*, 61 (January): 68–84; Biehal, G.J. and Sheinin, D.A. (1998), 'Managing the brand in a corporate advertising environment: a decision-making framework for brand managers', *Journal of*

Advertising, 27 (2): 99–111; Berens, G.A.J.M., Van Riel, C.B.M. and Van Bruggen, G.H. (2005), 'Corporate associations and consumer product responses: the moderating role of corporate brand dominance', *Journal of Marketing*, 69 (July): 35–48.

12 Grunig, L.A., Grunig, J.E. and Dozier, D.M. (2002), *Excellent Public Relations and Effective Organizations*. Hillsdale, NJ: Lawrence Erlbaum Associates.

13 Duncan, T. and Caywood, C. (1996), 'Concept, process, and evolution of IMC', in Thorson, E. and Moore, J. (eds), *Integrated Communication: Synergy of Persuasive Voices*. Mahwah, NJ: Lawrence Erlbaum Associates, pp. 13–34, quote on pp. 19–20.

14 Kotler and Mindak (1978), p. 18.

15 This perspective is associated with the IABC Excellence Study on strategic public relations. Work cited is Grunig, J.E. and Grunig, L.A. (1998), 'The relationship between public relations and marketing in excellent organizations: evidence from the IABC study', *Journal of Marketing Communications*, 4 (3): 141–162, quote on p. 141. See also Grunig, J.E. (1992), *Excellence in Public Relations and Communication Management*. Hillsdale, NJ: Lawrence Erlbaum Associates, and Grunig, et al. (2002).

16 Kotler and Mindak (1978), p. 18.

17 Gronstedt, A. (1996), 'Integrating marketing communication and public relations: a stakeholder relations model', in Thorson, E. and Moore, J. (eds), *Integrated Communication: Synergy of Persuasive Voices*. Mahwah, NJ: Lawrence Erlbaum Associates, pp. 287–304, quote on p. 302.

18 Heath, R.L. (1994), *Management of Corporate Communication: From Interpersonal Contacts to External Affairs*. Hillsdale, NJ: Lawrence Erlbaum Associates, p. 55.

19 See, for example, Scholes, E. and Clutterbuck, D. (1998), 'Communication with stakeholders: an integrated approach', *Long Range Planning*, 31 (2): 227–238; Fombrun, C. and Van Riel, C.B.M. (2004) *Fame and Fortune: How Successful Companies Build Winning Reputations*. London: FT Prentice Hall.

20 See, for example, Barwise, P. and Styler, A. (2003), *The MET Report 2003: Marketing Expenditure Trends* 2001–04 (http://www.london.edu/assets/documents/PDF/MET_Report_Exec_Summary_2.pdf).

21 Gronstedt, A. (1996), 'Integrated communications at America's leading total quality management corporations', *Public Relations Review*, 22 (1): 25–42, quote on p. 26.

22 Van Riel, C.B.M. (1995), *Principles of Corporate Communication*. London: Prentice Hall, p. 141.

Part 2

CONCEPTUAL FOUNDATIONS

This book is about organizations and the way in which they respond and adapt (or fail to adapt) to the world around them through managing communication with their stakeholders. Although the word 'management' often calls to mind a deliberate, rational process, communication programs and campaigns are not always shaped in that way. Sometimes, they come about by reactions to sudden crises, or as the result of political activity within the organization. The way in which organizations manage communication with their stakeholders is the subject of this part of the book.

In Part 2, we explore the basic themes and concepts that are used in discussing corporate communication, and provide the theoretical background to the management of corporate communication that will serve as a guide to the field (and the remainder of this book). Themes and concepts that are addressed include stakeholders, models for stakeholder communication and engagement, an organization's corporate identity, image and reputation, and corporate branding.

After reading Part 2, the reader should be familiar with the basic vocabulary and theoretical concepts in corporate communication and the importance of stakeholder communication for contemporary organizations.

3

Stakeholder Management and Communication

CHAPTER OVERVIEW

The need for companies to manage relationships with stakeholders is, both in theory and practice, one of the main purposes of corporate communication. The chapter starts with an introduction to the concept of stakeholders followed by an overview of different management and communication models that organizations use to communicate and collaborate with their stakeholders.

3.1 Introduction

This chapter together with Chapter 4 provides the theoretical background to the practice of corporate communication. There are three concepts that form the theoretical foundation of corporate communication: (1) stakeholder; (2) identity; and (3) reputation. These concepts provide the conceptual tools for understanding and practising corporate communication. The concepts of identity and reputation will be defined in the next chapter; and this chapter focuses on the concept of stakeholder. The chapter starts with outlining how stakeholder management is now central to the corporate strategies, operations and communication of many, if not all, contemporary organizations. Organizations have realized that now more than ever they need to listen to and communicate with a whole range of stakeholder groups successfully for their own as well as for society's sake and in order to avoid certain stakeholder groups raising issues that are potentially damaging to their reputations. This chapter is about the importance of stakeholder management to organizations and about how organizations can effectively communicate and collaborate with them.

3.2 Stakeholder management

Since the late 1980s, managers in many organizations have started to realize that their organizations are dependent upon a range of stakeholding groups instead of just a rather select group of financial investors or customers alone.[1] Instead of communicating with only investors or customers, they increasingly feel that groups such as members of the community, employees and government should also have a say in their organization and should be part of the communication loop. This realization was in part triggered by calls for organizations to demonstrate 'corporate citizenship' and by pressure from governments and the international community suggesting to organizations that the stakeholder perspective is the preferred option, if not the standard, for doing business in the first decade of the new millennium and beyond. There are now a range of stakeholder initiatives and schemes at the industry, national and transnational levels including Green Papers of the European Union (Promoting a European Framework for Corporate Social Responsibility 2001, Partnership for a New Organization of Work 1997), the UN Global Compact Initiative, the Global Reporting Initiative, the World Bank's Business Partners for Development, and the OECD's Guidelines for Multinational Companies. All these initiatives and schemes emphasize the wider responsibilities of organizations to *all* its stakeholders and indeed society at large, which stretch beyond financial performance alone. The Social Economic Council, a government think-tank and advisory body in the Netherlands, illustrates this 'wider' responsibility by stating that an organization 'has a visible role in society that extends beyond the core business and legal requirements, and that leads to added value to the organization as well as the society at large'.[2]

Theoretically, this widespread adoption of the stakeholder perspective in business marks a move away from the neo-classical economic theory of organizations to a socio-economic theory, within which the stakeholder perspective is embedded. The neo-classical economic theory suggests that the purpose of organizations is to make profits in their accountability to themselves and shareholders, and that only by doing so can business contribute to wealth for itself as well as society at large.[3] The socio-economic theory suggests, in contrast, that the notion of accountability in fact looms larger: to other groups outside shareholders who are important for the continuity of the organization and the welfare of society. This distinction between a conventional neo-classical perspective and a socio-economic or stakeholder perspective on the management of organizations is highlighted by the contrasting models displayed in Figures 3.1 and 3.2.[4]

In Figure 3.1, the organization is the centre of the economy, where investors, suppliers and employees are depicted as contributing inputs, which the 'black box' of the organization transforms into outputs for the benefit of customers.

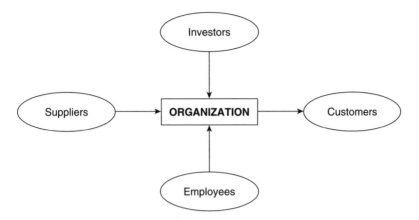

Figure 3.1 Input-output model of strategic management

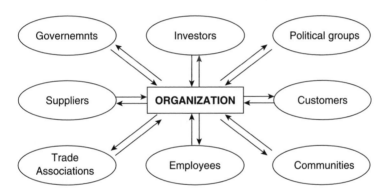

Figure 3.2 Stakeholder model of strategic management

Each contributor of inputs is rewarded with appropriate compensation, and, as a result of competition throughout the system, the bulk of the benefits will go to the customers. It is important to note that in this 'input-output' model, power lies with the organization, upon which the other parties are dependent, and that the interest of these other parties and their relationship to the organization are merely financial.

The stakeholder model (Figure 3.2) contrasts with the input–output model. Stakeholder management assumes that all persons or groups with legitimate interests in an organization do so to obtain benefits and there is in principle no priority for one set of interests and benefits over another. Hence, the arrows between the organization and its stakeholder constituents run in both directions. All those groups which have a legitimate stake in the organization, whether purely financial, market-based or otherwise, are recognized, and the relationship of the organization with these groups is not linear but one of interdependency. In other words, instead of considering organizations as immune to government or public opinion, the stakeholder management model recognizes the mutual dependencies between organizations and various *stakeholding* groups – groups that are themselves affected by the operations of the organization, but can equally affect the organization, its operations and performance.

The picture that emerges from the stakeholder perspective is a far more complex and dynamic one than the input–output model of strategic management that preceded it. More persons and groups with legitimate interests in the organization are recognized and accounted for, and these individuals and groups all need to be considered, communicated with and/or accommodated by the organization to sustain its financial performance and to secure continued acceptance for its operations. One further significant feat of the stakeholder model of strategic management is that it suggests that an organization needs to be considered 'legitimate' by both 'market' and 'non-market' stakeholding groups. This notion of legitimacy stretches further than financial accountability to include accountability for the firm's performance in social (social responsibility, community involvement, labour relations record, etc.) and ecological (e.g. the reduction of harmful waste and residues, the development of ecologically friendly production processes, etc.) terms.

True, organizations have always, even before the widespread adoption of the stakeholder philosophy in the early 1990s, dealt with so-called 'non-market' groups or publics (see also Chapter 2). However, before stakeholder management, such non-market groups were within the context of the input–output model seen as necessary to communicate with only because of their indirect or more direct capacity to block markets[5] or their ability to condition or effect customer relationships and sales. Igor Ansoff, an eminent strategy professor, illustrated this feat of the input–output model in his 1960 book, *Corporate Strategy* in which he made a distinction between economic or market objectives and social or non-market objectives. In Ansoff's view, social or non-market objectives are a secondary, modifying and constraining influence on economic or market objectives.[6] The stakeholder concept, in contrast, provides a drastically different view of the nature of the relationship of an organization with such non-market parties as governments, communities, and special interest groups. First of all, these non-market groups are credited as forces that need to be reckoned with. Second, the relationship of the organization with these non-market groups, as well as with market groups, is characterized by institutional meaning. In this institutional or socio-economic view, an organization is seen as being part of a larger social system that includes market and non-market parties, and as dependent upon that system's support for its continued existence. Organizational goals and activities must in this sense be found legitimate and valued by all parties in the larger social system, where every 'market' or 'non-market' stakeholder has to be treated by the organization 'as an end in itself, and not as a means to some other end'.[7]

Accountability of the organization towards all stakeholding groups stretches, as mentioned, further than financial performance alone into the social and ecological realms, and is captured with the roomier concept of *legitimacy*. This notion of legitimacy derives from norms and values of each of the stakeholder groups depicted in Figure 3.2 regarding what each deems acceptable and favourable in the organization. Having a *reputation* as a financially solid organization with a proven social and ecological track record (particularly in such areas as labour conditions, environmental performance and protection of human rights) normally provides sufficient ground to be found legitimate by most, if not all, stakeholder groups. Framing accountability through the concept of legitimacy also means that organizations engage with stakeholders not just for *instrumental* reasons when it leads to increases in revenue and reductions in costs and risks (as transactions are triggered by stakeholders or as a reputational buffer is created for crises or potentially damaging litigation) but also for *normative* reasons. Instrumental justification points to evidence of the connection between stakeholder management and corporate performance. Normative justification appeals to underlying concepts such as individual or group 'rights', 'social contracts', morality, and so on.[8] From this normative perspective, stakeholders are persons or groups with legitimate interests in aspects of corporate activity; and they are identified by this interest, whether the corporation has any direct economic interest in them or not. The interests of all stakeholders are in effect seen as of some intrinsic value to the organization, in this view. That is, each group of stakeholders merits consideration for its own sake and not merely because of its ability to further the interests of some other group, such as the shareholders.

Instrumental or normative motives for engaging with stakeholders, however, often converge in practice, as social and economic objectives are not mutually exclusive[9] and as 'doing good' for one stakeholder group delivers reputational returns which are easily carried over and may impact the views of other stakeholder groups. So, while certain initiatives and communication with particular stakeholder groups may have been started for normative, even altruistic reasons – to be a 'good corporate citizen' as an end in itself, so to speak – the gains that this delivers in terms of employee morale, reputation, and so on, are often considerable and clearly of instrumental value to the organization. Kotter and Heskett observed that highly successful companies such as Hewlett Packard and Wal-Mart, although very diverse in many ways, share a similar stakeholder perspective: 'almost all [their] managers care strongly about people who have a stake in the business – customers, employees, stockholders, suppliers, etc.'.[10] As HP's former chairman and CEO Lewis Platt once noted, many companies consider their shareholders to be far more important than their customers and employees. He suggested, however, that by doing so they lose their employees' support and the quality of their customer service declines. Kotter and Heskett also observed that although HP and Wal-Mart had originally adopted a stakeholder philosophy for both instrumental and normative reasons, this philosophy has turned out to be instrumental and successful overall.

3.3 The nature of stakes and stakeholding

Having sketched out some of the background to stakeholder management, it is helpful to devote a bit more space to discuss the concepts of 'stake' and 'stakeholding'. The standard definition of a stakeholder is the one provided by Freeman:

> **A stakeholder is any group or individual who can affect or is affected by the achievement of the organization's purpose and objectives.**[11]

A stake, which is central to this definition and to the notion of stakeholding in general, can be described as 'an interest or a share in an undertaking, [that] can range from simply an interest in an undertaking at one extreme to a legal claim of ownership at the other extreme'.[12] The content of stakes that are held by different persons and groups is varied, and depends on the specific interests of these individuals or groups in the organization. Special interest groups and NGOs who demand ever higher levels of 'corporate social responsibility' from an organization, in such instances exercise their societal stake in the organization, which at any one time may coincide with investors who for their part may apply relentless pressure on that same organization to maximize short-term profits. Stakes of different individuals and groups may thus be at odds with one another, putting pressure on the organization to balance stakeholder interests.

Freeman was among the first to offer a classification for all those groups who hold a stake in the organization. In his classic book, *Strategic Management: A Stakeholder Approach*, Freeman considered three groups of stakes: equity stakes, economic or market stakes, and influencer stakes. Equity stakes, in Freeman's terminology, are held by those who have some direct 'ownership' of the organization, such as shareholders, directors or minority interest owners. Economic or market stakes are held by those who have an economic interest, but not an ownership interest, in the organization, such as employees, customers, suppliers and competitors. Finally, influencer stakes are held by those who do not have either an ownership or economic interest in the actions of the organization, but who have interests as consumer advocates, environmental groups, trade organizations and government agencies. By considering these groups of stakes, Freeman specified the nature of stakes in terms of the interest of various groups in the organization—whether this interest was primarily economic or moral in nature—and whether this interest was bound in some form through a contract or (moral) obligation.

One way of looking at stakes is thus by assessing whether the interest of a person or group in an organization is primarily economic or moral in nature.

Clarkson suggests in this respect to think of primary and secondary groups of stakeholders, with primary groups being those groups that are important for financial transactions and necessary for an organization to survive.[13] In short, in Clarkson's view, a primary stakeholder group is one without whose continuing participation the organization cannot survive. Secondary stakeholder groups are defined as those who generally influence or affect, or are influenced or affected by, the organization, but they are not engaged in financial transactions with the organization and are not essential for its survival in strictly economic terms. Media and a wide range of special interest groups fall within the secondary group of stakeholders. They do, however, have a moral or normative interest in the organization and have the capacity to mobilize public opinion in favour of, or in opposition to, a corporation's performance, as demonstrated in the cases of the recall of Tylenol by Johnson&Johnson (favourable) and the *Exxon Valdez* oil spill (unfavourable).

A second way of viewing stakes is to consider whether stakeholder ties with an organization are established through some form of contract or formal agreement, or not. Charkham talked about two broad classes of stakeholders in this respect: contractual and community stakeholders.[14] Contractual stakeholders are those groups who have some form of legal relationship with the organization for the exchange of goods or services. Community stakeholders involve those groups whose relationship with the organization is non-contractual and more diffuse but their relationship is nonetheless real in terms of its impact. While community stakeholders are not contractually bound to an organization, groups such as the government, regulatory agencies, trade associations, professional societies, and the media are important in providing the authority for an organization to function, setting the general rules and regulations by which activities are carried out, and monitoring and publicly evaluating the conduct of business operations. Contractual groups, including customers, employees, and suppliers, on the other hand, are more formally tied to an organization because they have entered into some of form of contract; and the nature of their interest is often economic in providing services or extracting resources from the firm (Table 3.1).

Table 3.1   Contractual and community stakeholders

Contractual stakeholders	Community stakeholders
Customers	Consumers
Employees	Regulators
Distributors	Government
Suppliers	Media
Shareholders	Local communities
Lenders	Pressure groups

In summary, the notion of having a legitimate stake in an organization is rather 'inclusive' and ranges from economic to moral interests, and from formal, binding relationships as the basis of stakeholding to more diffuse and loose ties with the organization. This 'inclusiveness' implies that organizations ideally communicate and engage with all of their stakeholders. A particular way in which this 'inclusive' nature of the stakeholder concept is shown is in corporate social responsibility (CSR) initiatives that have been adopted by many organizations in recent years. These initiatives are a direct outcome of the shift from an 'input–output' model to a stakeholder model of strategic management (Figures 3.1 and 3.2). CSR includes philanthropy, community involvement, and ethical and environmentally friendly business practices.

3.4 Corporate social responsibility (CSR)

The drive for CSR came with the recognition of the need for business to deliver wider societal value beyond shareholder and market value alone. In recent years, CSR has become more pertinent through expectations voiced by the international community, NGOs, pressure groups, as well as many market parties. At the European Summit in Lisbon in March 2000, the European Council made a special appeal to companies' sense of responsibility, and linked CSR closely to the Lisbon 2010 strategic goal of a knowledge-based and highly competitive, as well as socially inclusive Europe. Internationally, the UN World Summit for Sustainable Development in Johannesburg, in 2002, voiced the need for businesses to contribute to the building of equitable and sustainable societies, wherever they work. Recognizing the urgency of this responsibility, many CSR schemes and standards have in recent years been developed and suggested by major international agencies. These schemes and standards should not merely be seen as an effort to support or judge companies' licence to operate in countries all over the world. Rather, they mark the priority that is now given to finding new ways to take up larger development and societal goals and towards establishing a new role for business in the twenty-first century.

On top of the momentum that has gathered around CSR in the international community and public policy arenas, organizations often also consider CSR in an effort to improve their reputations. With the media constantly reporting on their affairs, and because of the greater product homogeneity and competition in many markets, many organizations realize that doing business in a responsible and just manner offers strategic and reputational advantages. As with stakeholder management, CSR initiatives may in the first instance be initiated for either moral or instrumental reputational reasons. However, the actual reasons for CSR are often difficult to separate given the 'significant difficulties in distinguishing whether business behavior is truly moral conduct or instrumental adoption of an appearance of moral conduct as reputational strategy'.[15] However, regardless of the underlying motives, CSR initiatives often appear to be of a direct instrumental value to an organization. Research has found that these initiatives are related to reputational returns and an overall better financial performance.[16]

Case Study 3.1 discusses the Co-operative Bank in the United Kingdom, an organization that places CSR at the heart of its business operations and communication strategy.

CASE STUDY 3.1

THE CO-OPERATIVE BANK AND CORPORATE SOCIAL RESPONSIBILITY

The Co-operative Bank plc is a mid-size retail bank operating in the United Kingdom. By the mid-1980s, the environment and context of the Co-operative bank had changed dramatically because of the financial service revolution when deregulation removed barriers to entry (e.g. building societies), new technology had become the basis of competition and the consumer had become more sophisticated. In short, there was at that time an increase in competition both between the banks and within the financial sector as a whole within the UK. As a result, the major banks (including Barclays, Natwest, and the Bank of Scotland) turned to a more selective positioning strategy, thus placing the Co-operative Bank plc at a major competitive disadvantage because of the high awareness that these other banks enjoyed through size, high street presence and advertising expenditure. Hence, the Co-operative Bank plc needed to find itself a niche or secure a long-term positioning strategy.

The bank started a soul-searching exercise and re-interpreted the co-operative philosophy that lies at its foundation. The bank asked itself whether it was able to 'conduct its business in a socially and environmentally responsible manner while being consistently profitable at the same time' and concluded that it could. As the bank's website now states:

> In fact we believe that, in the years to come, the only truly successful businesses will be those that achieve a sustainable balance between their own interests, and those of society and the natural world ... The Co-operative Bank is seeking to achieve this balance.

The Co-operative Bank plc is indeed now well known within the financial and banking industry for its unique ethical positioning and CSR reporting that distinguishes it from its competitors. This ethical positioning strategy, according to some academic commentators, is not so much a moral affair but needs rather 'be seen as a pragmatic response to the Bank's conundrum relating to its positioning strategy', where 'the Bank could promote itself as a proponent of people's capitalism, an ethical bank, in contrast to the images of the big banks tainted by association with Third World debt, South African involvement, city scandals and huge profits'.

(Continued)

(Continued)

Whether its ethical policy is indeed based on more pragmatic and economic rather than purely moral reasons, the bank's strategy has nevertheless been successful on many accounts. Since launching its ethical positioning in May 1992, the bank has attracted large numbers of customers who do not wish their money to be used in ways that they ethically object to as the bank will not do business with certain organizations deemed 'unethical'. The bank also generally believes that it has sharply positioned itself within an increasingly homogeneous financial services industry and estimates that around 15–18 percent of annual profits is directly due to its responsible stance and behaviour.

Sustainability, a consultancy that evaluates CSR reporting of organizations worldwide, ranked the Co-operative Bank as the absolute number one in 2002: as a true 'expert' in stakeholder engagement. The bank was judged as an industry leader in setting CSR targets and being clear about how it has performed against previous ones; in having its social report independently verified, and in its discussion of financial exclusion that was seen as 'a good example of economic impacts well beyond the traditional understanding'. In the latest 2006 ranking, the Bank was ranked number two behind BT and again celebrated for its leadership in corporate sustainability reporting, transparency and disclosure.

Questions for reflection

1. What were the motives for the Co-operative Bank to adopt its ethical positioning strategy and place it at the heart of all its business operations? Were these motives economic or rather moral in nature?
2. What aspects of the CSR strategy followed by the Co-operative Bank have led to its success and acclaim in the business world? And what, in general, are sound and just tactics in CSR behaviour and reporting?

Note: * Wilkinson, A. and Balmer, J.M.T. (1996), 'Corporate and generic identities: lessons from the Co-operative Bank', *International Journal of Bank Marketing*, 14 (4): 22–35, quote on p. 29.

Many organizations define CSR in terms of the 'triple bottom line': people, planet and profits.[17] John Elkington introduced the term and suggested that organizations need to communicate their CSR activities; activities that include social ('people') and ecological ('planet') initiatives (see Case Study 3.2) alongside the generation of profits and healthy financial accounts ('profit'). 'People' stands for all social and labour issues both inside and outside the organization including employee support and compensation, gender and ethnic balance of the workforce, reduction of corruption and fraud in business transactions and health and safety codes. 'Planet' refers to the responsibility of organizations to integrate ecological care into their business operations, such as the reduction of harmful waste and residues and the development of ecologically friendly production processes. 'Profit' involves the conventional bottom line of manufacturing and selling products so as to generate financial returns for the organization and its shareholders. This latter category of responsibilities ('profit') is often considered as a baseline or requisite before an organization can even start considering how to meet its social ('people') and ecological ('planet') responsibilities. That is, these other responsibilities cannot be achieved in the absence of economic performance (i.e., goods and services, jobs, profitability) – a bankrupt firm will cease to operate.[18]

CASE STUDY 3.2

MANAGEMENT BRIEF: CORPORATE SOCIAL RESPONSIBILITY REPORTING*

The founders of Ben & Jerry's, the funky ice cream manufacturers now part of the Unilever group, believe that business should give something back to the community that supports it. But what makes Ben & Jerry's unique and from a CSR perspective interesting is that the company was one of the first organizations to acknowledge its shortcomings publicly, going so far as to print them as part of the social assessment in its annual report to shareholders. A growing number of organizations have since followed suit, and are among the elite that now publish rather frank society or social reports that appear alongside financial reports and in which they systematically report upon their social and ecological performance over the past year.

Yet, at the same time, most of the large organizations around the world still report little, if anything, about their impact upon society. And, what is worse, many who have pledged to take CSR reporting on board often put out glossy reports that are more about style than substance, according to Sustainability, the consultancy that evaluates CSR reporting of organizations worldwide. A recent report from think-tank Demos strengthens these observations through its comments that companies view social responsibility as a PR exercise instead of a refocusing and reshuffling of their business operations. The Institute of Public Policy Research in the UK equally controversially revealed that only 4 out of 10 company boards discuss social and environmental issues, routinely or occasionally, and that only a third of organizations have a board member with an environmental remit or with an interest in social issues. A survey by McKinsey in 2006 reported that organizations often simply focus on the media and on public relations tactics to manage their CSR initiatives without considering other ways to embed CSR within their organizations.

(Continued)

(Continued)

So what appears to be at stake is that, despite paying lip service to CSR, many organizations have not yet come round to developing and implementing fully-fledged CSR initiatives within their business operations. This may be due to the fact that it is still early days and that transparent standards and benchmarks of what constitutes social and ecological performance are lacking. As a result, many organizations pledge CSR, but take it rather easy and loosely when it comes down to implementing it in a substantial and comprehensive manner. In a recent article in *The Financial Times*, Schrage, an expert on social auditing, however, warned that these days may soon be over. On a worldwide scale, the public is demanding ever greater scrutiny and more evidence of CSR activities; and also governments are toughening their stance on what they endorse as good CSR reporting. Schrage writes, 'The message to multinational business – and to global regulators – is that social accountability demands the same kind of independent scrutiny as financial auditing.'

There are, however, difficulties with setting clear, unequivocal standards and with enforcing them, also because (transnational) authorities and institutions that would develop and guard such standards have not come forward yet. This of course plays in to the hands of the current CSR malpractice and the 'anything goes' strategy. Schrage acknowledges these difficulties, yet advocates that 'just as the Securities and Exchange Commission and Financial Accounting Standards Board establish a framework in the US for public accountants to evaluate corporate financial performance, a new reporting system is needed for independent review of corporate social performance'. Such a system, when governments and industries are ready for it, will at least need clear social standards (in areas such as labour conditions, environmental performance and promotion of human rights), a professional corps of social auditors (independent of corporate control and accountable to the public), and safe harbours that limit legal liability (so as to encourage companies to open their businesses to social audits).

Until that day comes, and in order to be ahead of the pack, here are five guidelines for CSR reporting that, according to Sustainability and others, have proven successful:

1. An organization needs to show that it is serious about CSR by setting clear objectives for social and ecological performance annually, and by systematically reporting on the results achieved afterwards.
2. Targets should include issues that are relevant to stakeholders and should be linked to benchmarks and standards (at the industry and policy levels) wherever possible.
3. Targets need to be progressive in bringing new aspirations and standards to bear upon business operations instead of regurgitating existing practices that may be seen as socially and ecologically viable.

4. Reporting needs to be an honest, transparent and full-scale self-assessment instead of merely polishing performance data.
5. Performance data need to be rigorously assessed and verified by credible auditors (accountants or consultants) wherever possible.

Note: *This management brief is based upon Fred Lager (1994) *Ben and Jerry's: The Inside Scoop, How Two Real Guys Built & Business with a Social Conscience and a Sense of Humour*. Crown Publisher, Schrage, E.J. (2001), 'A new model for social auditing', *Financial Times*, Maitland, A. (2006), 'The frustrated will to act for the public good', *Financial Times*, 26 January.

3.5 Stakeholder communication

The stakeholder model of the organization suggests that the various stakeholders of the organization need to be identified and they must be addressed for the stake that they hold. In practice, this comes down to providing stakeholders with the type of information about the company's operations that they have an interest in. Financial investors and shareholders, for instance, will need to be provided with financial information concerning the organization's strategy and operations (e.g., through annual reports and shareholder meetings), while customers and prospects need to be supplied with information about products and services (e.g., through advertising, sales promotions and in-store communication). Each of these stakeholder groups, on the basis of the stake(s) that an individual holds in an organization, looks for and is interested in certain aspects of the company's operations. While the interests of stakeholders are intricately varied, and at times even at odds with one another (e.g., staff redundancies are a blow to the workforce, but may be favoured by shareholders and investors who have an interest in the financial strength and continuity of the firm), it is important that an organization provides each stakeholder group with specific information and builds a strong reputation across exchanges with all of these stakeholders.

In order to do so, communication practitioners typically start with identifying and analyzing the organization's stakeholders and their influence and interest in the organization. In this way, they have a clearer idea what the information needs of stakeholders are, what specific positions they have on an issue or in relation to a corporate activity, and what kind of communication strategy needs to be used to maintain support or counter opposition. A basic form of stakeholder identification analysis involves answering the following questions that will capture the essential information needed for effective stakeholder communication:[19]

1. Who are the organization's stakeholders?
2. What are their stakes?
3. What opportunities and challenges are presented to the organization in relation to these stakeholders?
4. What responsibilities (economic, legal, ethical, and philanthropic) does the organization have to all its stakeholders?
5. In what way can the organization best communicate with and respond to these stakeholders and address these stakeholder challenges and opportunities?

A similar approach is to use a mapping or model to identify and position stakeholders in terms of their influence on the organization's operations or in terms of their stance on a particular issue related to the organization. There are two general mapping devices or tools that communication practitioners can use for this task: the stakeholder salience model and the power-interest matrix. Both mapping devices enhance practitioners' knowledge of stakeholders and their influence, and enable them to plan appropriate communication strategies. Such mapping exercises should be carried out on an ongoing basis, but can also be performed in relation to particular issues or corporate activities.

Stakeholder salience model

In this model, stakeholders are identified and classified based upon their salience to the organization. Salience is defined as how visible or prominent a stakeholder is to an organization based upon the stakeholder possessing one or more of three attributes: power, legitimacy, and urgency. The central idea behind the model is that the more salient or prominent stakeholders need to be given priority and need to be actively communicated with. Smaller or hardly salient stakeholders have less priority and it is less important for an organization to communicate with them on an ongoing basis.

The first step of the model is to classify and prioritize stakeholders according to the presence or absence of three key attributes: power (the power of the stakeholder group upon an organization); legitimacy (the legitimacy of the claim laid upon the organization by the stakeholder group); and urgency (the degree to which stakeholder claims call for immediate action)[20]. Together, these three attributes form seven different types of stakeholders as shown in Figure 3.3.

The three stakeholder groups on the edges of Figure 3.3 are classified as *latent* stakeholder groups which are groups possessing only one attribute:

1. *Dormant stakeholders*: Those who have the power to impose their will on others but because they do not have a legitimate relationship or urgent claim, their power remains dormant. Examples of dormant stakeholders include those who wield power by having a loaded gun (coercive), by spending a lot of money (utilitarian), or by commanding the attention of the news media (symbolic).

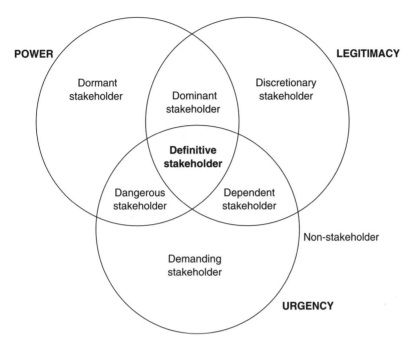

Figure 3.3   Stakeholder salience model

Dormant stakeholders, however, have little or no interaction with the organization, but because of their potential to acquire a second attribute (urgency or
legitimacy), practitioners should be aware of such stakeholders.

2. *Discretionary stakeholders*: Those who possess legitimate claims but have no
    power to influence the organization, nor urgent claims. Recipients of corpo-
    rate charity, for instance, fall within this group.
3. *Demanding stakeholders*: Those who have urgent claims, but neither the power nor
    legitimacy to enforce them. These groups can therefore be bothersome but do
    not warrant serious attention from communication practitioners. That is, where
    stakeholders are unable or unwilling to acquire either the power or the legiti-
    macy necessary to move their claim into a more salient status, the 'noise' of
    urgency is insufficient to move a stakeholder claim beyond latency. For example,
    a lone demonstrator who camps near a company's site might be embarrassing to
    the company or a nuisance to employees and managers of an organization, but
    the claims of the demonstrator will typically remain unconsidered.

Three further groups are considered and classified as expectant stakeholders and
are groups with two attributes present.

4. *Dominant stakeholders*: Those who have both powerful and legitimate claims giv-
    ing them a strong influence on the organization. Examples include employees,
    customers, owners and significant (institutional) investors in the organization.
5. *Dangerous stakeholders*: Those who have power and urgent claims, but lack
    legitimacy. They are seen as dangerous as they may resort to coercion and even

violence. Examples of unlawful, yet common, attempts at using coercive means to advance stakeholder claims (which may or may not be legitimate) include wildcat strikes, employee sabotage, and terrorism. The consumer electronics firm Philips, for example, was faced with such a dangerous stakeholder in March 2002, when an armed individual held several people hostage in the Rembrandt tower in Amsterdam (which is situated next to the company's main headquarters) to protest against the company's introduction of flat screen TVs which he thought communicated hidden codes.

6. *Dependent stakeholders*: those who lack power, but who have urgent, legitimate claims. They rely on others for the power to carry out their will, at times through the advocacy of other stakeholders. Local residents of a community in which a plant of a large corporation is based, for instance, often need to rely on lobby groups, the media or another form of political representation to have their concerns voiced and considered by the corporation.

The seventh and final type of stakeholder group that can be identified is:

7. *Definitive stakeholder*: those who have legitimacy, power and urgency. In other words, definitive stakeholders are powerful and legitimate stakeholders who by definition will need to be communicated with. When the claim of a definitive stakeholder is urgent, communication practitioners and other managers have a responsibility to give it priority and attention. Shareholders, for example, who are normally classified as dominant stakeholders, can become active when they feel that their legitimate interests are not being served by the managers of the company in which they hold stock, and then they effectively act as definitive stakeholders. When the actions of such powerful shareholders may, for example, imply the removal of senior executives, communication practitioners and managers of the organization urgently need to attend to their concerns.

Once all the organization's stakeholders have been classified according to their salience, communication practitioners will have an overview of which stakeholder groups require attention and need to be communicated with. Based on the classification, they can develop communication strategies to most appropriately deal with each stakeholder. For example, dominant and definitive stakeholders of the organization such as employees, customers and shareholders will need to be communicated with on an ongoing basis. Most organizations have ongoing communication programmes for these stakeholders including newsletters, corporate events and an intranet for employees, advertising and promotional campaigns for customers and financial reports, investor briefings and the annual general meeting for shareholders. In addition, many organizations will often communicate directly with members of the local community in which it operates (a dependent stakeholder) and will respond to dangerous stakeholders if the actions of those stakeholders affect others, including the company's employees. Organizations typically do not communicate on an ongoing basis with latent stakeholder groups including dormant, demanding and discretionary stakeholders.

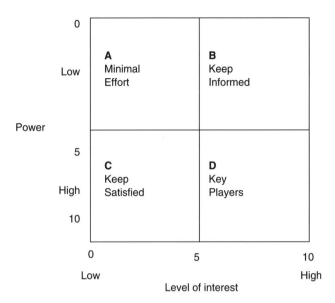

Figure 3.4 The power–interest matrix

The power–interest matrix

A second mapping device is based on the same principles as the stakeholder salience model. The general objective is to categorize stakeholders on the basis of the power that they possess and the extent to which they are likely to have or show an interest in the organization's activities. Practitioners would estimate stakeholders on these two variables and plot the location of the stakeholders in the matrix. Figure 3.4 displays these variables and the four cells in which stakeholders can be located.[21]

Similar to the stakeholder salience model, the idea again is that communication practitioners can formulate appropriate communication strategies on the basis of identifying and categorizing stakeholders. In particular, the reaction or position of 'key players' (quadrant D) towards the organization's decisions and operations must be given key consideration. They need to be constantly communicated with. Similarly, those with a high level of interest in the organization but with a low level of power or influence (quadrant B) need to be kept informed of the organization, so that they remain committed to the organization and may spread positive word-of-mouth to others. Stakeholders in quadrant C are the most challenging to maintain relationships with as, despite their lack of interest in general, these stakeholders might exercise their power in reaction to a particular decision or corporate activity. Practitioners should also remain sensitive to the possible movement of stakeholders from one quadrant to another when, for example, levels of interest in the organization change.

Stakeholder effects	awareness ———→	understanding ———→	involvement ———→	commitment
Tactics	Newsletters Reports Memos Free publicity	Discussions Meetings Advertising and educational campaigns	Consultation Debate	Early incorporation Collective problem-solving
Type of strategy	Informational strategy	Informational/ persuasive strategy	Dialogue strategy	

Figure 3.5 Stakeholder communication: from awareness to commitment

Both mapping devices provide an overview and ordering of the importance and influence of particular stakeholders to an organization in general terms (the stakeholder salience model and power–interest matrix) or in relation to a specific issue (the position–importance matrix). Based upon this ordering, organizations know how intensely they need to communicate with particular groups and also what the key messages should be. In other words, these mappings give an insight into whether stakeholders should only be kept informed of decisions of the organization or its stance on a particular issue, or instead whether stakeholders should be actively listened to and communicated with on an ongoing basis. In broad terms, stakeholders who are salient or have a powerful interest in the organization need to be communicated with so that they continue to support the organization. Important stakeholders such as customers, employees, suppliers and shareholders in any case need to be listened to and may also need to be actively involved in the decision-making of the organization. Figure 3.5 displays these differences between a strategy of simply providing information or disseminating information with stakeholders in order to raise their awareness, on the one hand, versus a strategy of actively communicating with stakeholders and incorporating them in the organization's decision-making, on the other.

An *informational strategy* is simply a strategy of informing someone about something. Press releases, newsletters and reports on a company website are often simply meant to make information available about the organization to its stakeholders. Such a strategy may create awareness of organizational decisions and may also contribute towards a degree of understanding of the reasons for these decisions. A second strategy that organizations can use is a *persuasive strategy* whereby an organization through campaigns, meetings and discussions with stakeholders tries to change and tune the knowledge, attitude, and behaviour of stakeholders in a way that is favourable to the organization. Corporate advertising and educational campaigns, for example, are often used to create a favourable image for the organization and to 'sell' a particular kind of understanding of the organization's decisions, its corporate values and its products and services. A third strategy that organizations may use is a *dialogue strategy* in which both parties (organizations and stakeholders) mutually engage in an exchange of ideas and opinions. A dialogue strategy involves active consultation of stakeholders and incorporation of important stakeholders into the organization's decision-making. It involves working towards a process of mutual understanding and/or mutual decisions rather than strategic self-interest on the part of the organization.

The use of each of these strategies will depend on the salience and power-interest of a stakeholder group and the need for active engagement with stakeholders to build long-term relationships with them and to provide them with opportunities to connect with the organization. For example, when powerful institutional shareholders challenge a company's executive payment and reward scheme, they become definitive stakeholders who not only need to be actively communicated with but ideally would also at the very least be consulted in future decisions about such matters (a dialogue strategy).

Schematically, these three strategies have been described as a one-way symmetrical model of communication (informational strategy), a two-way asymmetrical model of communication (persuasive strategy) and a two-way symmetrical model of communication (a dialogue strategy) as shown in Figure 3.6. In the first model, communication is always one-way, from the organization to its stakeholders. There is no listening to stakeholders or an attempt to gather feedback in this model. The aim is simply to make information available to stakeholders. However, the relationship between the organization and stakeholders is still 'symmetrical'. This means that communication practitioners aim to report objectively information about the organization to relevant stakeholders and do not try to persuade stakeholders regarding particular understandings, attitudes or behaviour. In other words, there is no explicit persuasive intent on the part of the practitioners which is labelled an 'asymmetrical' relationship between an organization and its stakeholders as that would involve a situation where the interests of the organization are emphasized at the expense of the interests of its stakeholders. In the second model, communication flows between an organization and its stakeholders and is thus labelled two-way communication. For example, an organization may gather feedback from stakeholders on how the organization is being perceived and understood. However, the two-way asymmetrical model is 'asymmetrical' because the effects of communication are unbalanced in favour of the organization. The organization does not change as a result of communicating with its stakeholders; instead, it only attempts to change stakeholders' attitudes and behaviours. The third model, the

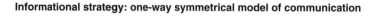

Figure 3.6   Models of organization–stakeholder communication

two-way symmetrical model, consists of a dialogue rather than a monologue. Communication again flows both ways between an organization and its stakeholders, but unlike the previous model, the goal is to exchange views and to reach mutual understanding between both parties. Both parties recognize the 'other' in the communication process and try to provide each other with equal opportunities for expression and for a free exchange of information.[22]

Each of these different strategies also requires different media or channels to communicate with stakeholders. Communication media or channels such as reports, adverts and face-to-face communication vary based on their capacity to process and channel 'rich' exchanges. A 'rich' exchange involves the ability to provide immediate feedback between the two parties, the ability to personalize and adapt messages based upon responses, and the ability to express and articulate the message in different ways.[23] Media that facilitate such 'rich' exchanges are central to a dialogue strategy and to some extent also feature in a persuasive strategy. These include face-to-face consultations and meetings and personalized documents such as letters or memos. Media which are less able to facilitate 'rich' exchanges, such as impersonal written documents (e.g. a financial report) are associated with an informational strategy where there is no direct need for the stakeholder to directly respond to the message. Face-to-face communication is the richest medium because it allows immediate feedback so that interpretations can be checked and subsequent communication can be adjusted. 'Rich' media are also useful for discussing ambiguous,

Table 3.2   Characteristics of the 'old' and 'new' approaches to organization–stakeholder relationships

Stakeholder management	Stakeholder collaboration
Fragmented among various departments	Integrated management approach
Focus on managing relationships	Focus on building relationships
Emphasis on 'buffering' the organization from stakeholders interfering with internal operations	Emphasis on 'bridging' and creating opportunities and mutual benefits
Linked to short-term business goals	Linked to long-term business goals
Idiosyncratic implementation dependent on department's interests and personal style of manager	Coherent approach driven by mission, values, and corporate strategies

sensitive, controversial or complex issues with stakeholders of the organization in order to overcome different frames of reference. Media of low 'richness' restrict immediate feedback and are therefore less appropriate for resolving ambiguous, sensitive, controversial or complex issues. However, an important point is that media of low richness are effective for reporting well-understood messages and standard data (such as, for example, reporting on financial performance).

3.6 Stakeholder engagement and collaboration

In recent years, communication practitioners have developed a focus on the importance of engaging stakeholders in long-term relationships. Rather than focusing on a simple instance of communication or of exchanging goods, recent efforts focus on changing the relationship between the organization and its stakeholders from 'management' to 'collaboration' and from 'exchange' to 'long-term relationships'. The emphasis has moved from a focus on stakeholders as being managed by companies to a focus on the interaction that companies have with their stakeholders on a continuous and relational basis. 'Collaboration' implies a two-way symmetrical model of dialogue and consultation through which communication practitioners build stakeholder relationships that are reciprocal, evolving and mutually defined, and that are a source of opportunity and competitive advantage.[24]

A summary of this change in focus is given in Table 3.2. The 'old' approach of stakeholder management consists of different practitioners and departments in the organization 'managing' interactions with stakeholders, often from the perspective of their own function or department. Another characteristic of the 'old' approach is the attempt to 'buffer' the claims and interests of stakeholders to prevent them from interfering with internal operations and instead trying to influence their attitudes and opinions. In this approach, in line with a persuasion strategy, an organization is trying either to insulate itself from external interference or to actively influence stakeholders in its environment through such means as contributions to political action committees, lobbying, and advocacy advertising. The 'new' approach of stakeholder collaboration, in contrast, involves an emphasis on stakeholder relationships across the organization. The aim here is to build long-term relationships and to seek out those stakeholders who are interested in collaboration. The 'new' approach is more in line with a dialogue strategy with its emphasis on 'bridging' stakeholder claims and interests. Bridging occurs when organizations seek to adapt their activities so that they conform with the external expectations and claims of important stakeholder groups. It suggests that an organization actively tries to meet and exceed regulatory requirements in its industry or that it attempts to quickly identify changing social expectations in order to promote organizational conformance to those expectations.

There are many examples of this change in approach to organization–stakeholder relationships. For example, many leading brands such as Saab, Lego and Harley Davidson now involve their customers in long-term relationships by incorporating them in their internal research and development (R&D) processes and through participation in branded on-line communities. Another good example is the way in which Merck, a pharmaceutical firm, engaged AIDS activist groups in the production and dissemination of vaccines and treatments for HIV sufferers.[25] Throughout the 1980s and 1990s, many AIDS activist groups had used aggressive tactics (e.g., demonstrations, disrupting trading at the New York Stock Exchange) aimed at pressurizing pharmaceutical companies to bring their treatments at the earliest possible date onto the market. Responding to these tactics, Merck enacted a series of relationship building tactics to pro-actively engage with these activist groups. First of all, the public affairs team at the company created an internal AIDS communication programme that helped members of the organization in their communication and relationship building with these activist groups. In order to educate employees about the issues, Merck developed educational programmes to teach employees (scientists and public affairs team members) how to best address the opportunities and challenges when dealing with members of the AIDS community. At the same time, Merck has on a continuous basis engaged with activists by organizing tours of research and development facilities and by arranging meetings with top researchers and public affairs staff so that activists can better understand the research process and will trust that the company is doing all it can to develop medicines and to get these approved by the US Food and Drug Administration. An important result of these meetings was that the activists, who were themselves often participating in clinical trials for the development of treatments, felt actively involved with the company and felt they had been given an opportunity to shape the company's drug trials and patient treatment guidelines.

CASE STUDY 3.3

STARBUCKS COFFEE COMPANY AND STAKEHOLDER COLLABORATION★

Starbucks, generally considered to be the most famous specialty coffee shop chain in the world, today has over 6,000 stores in more than 30 countries. Many analysts have credited Starbucks with having turned coffee from a commodity into an experience to savour.

Starbucks' aim has always been to be one of the most recognized and respected brands in the world. Since it made its IPO (initial public offering) in 1992, Starbucks has been growing at a rate of 20 per cent per annum with profits at a rate of 30 per cent per annum. Starbucks has always felt that the key to its growth and its business success would lie in a rounded corporate brand identity, a better understanding of its customers and a store experience that would generate a pull effect through word-of-mouth. Howard Schultz, Starbucks' founder and chairman, had early on in the company's history envisioned a retail experience that revolved around high-quality coffee, personalized, knowledgeable services and sociability. So Starbucks put in place various measures to make this experience appealing to millions of people and to create a unique identity for Starbucks' products and stores.

Schultz felt that the equity of the Starbucks brand depended less on advertising and promotion and more on personal communications, on strong ties with customers and with members of the local community and on word-of-mouth. As Schultz put it:

> If we want to exceed the trust of our customers, then we first have to build trust with our people. A brand has to start with the [internal] culture and naturally extend to our customers … Our brand is based on the experience that we control in our stores. When a company can create a relevant, emotional and intimate experience, it builds trust with the customer … we have benefited by the fact that our stores are reliable, safe and consistent where people can take a break.

Schultz regarded the baristas, the coffee makers in the stores, as his brand ambassadors and considered the company's employees as long-term 'partners' in making the company's strategic vision a reality. This commitment to employees is also anchored in Starbucks' mission statement which, among other things, states that the company aims to 'provide a great work environment and to treat each other with respect and dignity'.

From its founding onwards, Starbucks has looked upon each of its stores as a billboard for the company and as a contributor to building the company's brand and reputation. Each detail has been scrutinized to enhance the mood and ambience of the store, to make sure everything signalled 'best of class' and reflected the personality of the community and the neighbourhood. The company has gone to great lengths to make sure that the store fixtures, the

(Continued)

(Continued)

merchandise displays, the colours, the artwork, the banners, the music, and the
aromas all blend to create a consistent, inviting, stimulating environment that
evokes the romance of coffee and signals the company's passion for coffee.

Just as treating employees as 'partners' is one of the pillars of Starbucks' culture
and mission, so is contributing positively to the communities it serves and to the
environment. Each Starbucks store supports a range of community initiatives and
causes and aims to be a long-term 'partner' to the communities in which it trades.
At the community level, Starbucks store managers have discretion to make
money donations to local causes and to provide coffee for local fund-raisers.

Because of these initiatives, consumers and members of the community in
which Starbucks operate associate the Starbucks brand with coffee, accessible ele-
gance, community, individual expression, and 'a place away from home'. Besides
engaging in long-term relationships with customers, employees and communities, Starbucks has also tried to collaborate with non-governmental organizations
(NGOs) promoting the production and consumption of 'fair trade' coffee. Back
in 2000, Global Exchange, an NGO dedicated to promoting environmental,
political, and social justice around the world, had criticized the company for profiting at the expense of coffee farmers by paying low prices and not buying 'Fair
Trade' coffee beans. While the company is at times still being criticized for its
aggressive tactics in the coffee market, it has tried to collaborate with various
organizations to promote the consumption of fair trade coffee. Starbucks has
been an ongoing contributor to CARE, a worldwide relief and development
foundation, specifying that its support should go to coffee-producing nations.
The company also began a partnership in 1998 with Conservation International,
a non-profit organization that promotes biodiversity in coffee-growing regions,
to support producers of shade-grown coffee, which protects the environment.
Finally, in order to appease Global Exchange, Starbucks agreed to sell Fair Trade
coffee in all its stores. This decision has created a lot of goodwill from customers,
industry analysts, communities and NGOs worldwide.

However, Starbucks has recently (March 2007) come under fire for
attempting to block Ethiopia's desire to trademark some of its most famous
coffees. Premium coffee is a growing market, and to benefit from the rising
demand the Ethiopian government has set out to trademark three regions of
the country associated with its finest beans: Sidamo, Harar and Yirgacheffe.
The Ethiopian government asked Starbucks and other coffee companies to
sign a licensing agreement recognizing the brands. One large US coffee company, Green Mountain, has already done so. However, Starbucks objected to
the trademarks and has been working with its industry lobbyists (a buffering
tactic) to pressure the US Patent and Trademark Office to turn down
Ethiopia's trademark applications. As a result, the Office has refused to approve
two of the three trademarks. Oxfam has since taken up Ethiopia's cause in a
new media campaign, generating some 70,000 complaints against Starbucks
from consumers and the general public so far. In response, Starbucks has
launched a media counter-offensive, publicly rebuking Ethiopia's efforts. The
company claimed that licensing would be more appropriate than trademarking

the three coffee regions, and also argued that 'the trademark application is not based upon sound economic advice and that the proposal as it stands would hurt Ethiopian coffee farmers economically'. The active blocking of the Ethiopian government has led to a public realtions crisis for Starbucks with the normally ethically minded company accused of acting tough with one of the world's poorest countries.

Questions for reflection

1. Consider the importance for Starbucks of developing long-term relationships and alliances with different stakeholders. Should the company develop relationships and collaborate with all of its stakeholders or only a select few?
2. What strategies and models of communication should the company use for communicating with its different stakeholder groups?

Note: *This case study is based upon Holt, D. (2007), 'Brand hypocrisy at Starbucks' and 'Is Starbucks coffee that cares?' (http://www.sbs.ox.ac.uk/faculty/Holt+Douglas/) and Argenti, P.A. (2004), 'Collaborating with activists: how Starbucks works with NGOs', *California Management Review*, 47 (1): 91–116.

3.7 Chapter summary

This chapter has described the importance of stakeholder management within contemporary organizations. It has provided the theoretical background to the stakeholder theory of managing organizations and to different strategies and models which communication practitioners can use to identify and analyze the key stakeholders of the organization and to communicate and collaborate with them. The next chapter discusses how organizations use communication to build and maintain strong reputations with stakeholders.

KEY TERMS

Corporate social responsibility	Neo-classical economic theory
Dialogue strategy	Persuasive strategy
Economic/market stake	Socio-economic theory
Equity stakes	Stakeholder
Influencer stake	Stakeholder collaboration
Informational strategy	Stakeholder salience
Legitimacy	Triple bottom line

Notes

1 Preston, L.E. and Sapienza, H.T. (1990), 'Stakeholder management and corporate performance', *The Journal of Behavioral Economics*, 19: 361–375.

2 Social Economische Raad (2000), *De winst van waarden: ontwerpadvies over maatschappelijk ondernemen*. Den Haag: SER.

3 Friedman, M. (1970), 'The social responsibility of business is to increase its profits', *The New York Times Magazine*, September 13.

4 See Donaldson, T. and L.E. Preston (1995), 'The stakeholder theory of the corporation: concepts, evidence, and implications', *Academy of Management Review*, 20 (1): 65–91.

5 Freeman, R.E. (1984), *Strategic Management: A stakeholder approach*. Boston: Pitman; Kotler, P. (1986), 'Megamarketing', *Harvard Business Review*, March–April: pp.117–124; Baron, D.P. (1995), 'Integrated strategy: market and nonmarket components', *California Management Review*, 37 (2): 47–65.

6 Ansoff, I.A. (1960), *Corporate Strategy*. New York: Free Press.

7 Evan, W.M. and R.E. Freeman (1988), 'A stakeholder theory of the modern corporation: Kantian capitalism', in Beauchamp, T. and Bowie, N. (eds), *Ethical Theory and Business*. Englewood Cliffs, NJ: Prentice Hall, pp. 75–93, quote on p. 97; see also Drucker, P.F. (1980), *Managing in Turbulent Times*. New York: Harper and Row.

8 Berman, S.L., Wicks, A.C., Kotha, S. and Johnes, T.M. (1999), 'Does stakeholder orientation matter? The relationship between stakeholder management models and firm financial performance', *Academy of Management Journal*, 42 (5): 488–506; Jones, T. and Wicks, A. (1999), 'Convergent stakeholder theory', *Academy of Management Review*, 20: 404–437, quote on p. 206.

9 Jones and Wicks (1999), quote on p. 206, Porter, M.E. and Kramer, M.R. (2002), 'The competitive advantage of corporate philanthropy', *Harvard Business Review*, December: 5–16.

10 Kotter, J. and Heskett, J. (1992), *Corporate Culture and Performance*. New York: Free Press, p. 59.

11 Freeman (1984), p. 6.

12 Carroll, A.B. (1996), *Business and Society: Ethics and Stakeholder Management*. Cincinatti, OH: South-Western College Publishing, p. 473.

13 Clarkson, B.E. (1995), 'A stakeholder framework for analyzing and evaluating corporate social performance', *Academy of Management Review*, 20 (1): 92–117.

14 Charkham, J.P. (1992), *Keeping Good Company: A Study of Corporate Governance in Five Countries*. Oxford: Oxford University Press.

15 Windsor, D. (2001), 'The future of corporate social responsibility', *The International Journal of Organizational Analysis*, 9 (3): 225–256, quote on p. 226.

16 Berman et al. (1999); Margolis, J.D. and Walsh, J.P. (2003), 'Misery loves companies: rethinking social initiatives by business', *Administrative Science Quarterly*, 48: 268–305; and Orlitzky, M., Schmidt, F.L. and Rynes, S.L. (2003), 'Corporate social and financial performance: a meta-analysis', *Organization Studies*, 24: 403–441.

17 Elkington, J. (1997), *Cannibals with Forks: The Triple Bottom Line of the 21st Century Business*. London: Capstone Publishing Limited.

18 Carroll, A.B. (1991), 'The pyramid of corporate social responsibility: toward the moral management of organizational stakeholders', *Business Horizons*, 34 (4): 39–48.

19 Carroll, A.B. (1989), *Business and Society: Ethics and Stakeholder Management*. Cincinnati, OH: South-Western Publishing, p. 62.

20 Agle, B.R., Mitchell, R.K. and Sonnenfeld, J.A. (1999), 'Who matters to CEOs? An investigation of stakeholder attributes and salience, corporate performance, and CEO

values', *Academy of Management Journal*, 42 (5): 507–525; Mitchell, R.K., Agle, B.R. and Wood, D.J. (1997), 'Toward a theory of stakeholder identification and salience: defining the principle of who and what really counts', *Academy of Management Review*, 22 (4): 853–886.

21 Based upon Mendelow, A. *Proceedings of 2nd International Conference on Information Systems*, Cambridge, MA; also cited in Johnson, G. and Scholes, K. (1993), *Exploring Corporate Strategy: Text and Cases*, 3rd edn. London: Prentice Hall International, pp. 176–177.

22 Based upon Grunig, J.E. and Hunt, T. (1984), *Managing Public Relations*. New York: Holt, Rinehart and Winston; Deetz, S. (2006), 'Dialogue, communication theory, and the hope of making quality decisions together: a commentary', *Management Communication Quarterly*, 19: 368–375; Morsing, M. and Schultz, M. (2006), 'Corporate social responsibility communication: stakeholder information, response and involvement strategies', *Business Ethics: A European Review*, 15: 323–338.

23 Based upon Daft, R.L. and Lengel, R.H. (1986), 'Organizational information requirements, media richness and structural design', *Management Science* 32 (5): 554–571; and Kaplan, R.S. and Norton, D.P. (2001), *The Strategy-focused Organization: How Balanced Scorecard Companies Thrive in the New Business Environment*. Boston, MA: Harvard Business School Press.

24 Based on Svendsen, A. (1998), *The Stakeholder Strategy: Profiting from Collaborative Business Relationships*. San Francisco: Berrett-Koehler Publishers; Andriof, J., Waddock, S., Husted, B. and Rahman, S.S. (2002), *Unfolding Stakeholder Thinking: Theory, Responsibility and Engagement*. Sheffield: Greenleaf.

25 Based upon Taylor, M., Vasquez, G.M. and Doorley, J. (2003), 'Merck and AIDS activists: engagement as a framework for extending issue management', *Public Relations Review*, 29: 257–270.

4

Corporate Identity, Corporate Image and Corporate Reputation

CHAPTER OVERVIEW

One of the primary ways in which organizations manage relationships with stakeholders is through building and maintaining strong and differentiated corporate reputations. Such reputations are established when organizations consistently communicate and project an authentic, unique and distinctive corporate image towards stakeholders. Drawing on frameworks from theory and practice, the chapter discusses how organizations manage their corporate image and communication in order to establish, maintain and protect their corporate reputations with different stakeholder groups.

4.1 Introduction

Chapter 3 established the importance for organizations to communicate with different stakeholders for both moral (legitimacy) and instrumental (profit) reasons. It also discussed the challenges that organizations face in dealing with different expectations and demands of stakeholders. One way in which organizations have addressed this challenge is through strategically projecting a particular positive image of the organization, often labelled a corporate identity or corporate brand, to build, maintain and protect strong reputations with their stakeholders. Such strong reputations in turn lead to acceptance of the organization by different stakeholders and to the organization being found legitimate. Strong reputations also give organizations 'first-choice' status with investors, customers, employees and other stakeholder groups. For customers, for instance, a reputation serves as a signal of the underlying quality of an organization's products and services, and they therefore value associations and transactions with firms enjoying a good reputation. Equally, employees prefer to work for organizations with a good reputation, and will therefore work harder, or even for lower remuneration.

This chapter focuses on how organizations manage the process by which they project a particular corporate image of themselves and come to be seen and evaluated in a particular way by their stakeholders. The chapter starts by outlining traditional frameworks and principles of managing corporate identity, image and corporate reputation (Sections 4.2, 4.3 and 4.4) followed by more recent models to 'brand' the entire organization ('corporate branding') (Section 4.5).

4.2 Stakeholder communication, corporate identity and reputation

The emphasis that organizations, both in theory and practice, place on managing their corporate image suggests a preoccupation with how they *symbolically* construct an image (as a 'caring citizen', for example) for themselves through their communication and how in turn that image leads them to be seen in particular symbolic terms by important stakeholders. In other words, corporate image management adds an important symbolic dimension to corporate communication and the process by which organizations communicate with their stakeholders. Corporate communication is not only seen as a matter of exchanging *information* with stakeholders (an informational or dialogue strategy, see Chapter 3) so that they can make informed decisions about the organization, but also as a case of *symbolically* crafting and projecting a particular image for the organization. In many actual instances of corporate communication, the two dimensions may blend together and may be hard to separate. For example, when Tesco, a UK retailer, announced its sponsorship of Cancer Research UK, it provided people with information regarding the decision about its sponsorship (to fund research into the prevention, treatment and cure of cancer) and tied the sponsorship into the promotion of its Healthy Living range of products to support a healthy lifestyle. At the same time, through the sponsorship, the company aimed to project an image of itself as a caring and responsible corporate citizen contributing to the fight against one of the deadliest diseases around.

Investing in the development of a corporate image for the organization has further strategic advantages for organizations. These can be summarized under the following headings:

- *Distinctiveness*: a corporate image may help stakeholders find or recognize an organization. When consistently communicated, a corporate image creates awareness, triggers recognition, and may also instil confidence among stakeholder groups because these groups will have a clearer picture of the organization.[1] Inside the organization, a clear and strong image of the organization can

help raise motivation and morale among employees by establishing and perpet-
uating a 'we' feeling and by allowing people to identify with their organizations.

- *Impact*: a corporate image provides a basis for being favoured by stakeholders.
  This, in turn, may have a direct impact on the organization's performance when
  it leads to stakeholders supporting the organization in the form of buying its
  products and services, investing in the company or not opposing its decisions.
- *Stakeholders*: any individual may have more than one stakeholder role in relation
  to an organization. When organizations project a consistent image of themselves,
  they avoid potential pitfalls that may occur when conflicting images and messages are sent out. Employees, for example, are often also consumers in the marketplace for the products of the company that they themselves work for. When
  companies fail to send out a consistent image (often by failing to match all their
  internal and external communication), it threatens employees' perceptions of
  the company's integrity: they are told one thing by management, but perceive
  something different in the marketplace.

For these reasons, corporate image management is seen as an important objective
within corporate communication. In theory and practice, the original set of concepts that were introduced to describe this particular aspect of corporate communication involved corporate identity, corporate image and corporate reputation.

The concept of corporate identity grew out of a preoccupation in the design and
communication communities with the ways in which organizations present themselves to external audiences. Initially, the term was restricted to logos and other
elements of visual design, but it gradually came to encompass all forms of communication (corporate advertising, sponsorship, etc.) and all forms of outward-facing
behaviour in the marketplace. The German corporate design specialists Birkigt
and Stadler proposed one of the first models of corporate image management
(Figure 4.1).[2] Birkigt and Stadler's model put particular emphasis on the concept of
corporate identity which they defined as consisting of the following attributes:

- *symbolism*: corporate logos and the company house style (stationary, etc.) of an
  organization;
- *communication*: all planned forms of communication including corporate advertising, events, sponsorship, publicity and promotions;
- *behaviour*: all behaviour of employees (ranging from managers and receptionist
  to front-line staff such as sales people and shop assistants) that leaves an impression on stakeholders.

Through these three attributes, organizations communicate and project an
image of themselves to their stakeholders. Birkigt and Stadler also argued that
the image that organizations project through symbolism, communication and
behaviour is often also the way in which they are perceived by their stakeholders. The latter concept they called corporate image which involves the
image of an organization in the eyes of stakeholders.

One important implication of the Birkigt and Stadler model is that corporate identity has become quite a broad concept which encompasses more than

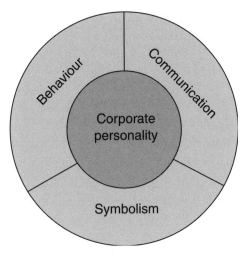

Figure 4.1   The Birkigt and Stadler model of corporate identity

corporate logos or corporate advertising campaigns. Because of its breadth, the concept also has a bearing upon different functional areas within the organization. Communication practitioners (including marketing communication professionals), while involved with senior management in the overall formulation of the corporate identity, often hold only the direct responsibility for corporate symbolism and communication, while product and brand managers are responsible for the positioning of products and services, and human resource staff and middle managers for the monitoring of employee behaviour.

A second important implication of the original Birkigt and Stadler model is that it suggests that corporate identity, as the outward presentation of an organization through symbolism, communication and behaviour, should emerge from an understanding of the organization's core mission, strategic vision and the more general corporate culture of an organization. The mission and vision represent the basic who and what of an organization; what business the organization is in and what it wants to be known and appreciated for. An organization's mission often already includes a statement on the beliefs that constitute the organization's culture, underpin its strategy and suggests how the organization wants to be known by stakeholder groups outside the organization. Birkigt and Stadler called the notion of core values in the organization's culture, mission and vision the concept of corporate personality. Design guru Wally Olins articulates the difference between corporate personality and corporate identity as follows:

> Corporate personality embraces the subject at its most profound level. It is the soul, the persona, the spirit, the culture of the organization manifested in some way. A corporate personality is not necessarily something tangible that you can see, feel or touch – although it may be. The tangible manifestation of a corporate personality is a corporate identity. It is the identity that projects and reflects the reality of the corporate personality.[3]

In other words, corporate identity involves the construction of an image of the organization to differentiate a company's position in the eyes of important stakeholder groups. Corporate personality, on the other hand, is based on deeper patterns of meaning and sense-making of people within that same organization and includes the core values that define the organization.

The French sociologists Larçon and Reitter added a further dimension to the concept of corporate identity when they similarly argued that it not only involves the visible outward presentation of a company, but also the set of intrinsic characteristics or 'traits' that give the company its specificity, stability and coherence.[4] In their view, a corporate identity is not merely a projected image in the form of visual design and communication, but is also fundamentally concerned with 'what the organization is' – the core of the organization as it is laid down in its strategies and culture. This notion of corporate identity 'traits' since then has often been referred to as an 'organizational' identity as opposed to a 'corporate' identity, again to make the distinction between core values that people share within the organization ('organizational identity' or 'corporate personality') and the outward presentation and communication of those values through symbolism, communication and behaviour ('corporate identity'). Albert and Whetten, who were among the first in 1985 to define this notion of 'organizational' identity, similarly talked about specific characteristics or 'traits' of an organization in all its strategies, values and practices that give the company its specificity, stability and coherence. They argued that just as individuals express a sense of personal distinctiveness, a sense of personal continuity, and a sense of personal autonomy, equally organizations have their own individuality and uniqueness. And just as the identity of individuals may come to be anchored in some combination of gender, nationality, profession, social group, life style, educational achievements or skills, so an organization's identity may be anchored in some combination of geographical place, nationality, strategy, founding, core business, technology, knowledge base, operating philosophy or organization design. For each organization, according to Albert and Whetten, its particular combination of identity anchors imbues it with a set of distinctive values that are core, distinctive and enduring to it.[5] For example, many would argue that Sony's differentiation in the marketplace is quality consumer products, and they certainly do have ability in that area. But what makes Sony truly distinctive is the company's core value of 'miniaturization'; of producing ever smaller technology. This feature of miniaturization, which goes hand in hand with a drive for technological innovation, is at the heart of Sony's organizational identity or corporate personality. At the same time, this organizational identity has been carried through in all products, services, and communications; that is, in Sony's corporate identity. Similarly, Virgin, a company that is active in very different markets (e.g., airlines, music stores, cola, and mobile phones) has meticulously cultivated the value of 'challenge' with all of its employees. Headed by its flamboyant CEO Richard Branson, Virgin has carried its core

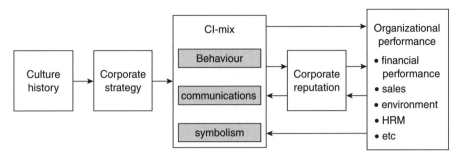

Figure 4.2 Corporate identity in relation to corporate reputation

Source: Based on C.B.M. Van Riel, and J. Balmer (1997), 'Corporate identity: The concept, its measurement and management', *European Journal of Marketing*, 31: 342.

organizational identity of 'challenge' through in its distinctive market position-ing of David versus Goliath; 'we are on your side against the fat cats'. This pro-jected corporate identity has led to the widespread perception that Virgin is a company with a distinctive personality: innovative and challenging, but fun.

Figure 4.2 summarizes the process of corporate image management as orig-inally articulated by Birkigt and Stadler. The aim of corporate image manage-ment is to establish a favourable reputation with the organization's stakeholders which it is hoped will be translated by such stakeholders into a propensity to buy that organization's products and services, to work for that organization, or to invest in it (organizational performance). In other words, a good corporate reputation has a strategic value for the organization that possesses it. It ensures acceptance and legitimacy from stakeholder groups, generates returns, and may offer a competitive advantage as it forms an asset that is difficult to imitate. A good corporate reputation, or rather the corporate identity upon which it is based, is an intangible asset of the organization because of its potential for value creation, but also because its intangible character makes replication by compet-ing firms more difficult.[6] Figure 4.2 shows the corporate identity mix (sym-bolism, communication and behaviour of members of the organization) as based on the organization's core values in its history and culture and which inform every part of its strategy.

The general principle for corporate communication practitioners is that they need to link the corporate identity – the picture of the organization that is pre-sented to external stakeholders – to the core values that members of the orga-nization themselves associate with the organization (culture) and define the organization's mission and vision (organizational identity or corporate person-ality). Making sure that the corporate identity is rooted in the organizational identity not only offers a distinctive edge in the marketplace, but also ensures that the image that is projected is authentic rather than cosmetic and actually carried and shared by members of the organization. In this context, corporate identity and organizational identity or corporate personality rather should be seen as two sides of the same coin within corporate communication. Developing a corporate identity must start with a thorough analysis and understanding of the organization's core values in its mission, vision and culture, rather than rushing into communicating what might be thought to be the company's core values in a superficial manner. Equally, whatever picture is projected to external stakeholders has an effect upon the beliefs and values of employees, and thus on the organizational identity or corporate personality, as employees mirror themselves in whatever messages are being sent out to external stakeholder groups.[7] The two sides to identity in organizations, organizational identity (or corporate personality) and corporate identity, therefore cannot and should not be seen as separate. This point is reinforced by studies into 'excellent' companies carried out over the past two decades. Writers such as Hamel and Prahalad, Peters and Waterman, and Collins and Porras, have found that what truly sets an 'excellent' company apart from its competitors in the marketplace in terms of the power of its image and products can be traced back to a set of values and related competencies that are authentic and unique to that organization and therefore difficult to imitate. Collins and Porras, in their analysis of companies that are industry leaders in the United States, argue that 'a visionary company almost religiously preserves its core ideology – changing it seldom, if ever'.[8] From this adherence to a fundamental set of beliefs or a deeply held sense of self-identity, as Collins and Porras point out, comes the discipline and drive that enable a company to succeed in the rapidly changing, volatile environments that characterize many contemporary markets.

In relation to the connections between corporate identity, organizational identity/corporate personality and corporate reputation, it is emphasized that it is strategically important for organizations to achieve 'alignment' or 'transparency' between them.[9] According to Fombrun and Rindova, transparency is 'a state in which the internal identity of the firm reflects positively the expectations of key stakeholders and the beliefs of these stakeholders about the firm reflect accurately the internally held identity'.[10] Along these lines, many practitioners, consultants and academic researchers stress the importance of alignment between (a) the organizational culture as articulated by senior managers and as experienced by employees (organizational identity and corporate personality); (b) corporate identity (i.e., the image projected by the organization); (c) corporate image (i.e., a stakeholder's immediate impression of an organization in relation to a specific message or image); and (d) corporate reputation (i.e., a stakeholder's collective representation of past images of an organization (induced through either communication or past experiences) established over time). Importantly too, where these elements are non-aligned (so that, for example, the rhetoric of corporate identity does not match the experienced reality), a range of sub-optimal outcomes are anticipated including employee disengagement, customer dissatisfaction and general organizational atrophy.

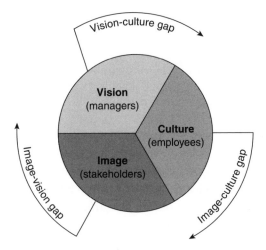

Figure 4.3 Toolkit to assess the alignment between vision, culture and image

4.3 Aligning identity, image and reputation

A useful way of analysing the alignment between an organization's culture, corporate identity and image or reputation is the toolkit developed by Hatch and Schultz.[11] The toolkit (Figure 4.3) consists of a number of diagnostic questions based on three elements:

- *vision*: senior management's aspirations for the organization;
- *culture*: the organization's values as felt and shared by all employees of the organization;
- *image*: the image or impression that outside stakeholders have of the organization.

The questions each relate to a particular interface between the three elements and are meant to identify the alignment between them. The first set of questions involves the interface between vision and culture; that is, how managers and employees are aligned. They are:

- Does the organization practise the values it promotes?
- Does the organization's vision inspire all its subcultures?
- Are the organization's vision and culture sufficiently differentiated from those of its competitors?

There is a potential for misalignment (*vision–culture gap*) here when senior management moves the organization in a strategic direction that employees do not understand or support. For example, senior managers may establish a vision that is too ambitious for the organization to implement and is not supported by its employees.

The second set of questions involves the interface between culture and image and is meant to identify potential gaps between the values of employees and the perceptions of stakeholders outside of the organization. The questions are:

- What images do stakeholders associate with the organization?
- In what ways do its employees and stakeholders interact?
- Do employees care what stakeholders think of the organization?

Misalignment between an organization's image and organizational culture (*image–culture gap*) leads to confusion among stakeholders such as customers and investors about what a company stands for. For example, employees of the organization may not practise what the company preaches in its advertising, leaving a tarnished image with its stakeholders. The final set of questions addresses the interface between vision and image. The key objective here is to find out whether management is taking the organization in a direction that its stakeholders support. The questions are:

- Who are the organization's stakeholders?
- What do the stakeholders want from the organization?
- Is the organization effectively communicating its vision to its stakeholders?

There is potential for misalignment (*image–vision gap*) here when organizations do not sufficiently listen to their stakeholders and create strategic visions that are not aligned with what stakeholders want or expect from the organization. These three sets of diagnostic questions help an organization meet the expectations of its stakeholders.

A classic example of an organization that failed to sufficiently align its vision, culture and image is British Airways (see Case Study 9.1). When Robert Ayling was CEO of British Airways, he and other senior managers articulated a vision for the company of becoming 'the undisputed leader in world travel'. This vision was coupled with a repositioning of the company in 1997 which involved blending the traditional British values of the company with new values of cosmopolitanism and global appeal. To give this repositioning shape, BA unveiled a striking new visual identity in June 1997. The 50 ethnic designs commissioned from artists around the world were meant to adorn the tailfins of BA's entire fleet, as well as ticket jackets, cabin crew scarves and business cards. Over the next three years, the idea was that the new look would gradually replace the sober blue and red livery and crest along with the traditional motto 'to fly, to serve' which dated back to 1984. The decision to change was based on market research in the early 1990s which had suggested that passengers viewed the airline as staid and stuffy. As Ayling commented at the time; 'We don't want to ram our Britishness down people's throats …There's no empire. We're just a small nation on an offshore island trying to make our way into the world.' The vision of senior managers within BA was that the repositioning presented the airline with an opportunity not just to tone down its national origins and project a more modern image, but also to reposition itself as a 'citizen of the world' in recognition of the fact that 60 per cent of BA's passengers came from outside the UK.

The colourful designs did attract tremendous free publicity at the time, with the front pages of most British newspapers featuring large colour photos. But they also generated more controversy than anticipated, many seeing the revamp as extravagant, confusing, or in the case of the then Prime Minister Margaret Thatcher, a national betrayal. At the launch of the new designs, Margaret Thatcher famously draped her handkerchief over one of the new designs. The backlash was disappointing, but Ayling hoped at the time that these emotionally charged reactions from the more conservative-minded sections of the British public would soon blow over. However, the negative news coverage of the new designs endured and carried over to BA customers and the general public in the UK who then voted with their feet (*vision–image gap*). BA customers appreciated the company's traditional values and British heritage which they felt were being lost with the new designs and repositioning. In addition to repainting the planes' tail fins, the company had also decided to remove the British flag from all its aircraft. This triggered a strike by cabin crew who apparently did not agree with the new corporate values and also felt that they had not been included in consultations on the new vision (*vision–culture gap*). Employees not only disagreed with the new vision, they also did not share and live the new values of a multicultural ethos as communicated in the new designs. Because they did not embody these values, there was thus a real potential for a gap between what the company communicated (cosmopolitanism) and employee behaviour which was still firmly rooted in a sense of Britishness and stakeholder images (*image–culture gap*). Before it came to that, Ayling and his senior management team acknowledged that they had made a wrong decision and abandoned the programme. When Rodd Eddington took over from Ayling as CEO in 2000, he announced a return to British livery and reintroduced the Union Flag on each tailfin of the BA fleet.

It is important for organizations to monitor the alignment between their vision, culture and image so that they can make adjustments accordingly. All three interfaces are equally important to an organization in order to make sure that images (corporate identity) are projected to stakeholders that are carried by both senior managers (vision) and employees (culture) and furthermore understood and appreciated by stakeholders (image).

When the image or reputation of stakeholders is broadly consistent with the projected images in communication, symbolism and behaviour, it also ensures that the organization is respected and understood in the way in which it wants and aims to be understood.[12] Alternatively, when there is a gap between the projected identity of an organization and the way in which it is regarded, an organization is not standing out on its own turf and may not have a strong enough reputation as a result. Its reputation is then rather based upon more general associations with the industry in which the organization is based or is informed by reports from the media. Shell, for instance, in the wake of the Brent Spar oil rig crisis (see Case Study 10.1) realized that its lousy reputation in the 1990s had more often than not been based upon media reports and the tainted image of the oil industry than its own identity and the values that were at the heart of its business and operations. Shell has since put considerable effort into a rethinking of its identity and values, redesigning systems for stakeholder management, and running a global identity campaign to close the gap between its identity and reputation.

Continuously measuring images or reputations with stakeholders is thus essential in order to understand what stakeholders think of an organization, whether this is in line with the projected corporate identity of the organization, and whether the organization is accepted and valued. Communication practitioners need to find out what values the company is respected for and whether the projected values in communication, symbolism and behaviour are actually salient in the minds of stakeholders. This will provide them with an important strategic indication as to whether the company's identity is at all valued and whether the company's identity has been successfully communicated. In the first scenario, when a company's identity in itself is not valued enough, managers may want to redefine their organization, strategies and operations with values that do matter to stakeholders and make a difference in the marketplace. Corporate giants such as BP (see Chapter 2) and Shell, in the oil sector, in the restyling of their identities into responsible businesses are a good example of this. When an identity is not effectively communicated or understood, the second scenario, management needs to rethink the company's stakeholder engagement programmes and the visibility and effectiveness of the communication tools that it has previously used (Chapter 3). Getting feedback from reputation research is an important step in the process of developing and refining corporate identity strategies including stakeholder engagement and communications programmes.

Such feedback can be gathered through two broad types of reputation research: (1) publicly syndicated rankings; and (2) company-specific reputation research. Table 4.1 provides a summary of three publicly syndicated reputation rankings. Each of these rankings enjoys popularity with managers but all have obvious limitations in that they fail to account for the views of multiple stakeholder groups, and appear to be primarily tapping a firm's financial performance and assets. The Fortune measure, for instance, is known for its financial bias and the high correlation between all of the measure's nine (previously eight) attributes (>0.60). This means that these nine attributes produce, when factor analyzed, one factor, so that a company tends to rate high, or average, or low, on all nine attributes.[13] These publicly syndicated rankings converge on a number of areas including financial performance, product quality, employee treatment, community involvement, environmental performance, and a range of other organizational issues (such as supporting equality of opportunity and diversity, good environmental performance, improved ethical behaviour, and so on).[14] But

Table 4.1 Overview of the *Fortune*, RepTrak Pulse and *Financial Times* Reputation Surveys

	Fortune's 'most admired corporations'	RepTrak Pulse	*Financial Times* 'world's most respected companies'
Method and sample	Annual survey of over 10,000 senior executives, outside directors and financial analysts	Annual survey of a large sample of consumers (approx. 60,000) who are asked to evaluate the 600 largest companies in the world	Annual questionnaire to 1,000 CEOs/senior executives in over 20 countries and 22 business sectors, complemented by a selected cross-section of fund managers, non-governmental organizations (NGOs) and media commentators
Measure	Ranking is based upon the compilation of assessments given by respondents of the ten largest companies in their own industry on nine criteria of 'excellence'	Ranking is based upon averaging perceptions of trust, esteem, admiration, and good feeling obtained from a representative sample of 100 local respondents who are familiar with the company.	Simple ranking on the basis of nomination by CEOs, and weighted by GDP of the respondent's country.
Attributes included	Quality of management, quality of products and services, innovativeness, long-term investment value, financial soundness, ability to attract, develop and keep talented people, responsibility to the community and the environment, wise use of corporate assets, global acumen	Four attributes: trust, esteem, admiration, and good feeling about a company	Most important unprompted reasons given behind nominations are business performance (growth and long-term profitability) clear leadership and people management, effective strategy of market capitalization, high quality products and services, and policies and procedures to assess business' environmental impact

these rankings do not take into account that stakeholder opinions vary and that stakeholder groups attend to very different cues when forming an opinion of an organization. Some stakeholder groups would not at all be interested in some of these areas, or would in any case not rate them in their evaluation of the company. Furthermore, the distinctive values that a company may project, and that are extracted from its organizational identity or corporate personality, are not necessarily captured by these publicly syndicated measures.

When communication practitioners plan to set up their own company-specific reputation research, they need to be conscious of the fact that a corporate reputation is not just a general impression but an evaluation of the firm by stakeholders. According to reputation expert Charles Fombrun, a corporate reputation is 'a perceptual representation of a company's past actions and future prospects that describe the firm's overall appeal to all of its key constituents when compared to other leading rivals'.[15] Whereas corporate images concern the immediate impressions of individual stakeholders when they are faced with a message that comes from an organization, reputations are more endurable evaluations that are established over time. Conceptually, a corporate image may be defined as the immediate set of associations of an individual in response to one or more signals or messages from or about a particular organization. In other words, it is the net result of the interaction of a subject's beliefs, ideas, feelings and impressions about an organization at a single point in time. Corporate reputation can be defined as a subject's collective representation of past images of an organization (induced through either communication or past experiences) that is established over time. Images might vary in time due to differing perceptions, but reputations are more likely to be relatively inert or constant, as individuals and stakeholders retain their assessment of an organization built in over time.[16] Gray and Balmer, two academics, illustrate this distinction between the image and reputation constructs:

> Corporate image is the immediate mental picture that audiences have of an organization. Corporate reputations, on the other hand, typically evolve over time as a result of consistent performance, reinforced by effective communication, whereas corporate images can be fashioned more quickly through well-conceived communication programs.[17]

These properties of the reputation construct provide the basis for developing operational measures and for surveying opinions of important stakeholder groups. First of all, the time dimension (as reputation is an established perception over time) needs to be factored into the measurement process by having respondents evaluate a company (vis-à-vis its nearest rivals) *generally* instead of having them reflect upon a single instant (e.g. a crisis) or image (e.g. campaign) in relation to that company. Second, reputation is a perceptual construct, so simple proxy measures of the assets, performance or output of a particular organization will not be enough. And third, measurement and also the sampling of respondents need to account for the various attributes upon which an organization is rated by different stakeholder groups.

Table 4.2 Corporate reputation research methods

Methodology	Techniques	Data collection	Number of respondents	Ease of analysis	Costs
Qualitative	Unstructured interview	Oral interview: each respondent is asked to reflect upon his/her views of an organization and explain why (with or without use of visual aids)	10–40	Moderate/low	Moderate
	Focus group	Group discussion: in a group, respondents discuss their views of the organization and explain why (with or without use of visual aids)	5–10 (each group)	High	Moderate
	Repertory grid	Oral interview: each respondent is asked to pick two out of three statements which match the organization best or worst and explain why	10–40	Moderate	Low
	Laddering	Oral interview: each respondent is asked to reflect upon beliefs about organization aimed at discovering means–ends relations	10–25	Low	High
Quantitative	Attitude scales/ attribute rating	Questionnaire: respondent ratings of attributes on Likert scales	50 or more	Moderate/ high	Moderate
	Q-sort	Oral interview: each respondent is asked to rate and rank statements about the organization written on cards	30–50	Low	Moderate

Different types of research techniques may be used to gather reputational data. These techniques exclude the publicly syndicated measures such as the Fortune 'most admired companies' and FT's 'most respected companies' which are a secondary source of research information that managers and communications practitioners can tap into to gain some information about the standing of their organizations (when these are included in the rankings). Better still is for a company to set up and conduct reputation research of its own with applied research techniques and its own stakeholder groups. In doing so, a company will be able to account for the diversity of opinions of its stakeholder groups and will have a clearer view of the attributes that these different groups actually find important and rate the organization on. Table 4.2 displays the two broad classes of research techniques, qualitative and

Companies X and Y compared						
Reputation factor	Very poor	Poor	Average	Good	Excellent	Factor importance
Quality of management team			X	Y		4.3
Quality and range of products					XY	3.8
Community and environmental responsibility				X	Y	4.1
Financial soundness			XY			4.0
Innovativeness of operations		X		Y		3.8
Industry leadership			Y	X		2.3

Figure 4.4   The corporate reputation of two companies compared

quantitative, that may be used either separately or in combination for reputation research.[18]

Qualitative research such as in–depth interviews with individual stakeholders or focus group sessions with selected groups of stakeholders are one option. These qualitative techniques are more open in nature; they allow selected stakeholders to delve into their associations with the organization as they see them. This usually provides very rich and anecdotal data of stakeholder views of the company. Quantitative research where stakeholders are asked to rate the organization (and its nearest rivals) on a number of pre-selected attributes is another option. Quantitative research leads to more discrete data that can be statistically manipulated, but is less rich and may also be less insightful (i.e. it reflects to a lesser extent the particular lens of the individual stakeholder). The choice of either qualitative or quantitative research techniques is based on content issues as well as pragmatic and political considerations. Qualitative techniques are chosen when the attributes upon which an organization is rated are simply not yet known, or when there is a need for a comprehensive, detailed, and rich account of stakeholders' perceptions and associations with the organization. Quantitative surveys are preferred when the attributes upon which an organization is rated are to a large extent known, allowing for a structured measurement across large sections of stakeholder groups. Many organizations also opt for quantitative surveys as these are relatively easy to administer and process and as they provide them with a 'tangible' indication (that is, a number). Figure 4.4 illustrates the reputations of two organizations through an attribute rating that produces such numerical values. A 'tangible' indication is also one of the motives for organizations to buy into panel studies such as the RepTrak Pulse, which provides them with a score that they can work with, and sets a benchmark for future years.

4.4 Identifying the distinctive nature of the organization's identity

Surveying the opinions of stakeholders regarding the organization is essential to capture their views of the organization and its relative standing in the sector in which it is operating; and to offset a strict view upon the company's core values in its organizational identity or corporate personality alone. Organizations cannot myopically focus internally on their identities alone and trust that on the back of their identity's strength they will achieve glowing reputations. Equally, organizations should not be led only by stakeholder opinions (and opportunistically manufacture and fashion a corporate identity for it), as such opinions may be fickle and can sometimes be short-lived. Therefore, an internal orientation on organizational identity, which may be a source of inspiration and differentiation, needs to be balanced with an external stakeholder orientation, so that a company avoids short-sightedly focusing on solely one.[19] Polaroid, for example, is a case in point. The company had from its beginning created a strong and distinctive identity around its business model and core competence of instant photography. Conforming to this identity, the focus was originally on self-developing film technology, garnering healthy profits on the film technology while earning relatively little on the cameras. This worked well until the advent of digital photography, which offered instant photographs but made film unnecessary. Digital photography altered investors' and consumers' expectations, and as Polaroid was rather slow in following suit (and redefining itself as an imaging company and moving into digital photography), it had to file for Chapter 11 bankruptcy protection in October 2001. Surveying and being attuned to the reputation that an organization has with its stakeholders provides an important strategic indication as to whether the company's identity is at all valued and whether it has been successfully communicated.

At the same time, communication practitioners and other managers within the organization need to open up the dialogue about the core values of the organization with employees and discuss them systematically and concretely.[20] This often results in a soul-searching exercise that senior managers and communications practitioners should engage in (see Table 4.3 overleaf) aimed at producing and triggering the attributes and values of the organization that are perceived as authentic, that characterize it, are unique to it, and set it apart from other companies in its sector. Wal-Mart offers a good example. Its credo of 'giving working people the opportunity to buy the same things previously available only to wealthier people' is wonderful, but is just a generic aspect of its positioning and pricing strategy; and is not the one specific feature that is differentiating or hard to imitate by rival firms. What is unique to Wal-Mart, however, are its core values of 'community' and 'partnership' that lie at the root of its founding and has led to the company's success. 'Community' and 'partnership' are values that are meticulously carried through in its stores, advertising campaigns, employee ownership schemes, and supply chain management. Wal-Mart has for instance changed the role of their suppliers into partners with them in their stores, thereby cunningly shifting inventory responsibilities back to the suppliers.

Without doubt, the values that an organization, through its members, considers to be true, authentic and differentiating stretch beyond corporate communication and the remit of communication practitioners alone. The CEO and the senior management team are the most obvious patrons of organization-wide identity questions as well as of the way in which these are translated into mission and vision documents and spread throughout the organization. When Carlos Ghosn, for instance, took the helm at Nissan in 1999 he personally led the restoration and strengthening of Nissan's identity, which had become sloppy, weak and insufficiently exploited.[21] Alongside a restructuring and cost-cutting programme to boost productivity and profitability (for which he took a lot of flak), Ghosn revamped Nissan's identity of quality engineering and the uniquely Japanese combination of keen competitiveness and a sense of community. He ensured that through his own performance and commitment as well as through internal communication these values trickled down through the ranks to embrace all employees.

As the example of Nissan shows, it is important that a sense of organizational identity is internalized by members of the organization, so that they can live and enact the company's values in their day-to-day work. Particularly those members of the organization who personally represent the organization in the eyes of stakeholders such as the CEO, front-office personnel and front-line staff (salespeople, retail staff), and those who are responsible for marketing and communication need to have a fine grasp of the organization's core ideology and values. Senior managers, with the help of senior communication practitioners, as experts on stakeholder management, can facilitate this understanding by articulating and actively communicating the company's values to all staff within the organization through policy documents and internal communication (see also Chapter 8).

A number of analytical tools are available to senior managers and senior communication practitioners for drawing out and articulating the organizational identity (Table 4.3). These different tools, ranging from management exercises to more psychological projective tests, can all be used to elicit the values within the organizational identity of the organization, but vary in measurement (open versus closed measurement) and in pragmatic considerations such as the ease of analysis and the costs involved in their use:

1. *Cobweb method*: this method consists of a group of senior managers coming together and sharing their views on the organization's key characteristics in a management session. At the beginning of the session, these managers are asked to name those attributes, which, in their opinion, best characterize and define

Table 4.3 Organizational identity research methods

Method	Participants	Data collection	Ease of analysis	Expert analysts needed	Costs
Cobweb method	Group of senior managers	Brainstorm session	High	No	Low
Focus group	Groups of senior managers and employees	Brainstorm session	High	No; but group facilitator (consultant)	Low–moderate
Projective tests	Groups of senior managers and employees	Interviews with use of visual aids	Low	Yes; trained psychologist/ researcher	Low–moderate
Laddering/critical incident	Groups of senior managers and employees	Open interviews	Low	Yes; trained researcher	Low–moderate
Audit/survey	Groups of senior managers and employees	Questionnaire	High	Yes; trained researcher	Low–moderate

the organization. This part of the session is a brainstorming exercise, so there are no true or false answers regarding the attributes that are mentioned. After this brainstorming session, managers have to choose eight attributes that they consider to be most relevant and to have most value in describing the organization. These eight attributes can then be visually displayed in the form of a wheel with eight scaled dimensions upon which, for further definition, the organization can be rated (and which can be further compared with stakeholder views of those attributes). The method is very easily carried out, but has obvious limitations in that it only captures the views of managers regarding the key characteristics of the organization.

2. *Focus group*: this method has the advantage over the cobweb method in that a broader group of representatives from the organization can be selected; and their views of the key characteristics of the organization can be captured in a more detailed manner. A focus group starts with a brainstorming session in which all participants are asked to write down (on oval cards) and share their views on the identity of the organization. After each participant has articulated his or her views, these ovals are grouped and structured into a map on a blackboard, providing a synthesis of each participant's views upon the identity of the organization. Further analysis and groups discussions then follow to select the key characteristics that, according to the group, best define the organization.

3. *Projective techniques*: These techniques (including cognitive mapping and repertory grids) stem from psychotherapy and aim to generate rich ideas and to involve individual members of the organization in a discussion of a subject such as organizational identity that may be difficult to verbalize in discrete terms. Visual aids such as pictures, cards, diagrams or drawn out metaphors may be used to elicit a response. These visual aids are usually designed to be ambiguous so that respondents will 'project' their own meaning and significance onto the visuals. By doing so, they will declare aspects of their deeper

values, beliefs and feelings concerning the organization, and this can be used for a further discussion of the key aspects of the organization. A common form of projective technique is the thematic apperception test (TAT). This approach asks individuals to simply write a story about an image that depicts a work situation; the researcher's task is then to find themes in what people say about their organization.[22]

4. *Laddering/critical incident*: this widely used management technique can also be applied to organizational identity, where it is used to infer the basic values that guide people's work in an organization. The method involves open interviews where employees are asked to describe what they do on a daily basis and how they look upon their work. Such descriptions of critical work incidents can then be further analyzed to decipher the underlying values. The method can, when aggregated, give important insights into the general values that people working within an organization seem to share.[23]

5. *Audit or survey*: a more structured research method involves an audit or survey that asks members of the organization to select from lists of attributes those characteristics that best define the organization. The selected characteristics can then be further screened by asking respondents in the same survey to evaluate the importance and value of each of the selected characteristics in describing the organization. Surveys are easy to administer, but may not be able to capture the richness and detail of organizational identity which more open methods can.

Once the values and attributes that make up an organizational identity are drawn out and made explicit, senior managers and communication practitioners need to consider whether the identified values are inspiring and stand out, whether they offer potential for differentiation in the marketplace, and whether they are likely to be appreciated by stakeholders of the organization. In other words, it needs to be decided whether the elicited core values are to play a role in the corporate identity mix and are to be made public through products and services, through communication and through employee behaviour. Some of the values expressed through the corporate identity mix will in fact derive from the organizational identity; other values may be included because of the sector in which the organization is operating or because of the expectations of its stakeholder groups.

Reputation scholars Fombrun and Van Riel have carried out comparative analyses of corporate reputations of the most visible organizations across the world. Based upon stakeholder evaluations of the strongest corporate reputation within different countries, Fombrun and Van Riel inferred that organizations with the strongest reputations are on average characterized by high levels of *visibility* (the degree to which corporate themes are visible in all internal and external communication), *distinctiveness* (the degree to which the corporate identity or positioning of the organization is distinctive), *authenticity* (the degree to which an organization communicates values that are embedded in its culture), *transparency* (the degree to which an organization is open and transparent about its behaviour), and *consistency* (the degree to which organizations communicate consistent messages through all internal and external communication channels) in corporate communication.[24] In other words, a key driver for the strength of an organization's reputation is the degree to which the values that it communicates are not only authentic but also distinctive.

Many brand managers and communication practitioners indeed draw heavily on the idea of uniqueness of distinctiveness because it encapsulates the idea that the organization needs to express its uniqueness in the market and with other stakeholders. The idea is that this enables an organization to differentiate itself from its competitors and to attain a preferred 'position' in the consciousness of consumers and other stakeholders. While differentiated corporate values are seen as important in communicating a unique or distinct identity to stakeholders, recent research has also demonstrated that organizations in specific industry sectors may become more similar in the kinds of corporate identity that they project and that such convergence may be more or less appreciated by stakeholders dependent upon their expectations regarding appropriate corporate behaviour in a particular industry.[25] Communication scholars Deephouse and Carter have demonstrated that isomorphism (i.e., the similarity of an organization to others in its industry) improves the degree to which an organization is deemed legitimate (socially acceptable) by stakeholders, presumably because organizations converge on images and behaviours that are expected of them by stakeholders.[26]. They also found that organizations with stronger corporate reputations were able to deviate from such pressures to communicate similar images and improve their distinct status without loosing their legitimacy. Management scholars Lamertz, Heugens and Calmet similarly identified social pressures which stimulated organizations in the Canadian beer brewing industry to construct similar images (corporate identity) of themselves to meet stakeholder expectations. At the same time, they also found that alongside such similar images these beer brewing organizations also claimed distinctive attributes as part of their corporate identity.[27]

What this evidence suggests is that it is, first of all, important for organizations to claim the same generic values (e.g., technological innovation, customer care, ethical conduct) as its rivals in order to meet expectations of stakeholders that the organization is financially solid, socially engaging and ecologically sound in its business practices. At the same time, it remains crucial for organizations to claim some distinctive values in order to differentiate the organization from rival companies in the eyes of stakeholders. HSBC, for example, has claimed a distinctive value of being 'the world's local bank' whereby the company claims to tune its global scale to the local demands of individual customers. At the same time, HSBC has claimed very similar values as its competitors (Barclays, Citigroup, BNP and ING) regarding being a global or international institution that is focused on 'customer service', 'value creation', 'professionalism' and 'technological and financial innovation'.

4.5 Corporate communication as corporate branding

In recent years, many writers in academic and practitioner circles have started to use the term 'corporate branding' and have proposed it as a guiding concept in corporate communication. For many of these writers, the idea of an organization as a brand was a logical extension of the product branding approach, with a focus on product and brand benefits and on individual consumers. The distinction between the two followed from Olins' framework on monolithic, endorsed and branded identities. Figure 4.5 displays these three types of identities. The monolithic identity refers to a corporate brand: a structure where all products and services, buildings, official communication and employee behaviour are labelled or branded with the same company name. Examples include Disney, Coca-Cola, Nike, McDonald's, Wal-Mart and BMW (see Case Study 4.1). The branded identity refers to a structure whereby products and services are brought to the market each with their own brand name and brand values. Companies such as Unilever and Procter & Gamble have traditionally followed this branded identity structure where neither the company's name nor its core values figured in the positioning and communication of its products. This branded strategy traditionally made sense for Unilever and Proctor & Gamble as they were addressing very different market segments through the different products in their product portfolio.

Many large organizations that were previously branded giants are changing their organizations into monolithic corporate brands. Kingfisher and Unilever are good examples of organizations that have moved towards endorsed and monolithic identities and aim to have their product brands more strongly associated with their company name. Kingfisher, a leading home improvement company in Europe and Asia traditionally had a branded structure around retail brands such as B&Q and Castorama. Since 1998, the company has been strengthening its Kingfisher corporate brand, which originally was only a name for its financial holding and was used to communicate with the financial community and investors. One central part of its corporate branding strategy has been to sponsor the sailor Ellen MacArthur and her successful attempts to sail around the world in record-breaking times. MacArthur's sailboat was badged with the Kingfisher name and increased awareness of the corporate brand with consumers and other stakeholders across the world. Similarly, Unilever announced in 2005 that the corporate brand will appear more prominently on all of its products. The announcement forms part of the company's 2010 strategy and is driven by the company's belief that many consumers are demanding more and more from the companies behind the brands, increasingly bringing their views as citizens into their buying decisions. The logo of the company has been redesigned and brings together 25 different icons representing Unilever

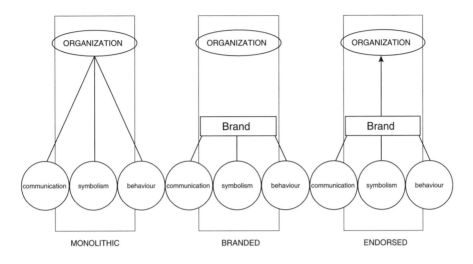

Identity structure	Definition	Example
Monolithic	Single all-embracing identity (products all carry the same corporate name)	Sony, BMW, Virgin, Philips
Endorsed	Businesses and product brands are endorsed or badged with the parent company name	General Motors, Kellogg, Nestlé, Cadbury
Branded	Individual businesses or product brands each carry their own name (and are seemingly unrelated to each other)	Procter & Gamble (Ariel, Ola), Electrolux (Zanussi), Unilever (Dove)

Figure 4.5   Monolithic, endorsed and branded identities

and its brands. The redesigned logo and its more prominent place on products and in advertising are meant to highlight the company behind the products to consumers, employees, investors and other stakeholders.

One important reason for organizations to move from branded to endorsed and monolithic identities is that monolithic identities have become enormously valuable assets – companies with strong monolithic identities, and the reputations associated with it, can have market values that are more than twice their book values[28] – and can save money as marketing and communication campaigns can be leveraged across the company. Many brand rankings such as the ones published by Interbrand and *Business Week* confirm the impact of monolithic identities on companies' financial performance. Not surprisingly, therefore, many academic writers and communication professionals have started to emphasize the importance of branding the entire organization and of focusing communication and marketing on the organization rather than on individual products and services.

The idea of corporate branding is, however, in principle not that different from the idea of corporate image management as discussed above. As Majken Schultz, one of the leading writers on corporate branding puts it, the focus in corporate branding is on how an organization can formulate an enduring identity that is relevant to all its stakeholders.[29] Similar to corporate image management, the approach in corporate branding is cross-disciplinary and includes input from communication, marketing and other functional areas within the organization. It is also aimed at all stakeholders of the organization, which contrasts the concept with product branding which is exclusively focused on (prospective and current) customers and consumers.

Schultz emphasizes that the core of corporate branding is the alignment between vision, culture and image. Central to this alignment (see Section 4.3) is the idea of organizational identity – who we are as an organization – and what that means to external stakeholders (image) and different cultures of employees within the organization (culture). The vision of senior managers then adds a strategic dimension to this process by setting directions for possible ways of further development or transforming who we are as an organization. For example, the vision of senior managers in Unilever of strengthening and highlighting the corporate brand behind its products is one that sets a strategic direction for the company. It fundamentally changes the identity of the organization and how it is seen by customers and stakeholders (image). Importantly, it also presents a break from the company's past strategy and internal culture where brand and product managers had executive responsibility to plan communication and marketing strategies (culture). The new identity would have to go hand in hand with a new culture that fosters collaboration between communication and marketing practitioners and a commitment to a monolithic Unilever identity.

Accordingly, the role of all employees (not just communication and marketing staff) becomes much more important in corporate branding (or corporate image management) as employees are central as brand ambassadors to the credibility and coherence of the corporate brand. Ideally, the identity behind the corporate brand would pervade the entire organization, from top to bottom, and would be an integral part of the mission and vision statements and of the values that employees associate with their organization. Internal communication with employees is crucial in this respect (see Chapter 8) in order to make sure that employees know of upcoming communication and marketing campaigns. Many organizations provide additional support to employees in the form of brand manuals, intranet resources and brand briefings or workshops. This support is meant to ensure that employees do not just know about the corporate brand but also live and enact it as part of their day-to-day jobs, regardless of whether those jobs involve direct contact with stakeholders or not.[30]

CASE STUDY 4.1

BMW: AN EXERCISE IN ALIGNING IDENTITY, BRAND AND REPUTATION*

BMW, the German car manufacturer, has been strategically focused on premium segments in the international car market. With its BMW, Mini and Rolls-Royce brands, the company has become one of the leading premium car companies in the world. BMW's strong identity and marketing campaigns are often credited as the building blocks of the company's continuing success. There are four values that define the BMW identity inside the organization (organizational identity) and its corporate brand and communication to external stakeholders: dynamism, aesthetics, exclusivity and innovation. These values have been central to BMW's success in terms of the company's leadership in design and are consistently communicated across all its corporate communication, corporate design, consumer advertising as well as through the behaviour of managers, designers, and retail staff. The brand consultancy Interbrand argues that these four brand values align customers' images and associations with the vision and culture of BMW.

BMW has long focused on innovation but made it the driving force for its product development process and its philosophy at the end of the 1990s. Since then, the company has put a lot of emphasis on its research and development (R&D), making it a core element of its corporate strategy. BMW's success has been its ability to nurture new ideas, short-list the potential ones and process them till the end stage through an integrated innovation process. The innovation process within BMW is aimed at systematically channelling potential innovations to the actual product development stage. The process focuses on three major areas: unique selling propositions for each car to be launched, breakthrough innovations, and concept cars to convey BMW's brand image at automobile shows. For this purpose, the company has implemented systems to search for and filter innovative ideas from across the world (within and outside of the company), which after further development can be carried over into actual product development and car vehicle manufacturing processes. Besides its focus on innovation, the company has also been a powerhouse of creative and aesthetic designs of cars. According to Christopher Bangle, global chief of design for BMW, 'our fanaticism about design excellence is matched only by the company's driving desire to remain profitable'. Bangle sees the company's core value as being 'an engineering-driven company whose cars and motorcycles are born from passion'. In his words; 'We don't make "automobiles", which are utilitarian machines you use to get from point A to point B. We make "cars", moving works of art that express the driver's love of quality'.

The values of dynamism, aesthetics, innovation and exclusivity are carried through in all of the company's communication to consumers and to other

(Continued)

(Continued)

stakeholders. They feature as brand promises in dealer and customer materials including showroom interior design, tradeshow materials, advertising and customer promotion packages. These values also featured as part of the company's branded entertainment strategy. This strategy consisted of product placement in movies (including a series of James Bond films) and an initial set of five short promotional films in 2000 that were made available online on the BMW website. The online films cleverly built BMW's brand image and were promoted using trailers on television, print and online advertisements that drove customers to visit the website. In 2002, BMW produced three more promotional films inspired by the success of the first five films.

Particularly because of its creative advertising, the BMW brand has come to be associated with the words 'driving' and 'performance'. The company's taglines in many adverts were 'The Ultimate Driving Machine' and 'Sheer Driving Pleasure'. According to marketing guru Al Ries, this association with 'driving' was a very powerful component of BMW's brand as it led consumers to associate BMW with high-performing cars.

However, a study commissioned by BMW in 2005 revealed that in the USA a large percentage of luxury car buyers did not consider BMW at the point of purchase. The management of BMW in the USA realized that some kind of change was needed in the company's communication. In the words of US Marketing Director Jack Pitney: 'We're entering new product segments all the time, and we can't afford to not be on the shopping lists of this many people ... People think we have a cool persona as a brand, but say we lack humanity.' Pitney felt that BMW needed to draw upon its brand history and particularly its four identity values to add a sense of humanity to the brand.

Pitney and his colleagues in the USA felt that the situation faced by BMW was actually a direct result of the company's overemphasis on 'performance driving' over the past 33 years. He felt that consumers instead were looking for brands that stood for larger values. In the company's brief to ad agencies pitching for the account, the company said that 'BMW wants to bring the excitement back to the brand and restore the equilibrium between its products and its marketing communications. Remember your challenge is not to reinvent the brand but to evolve the marketing from its current one-dimensional focus on performance.'

A new agency was successfully recruited and in May 2006, the North American arm of BMW released a new advertising campaign promoting itself as a 'company of ideas'. The tone and tenor of the new campaign were different from previous adverts in the past. The series of new ads no longer stressed the BMW car's performance, but were intended to project the company's competence in design and its corporate culture that fostered innovation. In doing so, BMW wanted to build demand by reaching out to consumers who had until now not considered purchasing a BMW vehicle. At the same time, the company wanted to make the existing BMW loyal customers proud of the company's success story. The ad campaign was unveiled through various media including adverts in magazines, on television, on outdoor billboards and on the internet. The campaign tried to communicate BMW's independence and freedom to pursue innovative ideas, as it was neither owned by nor part of a division of another company. The ads still featured the tagline 'The Ultimate Driving Machine', but placed little emphasis on its high performance features. The focus instead was on the theme of BMW as a 'company of ideas', where radical design and ideas are encouraged as a way of supporting the tagline around performance. According to Pitney, the idea was to draw upon the company's distinctive identity based on aesthetics and innovation and show consumers and the general public how a BMW car actually becomes an ultimate driving machine.

Questions for reflection

1. Describe the alignment between vision, culture and image for BMW and discuss the potential for gaps between them.
2. Consider the four values of the identity and brand positioning of BMW. Are these values, authentic, distinctive and unique from the perspective of consumers and other stakeholders in the premium car market?

Note: *This case study is based upon Bangle, C. (2001), 'The ultimate creativity machine: how BMW turns art into profit', *Harvard Business Review*, January, 5–11; Ries, A. and Ries, L. (2000), *The 22 Immutable Laws of Branding*. Harper Collins: New York, Kiley, D. (2006), 'BMW targets new drivers', www.businessweek.com, 5 May.

4.6 Chapter summary

The chapter has outlined the theoretical background to frameworks and approaches that organizations use to build strong and distinctive reputations with their stakeholders. One important observation that was made is that communication practitioners (and managers in other areas) need to look inside their organizations for core values that define their organization and that can give them a competitive edge in contacts with internal and external stakeholders. Indeed, many organizations which have not thought seriously about their corporate identity and whether their profile is appreciated by stakeholder groups, often appear to hire and fire outside agencies with regularity, trying to find the one with the ability to 'sell' a message that people do not seem to be 'buying'. In other words, such organizations have not given enough care to crafting an identity that is authentic and distinctive, and also meaningful to stakeholders. The following chapters in Part 3 draw upon the overview of theoretical concepts (stakeholder, identity and reputation) that were presented in Chapters 3 and 4. Part 3 involves the theory and practice of operational issues such as developing a communication strategy and communication programmes (Chapter 5), organizing and coordinating communication activities within an organization (Chapter 6), and enacting the role of a communication professional (Chapter 7).

KEY TERMS

Brand(ed) identity	Focus group
Cobweb method	Laddering
Corporate brand	Organizational identity
Corporate identity	Projective technique
Corporate image	Publicly syndicated rankings
Corporate personality	Q-sort
Corporate reputation	Repertory grid
Culture	Vision

Notes

1   Dowling, G.R. (2001), *Creating Corporate Reputations*. Oxford: Oxford University Press.

2   Birkigt, K. and Stadler, M. (1986), *Corporate Identity: Grundlagen, Funktionen und Beispielen*. Landsberg an Lech: Verlag Moderne Industrie.

3   Olins, W. (1978), *The Corporate Personality: An Inquiry into the Nature of Corporate Identity*. London: Design Council, p. 212.

4   Larçon, J.P. and Reitter, R. (1979), *Structures de pouvoir et identité de l'enterprise*. Paris: Nathan.

5   Albert, S. and Whetten, D.A. (1985), 'Organizational identity', in Cummings L.L. and Staw B.M. (ed.), *Research in Organizational Behavior*. Greenwich, CT: JAI Press, pp. 263–295.

6   Weigelt, K. and Camerer, C. (1988), 'Reputation and corporate strategy: a review of recent theory and applications', *Strategic Management Journal*. 9: 443–454.

7   Dutton, J.E. and Dukerich, J.M. (1991), 'Keeping an eye on the mirror: image and identity in organizational adaptation', *Academy of Management Journal*, 34: 517–554.

8   Hamel, G. and Prahalad, C.K. (1994), *Competing for the Future*. Boston, MA: Harvard Business School Press; Peters, T.J. and Waterman, R.H. (1982), *In Search of Excellence: Lessons from America's Best Run Companies*. New York: Harper & Row; Collins, J.C. and Porras, J.I. (1997), *Built to Last: Successful Habits of Visionary Companies*. New York: Harper Business.

9   See, for example, Hatch, M.J. and Schultz, M. (2000), 'Scaling the tower of Babel: relational differences between identity, image and culture in organisations', in Schultz, M., Hatch, M.J. and Larsen, M.H. (eds), *The Expressive Organization*. Oxford: Oxford University Press; Ravasi, D. and Schultz, M. (2006), 'Responding to organizational

identity threats: exploring the role of organizational culture', *Academy of Management Journal*, 49: 433–458.

10 Fombrun, C. and Rindova, V. (2007), 'The road to transparency: Reputation management at the Royal Dutch/Shell', in M. Schultz, M.J. Hatch and M.H. Larsen (eds) *The Expressive Organization*. Oxford: Oxford University Press. pp. 76–96.

11 Hatch, M.J. and Schultz, M. (2001), 'Are the strategic stars aligned for your corporate brand?' *Harvard Business Review*, February: 128–135, and Schultz, M. and Hatch, M.J. (2003), 'Cycles of corporate branding: the case of the LEGO Company', *California Management Review*, 46: 6–26.

12 Peteraf, M. and Shanley, M. (1997), 'Getting to know you: a theory of strategic group identity', *Strategic Management Journal*, 18: 165–186; Whetten, D.A., Lewis, D. and Mischel, L.J. (1992), 'Towards an integrated model of organizational identity and member commitment', paper presented at the Academy of Management Annual Meeting, Las Vegas.

13 Fryxell, G.E. and Wang, J. (1994), 'The Fortune Corporate Reputation Index: reputation for what?', *Journal of Management*, 20: 1–14.

14 Fombrun, C. (1998), 'Indices of corporate reputation: an analysis of media rankings and social monitors ratings', *Corporate Reputation Review*, 1 (4): 327–340.

15 Fombrun, C. (1996), *Reputation: Realizing Value from the Corporate Image*. Cambridge, MA: Harvard University Press, p. 72.

16 Wartick, S.L. (1992), 'The relationship between intense media exposure and change in corporate reputation', *Business & Society*, 31: 33–49.

17 Gray, E.R. and Balmer, J.M.T. (1998), 'Managing image and corporate reputation', *Long Range Planning*, 31 (5): 685–692, quote on p. 687.

18 Dowling, G.R. (1988), 'Measuring corporate images: a review of alternative approaches', *Journal of Business Research*, 17: 27–34, Van Riel, C.B.M., Stroeker, N.E. and Maathuis, O.M. (1998), 'Measuring corporate images', *Corporate Reputation Review*, 1 (4): 313–326.

19 Bouchikhi, H. and Kimberly, J.R. (2003), 'Escaping the identity trap', *Sloan Management Review*, Spring: 20–26; see also Hatch and Schultz (2001); Cheney, G. and Christensen, L.T. (2001), 'Organizational identity: linkages between "internal" and "external" organizational communication', in Jablin, F. and Putnam, L. (eds), *The New Handbook of Organizational Communication*. Thousand Oaks, CA: Sage, pp. 231–269.

20 Edmonson, A.C. and Cha, S.E. (2002), 'When company values backfire', *Harvard Business Review*, November: 2–3.

21 Ghosn, C. (2002), 'Saving the business without losing the company', *Harvard Business Review*, January: 37–45.

22 Thorpe, R. and Cornelissen, J.P. (2002), 'Visual media and the construction of meaning', in Holman, D. and Thorpe, R. (ed.), *Management and Language: The Manager as a Practical Author*. London: Sage, pp. 67–81.

23 Van Rekom, J. (1997), 'Deriving an operational measure of corporate identity', *European Journal of Marketing*, 31 (5/6): 410–422.

24 Fombrun, C. and Van Riel, C.B.M. (2004), *Fame and Fortune: How Successful Companies Build Winning Reputations*. London: FT Prentice Hall.

25 Brammer, S.J. and Pavelin, S. (2006), 'Corporate reputation and social performance: the importance of "fit"', *Journal of Management Studies*, 43: 435–455.

26 Deephouse, D.L. and Carter, S.M. (2005), 'An examination of differences between organizational legitimacy and organizational reputation', *Journal of Management Studies*, 42: 329–360.

27   Lamertz, K., Heugens, P.P.M.A.R. and Calmet, L. (2005), 'The configuration of organizational images among firms in the Canadian beer brewing industry', *Journal of Management Studies,* 42: 817–843.

28   Hatch and Schultz (2001),

29   Schultz, M. (2005), 'A cross-disciplinary perspective on corporate branding', in Schultz, M. Antorini, Y.M. and Csaba, F.F. (eds), *Corporate Branding: Purpose/People/Process.* Copenhagen: Copenhagen Business School Press, pp. 23–55.

30   Mitchell, C. (2002), 'Selling the brand inside', *Harvard Business Review,* January: 99–105.

Part 3

CORPORATE COMMUNICATION IN PRACTICE

Corporate communication, as an area of practice, involves communication professionals developing, planning and executing communication programmes on a day-to-day basis. The process by which professionals develop such programmes and communicate corporate messages to stakeholders is often labelled a communication strategy. The effectiveness of a communication strategy depends on both professionals having the right competencies and skills to perform their job, as well as on organizational structures that support these professionals in coordinating and aligning different communication programmes into a coherent whole.

Part 3 explores these three operational issues in corporate communication: how communication strategies are developed and communication programmes planned and executed; how communication professionals and their various activities are organized within different types of organizations; and how professionals can develop competencies and skills to become more effective in their various roles within the organization.

After reading Part 3, the reader should be familiar with effective approaches to these three areas and know how to develop communication strategies, how to organize and manage communication and how to support themselves and others in their professional development as communication professionals.

5

Communication Strategy and Planning

CHAPTER OVERVIEW

The chapter describes the process and content of developing a communication strategy for an organization. The process refers to the procedures for developing a communication strategy across communication disciplines and stakeholders and in line with the overall corporate strategy of an organization. The content refers to the actual message style and themed messages that feature in communication programmes for stakeholders. The chapter ends with a practical model of how organizations develop communication strategies and plan specific communication programmes and campaigns.

5.1 Introduction

Managing corporate communication requires a communication strategy that describes the general image that an organization aims to project through themed messaging to stakeholders. A communication strategy also provides guidance to specific communication programmes (for example, a product launch or investor meeting). This chapter describes how communication strategies are developed in practice and how in line with such strategies specific communication programmes and campaigns can be planned and executed.

The first part of the chapter (Section 5.2) discusses the process of strategy making in corporate communication. A comprehensive communication strategy is often developed in interactions between practitioners from different communication disciplines and the CEO and members of the executive team within the organization. The second part of the chapter (Section 5.3) elaborates on the content of a communication strategy in terms of what such strategies normally consist of and how they guide the design of particular communication programmes. The content often involves identified themed messages or message styles that are adopted throughout communication with stakeholders. The final part of the chapter (Section 5.4) illustrates how organizations plan specific communication programmes and campaigns as part of a wider communication strategy.

5.2 The process of developing a communication strategy

A communication strategy involves the formulation of a desired position for the organization in terms of how it wants to be seen by its different stakeholder groups. Based upon an assessment of the gap between how the company is currently seen (corporate reputation) and how it wants to be seen (vision) (see Chapter 4), a communication strategy specifies a strategic intent, on which possible courses of action are formulated, evaluated and eventually chosen. Communication strategies often involve a process of bringing stakeholder reputations in line with the vision of the organization in order to obtain the necessary support for the organization's strategy. In other cases, a communication strategy may be about reinforcing existing reputations of stakeholders if those are broadly in line with how the organization wants itself to be seen.

To illustrate, Wal-Mart wants to be known as a market-driven retailer that has the interests of its customers, employees, suppliers and local communities at heart. The company had for a long time been able to frame its low-cost market strategy in terms that not only fitted with its own customer-focused identity, but was also acceptable to consumers and the general US public. However, more recently, Wal-Mart has faced criticism for the way in which it engages with, and cares for, important stakeholder groups such as employees and members of the local communities in which the company operates. The State of Maryland, for example, passed the so-called 'Wal-Mart Healthcare Bill' early in 2006, introducing a law that would fine big companies, and particularly Wal-Mart, for not picking up their fair share of employee healthcare coverage. The result is a gap between the company's vision of how it wants to be seen and the actual reputation that it currently has with employees, local communities, government and the general public in the United States. Because of this gap, Wal-Mart executives have realized that its poor reputation could eventually pose a threat to its growth in the USA and elsewhere. The company has therefore decided to recruit a senior director of stakeholder management to 'help pioneer a new model of how Wal-Mart works with outside stakeholders, resulting in fundamental changes in how the company does business'.[1] The company has started to formulate a communication strategy aimed at raising awareness of its environmental and social contributions and of its support for employees in the hope that stakeholder opinions will again become more favourable towards the company.

As in the case of Wal-Mart, the assessment of the gap between reputation and vision leads to the formulation of a *strategic intent* within the communication strategy. A strategic intent sets the general direction, often articulated in objectives, and defines the general pattern of actions that will be taken to achieve these objectives. As Hamel and Prahalad put it:

> On the one hand, strategic intent envisions a desired leadership position and establishes the criterion the organization will use to chart its progress … At the same time, strategic intent is more than simply unfettered ambition. The concept also encompasses an active management process that includes: focusing the organization's attention on the essence of winning; motivating people by communicating the value of the target; leaving room for individual and team contributions; sustaining enthusiasm by providing new operational definitions as circumstances change; and using intent consistently to guide resource allocations.[2]

Based upon an analysis of the current reputation of the organization with its stakeholders, strategic intent sets a general direction for communication in terms of the change or consolidation of that reputation that is aimed for. The strategic intent also suggests a particular set of communication activities that aim to affect the awareness, knowledge, reputation and behaviour of important stakeholders. Before the next section outlines in detail what the content of a communication strategy consists of, the present section continues by discussing the process by which a communication strategy is developed. In particular, the focus here is on the different parties (communication managers, the CEO and executive directors of other functional areas in the organization) that are involved in this process and the way in which they work together to shape and formulate a communication strategy.

A range of paradigms or schools of thought[3] exist on the *process of strategy-making*. How strategies are formed within organizations has become variously depicted in these different paradigms as following a rational planning mode, in which objectives are set out and methodically worked out into comprehensive action plans, as a more flexible intuitive or visionary process, or as rather incremental or emergent in nature, with the process of strategy formation being rather continuous and iterative. Each of these paradigms thus varies in whether the process of strategy formation is characterized and described as 'top-down' or 'bottom-up', as deliberate and planned or as ad hoc and spontaneous and as analytical or visionary.

Besides the diversity and the distinct views presented by each of these different schools of thought there is also consensus on the following three points:

1. *Strategy formation often consists of a combination of planned and emergent processes.* In practice, strategy formation involves a combination of a logical rational process in which visions and objectives are articulated and systematically worked out into programmes and actions, as well as more emergent processes in which behaviours and actions simply arise ('emerge') yet fall within the strategic

scope of the organization. The same combination of planned and emergent processes of strategy formation can also be observed at the level of communication strategy. In practice, communication strategy typically consists of pre-structured and annually planned programmes and campaigns, as well as more ad hoc, reactive responses that 'emerge' in response to issues and stakeholder concerns in the environment (Chapter 10).

2. *Strategy involves a general direction and not simply plans or tactics.* The term strategy is itself derived from the Greek 'strategos' meaning a *general* set of manoeuvres carried out to overcome an enemy. What is notable here is the emphasis on *general*, not *specific*, sets of manoeuvres. Specific sets of manoeuvres are seen as within the remit of those concerned with translating the strategy into programmes or tactics. In other words, strategy embodies more than plans and tactics, which often have a more immediate and short-term focus. Instead, strategy concerns the organization's direction and positioning in relation to its environment for a longer period of time.

3. *Strategy is about the organization and its environment.* Related to the previous point, the strategy literature is permeated with the concepts of 'mission', 'vision' and 'environment'. Together, they suggest that organizations must make long-term, strategic choices that are feasible in their environments. According to Steiner and his colleagues, 'strategic management' can be distinguished from 'operational management' (or input–output management, see also Chapter 3) by 'the growing significance of environmental impacts on organizations and the need for top managers to react appropriately to them'.[4] Managers who manage strategically do so by balancing the mission and vision of the organization – what it is, what it wants to be, and what it wants to do – with what the environment will allow or encourage it to do. Often therefore, strategy is characterized as continuous and adaptive in that it needs to be responsive to external opportunities and threats that may confront an organization. A broad consensus exists in the strategy literature that strategy is essentially concerned with a process of managing the interaction between an organization and its external environment so as to ensure the best 'fit' between the two.

Given that the central concern of strategy is with matching or aligning the organization's mission, its resources and its capabilities with the opportunities and challenges in the environment, one would perhaps expect lengthy discussions in the strategy literature about the stakeholders that constitute the 'environment'. But this, unfortunately, has not been the case. Although the concept of environment pervades the literature on strategy, until recently it has been conceptualized in 'general, even rather vague' terms.[5] Environments were and often still are characterized, as Chapter 3 outlined, in terms of markets or operating domains, which ignores the whole range of other stakeholder groups that nowadays have a profound impact upon an organization's strategic scope and operations. One would perhaps also expect acknowledgement by strategy scholars that corporate communication is an important 'boundary-spanning' function between the organization and the environment.[6] As a boundary-spanning function, corporate communication operates at the interface between the organization and its environment; to help gather, relay and interpret information from the environment as well as represent the organization to the outside world.

But this role of corporate communication is, as said, not reflected in most strategy theories. In these theories, communication is often still seen as a largely tactical activity with practitioners acting as communication 'technicians' (Chapter 7). In such a view, communication is concerned primarily with sending out messages and publicizing a favourable image for an organization with little, if any, involvement in more strategically important activities such as environmental scanning, analysis or counselling of senior managers. Moving beyond these strategy theories, the academics White and Dozier argue that this picture is also reflected in practice with their suggestion that for the vast majority of organizations, the strategic potential of corporate communication in its boundary-spanning role appears to go largely unrealized. This is the case, White and Dozier argue,[7] as senior management equally tends to treat communication largely as a tactical function, concerned primarily with the technical gathering of information and with carrying out publicity and promotional campaigns to external audiences.

Seeing corporate communication as a strategic function, in contrast, requires that communication practitioners are involved in decision-making regarding the corporate strategy. Such a view of communication means that communication strategy is not just seen as a set of goals and tactics at the functional or operational level – at the level of the corporate communication function – but that its scope and involvement in fact stretch to the corporate and business-unit levels of the organization as well. At the corporate level, where strategy is concerned with the corporate mission and vision, communication practitioners can aid managers in developing strategies for interaction with the environment. In this sense, communication practitioners are directly involved and support strategic decision-making through their 'environmental scanning' activities. Environmental scanning may assist corporate strategy-makers in analyzing the organization's position and identifying emerging issues which may have significant implications for the organization and for future strategy development. Communication practitioners can at this corporate level also bring identity questions and a stakeholder perspective into the strategic management process, representing the likely reaction of stakeholders to alternative strategy options, and thereby giving senior management a more balanced consideration of the attractiveness and feasibility of the strategic options open to them. Finally, communication practitioners, of course, may also implement the corporate strategy by helping to communicate the organization's strategic intentions to both internal and external stakeholders, which can help avoid misunderstandings that might otherwise get in the way of the smooth implementation of the organization's strategy. With such involvement in the corporate strategy of an organization, the communication strategy itself will also be more substantial instead of being just a tactical ploy.[8] In other words, in an era of stakeholder management, a corporate communication strategy cannot be divorced from the organization's corporate strategy, to which it must contribute if it is to have a genuine strategic role.[9] As one practitioner put it, '[communication] must pass one basic test: at minimum; everything done must be aligned with the corporate vision or mission … and must substantially contribute to achieving the organization's objectives'.[10]

In summary, a corporate strategy is concerned with the overall purpose and scope of the organization to meet its various stakeholders expectations and needs. A corporate strategy provides a strategic vision for the entire organization in terms of product, market or geographical scope or matters as fundamental as ownership of the organization. A vision often also articulates how the company wants to be seen by its various stakeholder groups. A communication strategy in turn is a functional or operational strategy concerned with how corporate communication can develop communication programmes towards different stakeholders to achieve that vision and to support the corporate objectives in the corporate strategy. Figure 5.1 illustrates this dynamic between the corporate strategy and the corporate communication strategy. On the one hand, the decisions that are made at the level of the corporate strategy need to be translated into specific communication programmes for different stakeholders. In the words of Kevin Rollins, CEO of Dell: 'The job of a senior manager is to determine which elements of the overall strategy you want to communicate to each constituency.' Rollins, together with Dell's senior communication managers, decides how they 'break messages up into pieces and try to give the right piece to the right audience'.[11] At the same time, corporate communication and communication strategies need to be linked to the corporate strategy. This link consists of counselling and informing the CEO and senior executives on stakeholder and reputation issues so that these can be factored into the overall corporate strategy and the company's strategic vision. Michael Dell, the founder of Dell, articulates this link by saying that 'communications are an essential part of what you have to offer to customers and shareholders'. In his view, 'communications has to be in the centre to be optimally effective' and for it to support the corporate strategy.[12]

This nested model of strategy formation, in which a corporate strategy and communication strategy are seen as interrelated layers in the total strategy-making structure of the organization, depends on a number of conditions. First of all, a conventional view of strategy formation where strategy is seen to cascade down from the corporate to the business unit and ultimately to the functional level of corporate communication, with each level of strategy providing the immediate context for the next, 'lower' level of strategy making, needs to be rejected. As scholars such as Mintzberg and Whittington[13] have suggested, strategy-making fares better when it does not strictly follow such a rigid, hierarchical top-down process. Instead, it should be more flexible and at least in part decentralized so that business unit and functions such as corporate

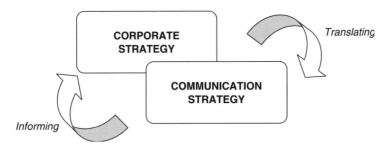

Figure 5.1 The link between corporate strategy and communication strategy

communication are encouraged to initiate ideas that are then passed upward for approval at the appropriate senior management level. From this perspective, business units and functions may be responsible not only for developing strategic responses to the problems or opportunities encountered at their own level, but may sometimes initiate ideas that then become the catalyst for changes in strategy throughout the organization. Communication practitioners, for instance, may relay their understanding of stakeholders at the functional level to the CEO and senior management level and may as such initiate a revision of corporate strategy in terms of how the organization needs to build and maintain relationships with those organizational stakeholders who have the power to influence the successful realization of its corporate goals.

The implementation of a corporate calendar system within Siemens provides a good example of the interconnections between a corporate strategy and a communication strategy. The corporate calendar (Figure 5.2) lists events throughout the year at which the corporate strategy and corporate objectives are communicated to employees from different parts of the company. The calendar was developed by corporate communication professionals who realized that employees were not always informed about the company's strategy in a timely and consistent manner. Communication professionals raised the issue with the CEO and senior executives (*informing* in Figure 5.1) who agreed that the calendar system could be usefully incorporated into the corporate strategy as a way of implementing the strategy. The CEO and senior executives felt that the calendar would make an important contribution to the achievement of the corporate objectives as it provides a medium to report on the past year's targets and for setting binding priorities and objectives for the new fiscal year (*translating* in Figure 5.1). As displayed in Figure 5.2, the Siemens Business Conference (SBS) marks the start of each fiscal year. This central event provides a platform for senior managers to report on the past year's targets and to set priorities and objectives for the new fiscal year. The SBS event is followed by management conferences in the business divisions, regions and corporate units

(Figure 5.2). By streamlining management events, the corporate calendar ensures that all managers and employees hear about the past year's results and are given objectives for the coming period. In this way, a corporate communication medium (the corporate calendar) directly contributes to the achievement of the company's corporate objectives.

			AM				PM						
			8:00	10:00	12:00	2:00	4:00	6:00	8:00	10:00	12:00		
Events and corporate calendar	Oct	Nov	Dec	Jan	Feb	Mar	Apr	May	Jun	Jul	Aug	Sep	Oct
Siemens Business Conference (incl. top+ award)		Oct. 29-31 2003											Oct. 6-8, 2004
Communication of key topics for the new fiscal year		Groups, Regions, Corporate Units											
Target achievement, target agreements, staff dialogs, management dialogs													
Structuring and integration of initiatives in the Group/Region planning process													
Approval of Regional business plans													
Review of Group plans by the Corporate Executive Committee													
Quarterly reviews (Q2 with expanded circle of attendees)		Q4		Q1			Q2			Q3			
Regular reviews of initiatives in the Corporate Executive Committee													
Best practice sharing/ Best Practice Days													
Training to support initiatives													

Figure 5.2   The Corporate Calendar System in Siemens (Calendar dating from 2003). Reprinted with permission.

5.3 The content of communication strategy

The content of a communication strategy is influenced by the process by which it is formed and by the different parties who have had a stake in it. Ideally, the content of the strategy starts from an organization-wide assessment of how the organization is seen by different stakeholders (reputation) in the light of the organization's vision (vision) at a particular point in time. The gap between the reputation and vision, as mentioned, forms the basis for the formulation of a strategic intent: the change or consolidation in the company's reputation that is intended. The strategic intent in turn is translated into themed messages that are designed to change or reinforce perceptions in line with the vision of how the organization wants to be known.

For example, Philips, the international electronics firm, in 2004 announced a new vision of wanting to become recognized as a market-driven company known for the simplicity of its products, processes and communication. This new vision was announced with its 'Sense and simplicity' slogan which is both a brand promise to customers as well as a potential differentiator from the company's competitors in the marketplace. While companies like Samsung and Apple are also working towards simplifying technology for customers, Philips is among the first to make it part of its brand positioning and as core to its product design. The new vision also articulates a broad-based corporate reputation for Philips (as a monolithic corporate brand) instead of a product-based image based on particular products (such as Philishave) and one that is based on the company's strong leadership in innovation, the strengths of its management and strategy and the care that it shows for employees. Recent reputation research with stakeholders, however, demonstrated that the company still has a narrow consumer product based image, that the company is seen as reliable but not as innovative, as lacking a clear strategy and vision and with doubts surrounding its management capabilities.

Based upon these results, the strategic intent within Philips' communication strategy is defined as changing stakeholder reputations of the company from a product-based image to a broad-based reputation that is rooted in a view of the company as a leader in innovation with a clear strategy and vision and capable management. To achieve its strategic intent, Philips has identified a number of themed messages that the company consistently communicates to different stakeholders. These include leadership in innovation (on the ability of the company to develop new and exciting products), performance management (on the strong leadership and management within the organization), care for employees (on the care and support that the organization gives to its employees), quality products and services (on the reliable and high quality products of the company), leadership in sustainability (the track record of the company in environmental and social performance), market orientation (the focus of the company on customer needs) and strong communication (the ability of the company to communicate and engage with its stakeholders). The themed messages are specifically designed to address the company's reputation in a number of areas and in line with the company's vision.

Themed messages, in other words, are messages that relate to specific capabilities, strengths or values (as 'themes') of an organization. These messages are continuously and consistently communicated to stakeholders to achieve the strategic intent of changing or consolidating the company's reputation. A themed message may involve a company's specific capability such as the ability of an organization to develop innovative products (e.g., Philips), its general strengths or achievements such as the care that it has demonstrated in support to its employees and the general community in which it operates (e.g., Co-operative Bank) or particular values associated with the company's identity such as its claimed integrity or transparency (e.g., AstraZeneca). These messages in turn are translated into different message styles that communicate the claim

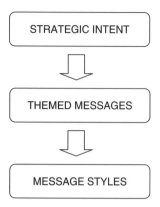

Figure 5.3   Stages in formulating the content of a communication strategy

Table 5.1   Alternative message styles

Functional orientation	Symbolic orientation	Industry orientation
Rational message style	Symbolic association message style Emotional message style	Generic message style Preemptive message style

about the company's capabilities, strengths or values in a convincing way (Figure 5.3).

There are various ways to communicate themed messages. Several relatively distinct message styles have developed over the years and represent the various ways in which corporate messages are communicated to different stakeholder groups.[14] Table 5.1 summarizes six message styles and groups them into three categories: functional orientation, symbolic orientation and industry orientation. Functionally oriented messages refer to tangible, physical or concrete capabilities or resources of an organization. Symbolically oriented messages appeal to psychosocial needs, preferences and experiences of stakeholders. An industry orientation message style does not necessarily use any particular type of functional or psychosocial appeal but is designed to achieve an advantage over competitors in the same industry. Finally, it is important to note that, as is the case with most categorization schemes, the message styles covered in the following section sometimes overlap in specific examples of corporate communication practice. In other words, distinctions are sometimes very fine rather than perfectly obvious, and a particular corporate communication strategy may simultaneously use multiple message styles in relation to themed messages.

1. ***Rational message style***. In this approach, an organization makes a superiority claim about its products or achievements based upon a distinctive advantage in its capabilities, size or resources (including technology). The main feature of this message style is identifying an important difference that can be highlighted and

then developing a claim that competitors either cannot make or have not chosen to make. The claim is seen as 'functional' because it addresses a basic need or expectation of stakeholders. The message style is labelled rational because it follows a basic argumentation structure where the grounds for the claim for superiority are supplied through supporting information. For example, when Lucent Technologies, a communication network provider, claims a superior ability to develop and deliver network solutions to clients, it is based upon its distinctive and proven track record in research and development in network technology (the company is associated with the world-renowned AT&T Bell Labs and the company's engineers have won many prizes for their ground-breaking technologies including Nobel Prizes) (Case Study 5.1). Similarly, BMW claims a superior ability in engineering aesthetically pleasing, high performance cars that is backed up by the company's long-standing emphasis on innovation and aesthetics in the design process (Case Study 4.1). The rational message style can be effective in cases where the organization can claim a distinctive advantage in its capabilities, size or resources. In cases where the organization cannot claim such an advantage or where such an advantage is easily matched, alternative message styles are used. For example, organizations typically do not use a rational message style when they communicate about their corporate social responsibility (CSR) because standards for performance in such areas are not obvious and transparent (Chapter 3) and as such performance can often be easily matched by competitors. In addition, a hard-hitting rational message style may also be seen as socially unacceptable for communicating about CSR.

Rational message style

Definition: superiority claim based upon actual accomplishments or delivered benefits by the organization
Conditions: most useful when point of difference cannot be readily matched by competitors
Content: informational in the form of a claim that is supported with information as the grounds for the claim

---

2. *Symbolic association message style*. Whereas the rational message style is based on promoting physical and functional differences between an organization and its competitors, a symbolic association message style involves psychosocial, rather than physical differentiation. The aim with this message style is to develop an image for the organization and to differentiate the organization psychologically from its competitors through symbolic association. In imbuing the organization with a symbolic image, communicators draw meaning from the culturally constituted world (that is, the world of symbols and values) and through communication transfer that meaning to the organization. The core of this message style consists of identifying a set of symbols and values that

through repeated linkage with the organization may come to be associated with that organization. One example of this message style is the way in which organizations link themselves through sponsoring to values associated with a sport or certain cause. Kingfisher, for example, has associated itself with Ellen MacArthur's record-breaking sailing attempts around the world, which, through association, created a positive image of the organization with attributes of freedom, challenge, ambition and leadership. Similarly, Tesco's support of Cancer Research UK associates the company with caring for one of the deadliest diseases and with healthy living. Another example of this message style involves corporate value statements whereby an organization explicitly states values or moral attributes that guide its conduct. Astrazeneca, for instance, lists the values of integrity, honesty and trust as central to how the company engages with its different stakeholders. These values express the moral sentiments and social capital that make organizations legitimate in the eyes of stakeholders. Astrazeneca also gives examples of how the company tries to live up to its values in specific practices. Similar to sponsorship, these value statements are meant to link the company with general (culturally shared and recognized) moral values and sentiments which may then become associated with the organization.

A symbolic association message style may also be described as 'transformational' because it associates the organization with a set of culturally shared experiences and meanings which without corporate communication would not typically be associated with the organization to the same degree. Such communication is transforming (versus informing) by virtue of endowing the organization with a particular symbolic image that is different from any of its competitors.

Symbolic association message style

Definition: claims based on psychological differentiation through symbolic association
Conditions: best for homogeneous organizations where differences are difficult to develop or easily duplicated or for messages around areas such as CSR or social capital that are difficult to communicate in concrete and rational terms
Content: transformational in the form of endowing the organization with a particular image through association with culturally shared and recognized values or symbols

---

3. *Emotional message style*. An emotional message style is another form of symbolically oriented communication. By using this message style, organizations aim to reach stakeholders at a visceral level. One approach may be to use emotional appeals in corporate communication to regulate the emotional responses of stakeholders. The display of emotions may, for example, lead to greater levels of involvement and affiliation with an organization. Starbucks, for example, incorporates emotional appeals around love, joy and belonging into its in-store communication which has led to consumers associating the Starbucks brand with community, individual expression, and 'a place away from home'. Displays

of positive emotions may also stimulate supportive, sharing and expansive behaviours of stakeholders while the display of negative emotions may lead to distancing and avoidance.[15] A good example of this message style involves the launch of Orange back in 1994 (Case Study 1.1). At the time, the mobile phone market in the United Kingdom was a confusing place for customers. Digital networks had just been introduced, but few people yet understood the benefits and most members of the general public were worried about the safety of mobile technology. On top of this, Orange also faced an uphill task in differentiating itself in this market as the last entrant in a market which already included BT Cellnet and Vodafone. In response, Orange launched an advertising campaign which communicated the positive emotions afforded by using mobile phones (friendship, love, freedom) and assured people that the negative emotions (fear, safety) that they may have had concerning the introduction of this new technology were unfounded. In considering an emotional message style, it is important for organizations to make sure that the display of emotions is seen as authentic. If stakeholders perceive references to emotions to be inauthentic, an emotional message style may backfire. In the case of Starbucks, for example, the company's emotional message style has been verified as authentic by stakeholders because of the genuine enthusiasm, friendliness and professionalism conveyed by employees.

Emotional message style

Definition: attempts to provoke involvement and positive reactions through a reference to positive (or negative) emotions
Conditions: effective use depends on the perceived authenticity of the professed emotion and on the relevance of the emotion to stakeholders
Content: appeals to specific positive or negative emotions (e.g., romance, nostalgia, excitement, joy, fear, guilt, disgust, regret)

---

4.   *Generic message style*. An organization employs a generic strategy when making a claim that could be made by any organization that operates in the same industry. With this message style, the organization makes no attempt to differentiate itself from competitors or to claim superiority. This message style is most appropriate for an organization that dominates a particular industry. For example, Campbell's soup dominates the prepared-soup market in the United States, selling nearly two-thirds of all soup. Based upon its market dominance the company has run advertising campaigns that stimulate demand for soup in general, rather than Campbell's soup in particular. The rationale behind this message style was that any advertising that increased overall soup sales would also naturally benefit Campbell's sales. Along similar lines, Novo Nordisk's 'leading the fight against diabetes' campaign emphasized the company's long-standing leadership in developing products for the diagnosis and treatment of diabetes. Given Novo Nordisk's grasp on the diabetes market, the campaign communicated in the company's words 'a clearly differentiated corporate position in the global diabetes market'.

> **Generic message style**
> *Definition*: straight claim about industry or cause with no assertion of superiority
> *Conditions*: monopoly or extreme dominance of industry
> *Content*: general claim (stimulate demand for product category or raise awareness of cause)

5.   **Preemptive message style**. A second message style that involves an industry-wide orientation is employed when an organization makes a generic-type claim but does so with a suggestion of superiority. Preemptive communication is a clever strategy when a meaningful superiority claim is made because it precludes competitors from saying the same thing. For example, many electronics firms can potentially claim to be about developing technological products that are advanced but easy to operate and designed around the needs of the customer, but no other firm could possibly make such a claim after Philips made it as part of its generic 'sense and simplicity' campaign. This claim could potentially have been made by many other electronics firms such as Sony and Samsung, but in appropriating this claim with its implicit assertion of superiority Philips has preempted competitors from using the simplicity tact in promoting their own organizations. Another example of the preemptive message style involves BP's restyling of itself as being 'beyond petroleum' in its focus on renewable energies and on the reduction of carbon emissions within its business operations. When the company recognized the changing expectations of stakeholders towards the petroleum industry, BP was the first to take up an industry-wide position on climate change and on the industry's responsibilities in reducing carbon emissions. In doing so, the company has come to be seen as an environmental leader in its industry ahead of Shell and Exxon-Mobil.

> **Preemptive message style**
> *Definition*: generic claim with suggestion of superiority
> *Conditions*: changing industry allowing a company to take a position on an issue connected to that industry
> *Content*: claim of industry-wide leadership on a relevant issue or capability

Five general message styles have been discussed and categorized as functional, symbolic or industry-oriented. These strategic alternatives to communicating corporate messages provide a useful aid to understanding the different approaches available to communicators and the factors influencing the choice for a particular message style. The message styles should, however, not be seen as mutually exclusive. In fact, organizations may use different message styles to communicate different messages to different stakeholders. The following section illustrates how organizations develop and plan particular communication programmes and campaigns as part of their communication strategy. These programmes and campaigns include different themed messages that may be communicated through multiple message styles.

5.4 Planning communication programmes and campaigns

Once the content of a communication strategy has been roughly drawn out, communication professionals translate that content into specific communication programmes and campaigns towards both internal and external audiences. A communication programme is defined as a formulated set of activities towards targeted internal and external audiences, which may include outreach activities, community initiatives and other ways in which organizations and their employees communicate with stakeholder audiences. A communication programme is thus a broader concept than the idea of a communication campaign which is restricted to the use of a mediated form of communication (e.g., mass media advertising) towards stakeholder audiences. Both programmes and campaigns start from the basic model presented in Figure 5.3 but with added detail on communication objectives, the segmentation of target audiences, the media strategy and the budgeting of the programme or campaign. Figure 5.4 presents communication professionals with a framework for identifying the broad targets of their communication and for planning effective communication programmes and campaigns. The framework consists of seven steps, starting with the strategic intent.

Step 1: Strategic intent

At the onset of a communication programme or campaign, it is important to refer back to the organization's overall communication strategy and the identified strategic intent. Roughly speaking, the strategic intent formulates a change or consolidation of stakeholder reputations of the organization. It is based upon the gap between how the organization wants to be seen by important stakeholder groups and how it is currently seen by each of those groups.

Step 2: Define communication objectives

Based upon the strategic intent, communication professionals need to set specific communication objectives for each communication programme or campaign. Here, professionals may decide to develop specific programmes or campaigns for particular stakeholder groups (e.g., employees, shareholders and investors, customers) or instead to develop a general corporate programme or campaign that addresses all of them. In both cases, however, professionals need

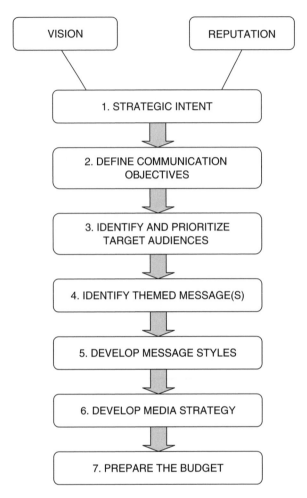

Figure 5.4 The process of planning communication programmes and campaigns

to define objectives in terms of whether they are seeking to change or consolidate a particular stakeholder's awareness, attitude, more general reputation, or behaviour. In line with the strategic intent, successful communication consists of appealing to stakeholders with a particular message so that they react favourably to it and change or consolidate a specific supportive behaviour towards the organization such as investing in an organization or buying its products. Communication objectives should be as tightly defined as possible: specific, measurable, actionable, realistic and timely (SMART):

1. *Specific*: objectives should specify what it is that the professional wants to achieve (e.g., knowledge change, change in reputation) of a particular stakeholder group.

2. *Measurable*: professionals should be able to measure whether they are meeting the objectives or not. This often consists of identifying clear indicators (e.g., a percentage change in supportive behaviours towards the organization) that can be measured and afterwards used to evaluate the success of the programme or campaign.
3. *Achievable*: objectives should be achievable and attainable in the light of current stakeholder reputations of the organization and the competitive landscape.
4. *Realistic*: objectives need to be realistic in the light of the resources and budget that is provided for a particular programme or campaign.
5. *Timely*: objectives should also specify the time-frame in which they need to be achieved. Communication objectives often include a 'window' of 1–2 years after the programme or campaign to measure the direct impact of a programme or campaign.

Step 3: Identify and prioritize target audiences

Organizations have many stakeholder groups. Obviously, organizations cannot communicate with all of them, and professionals therefore use the stakeholder salience model and the power–interest matrix (Chapter 3) to identify the most important stakeholder groups. Once important stakeholder groups have been identified, professionals need to segment those groups into more specific target audiences that are prioritized for a particular programme or campaign. For example, the stakeholder group of 'employees' includes many segments of different groups (e.g., top management, middle management, front-line staff, back-office personnel, administrative staff, etc.) which may not all need to be addressed within a particular programme or campaign. A target audience is defined as the segment of individuals (from a particular stakeholder group) that is the focus ('target') of a particular programme or campaign.

Step 4: Identify themed messages

Based upon the identified communication objectives and selected target audiences, professionals need to decide what the core message should be. The core message towards a particular target audience often evolves directly from how the organization wants to be seen. For example, Philips' vision of wanting to be seen as a leader in innovation provides a core message that can be translated into a specific campaign format and message style (Step 5 below). Themed messages may relate to the organization as a whole or to more specific areas such as products and services, CSR or financial performance, in which case they may be primarily relevant to particular stakeholder groups.

Step 5: Develop message styles

A message can be told in different ways using one of the five message styles (Section 5.3). The message styles involve the creative concept that articulates the appeal of the message and brings it to life through the use of catchy slogans and visual stimuli (pictures, images, logos and the typographic setting of a message). As mentioned above, the use of a particular message style depends on certain conditions and expectations of stakeholders: for example, an organization may adopt a rational message style when it communicates its financial growth and potential to investors at the annual general meeting by referring to its recent fiscal results and the growth of the market in which it operates. Simultaneously, an organization may adopt a symbolic association style by sponsoring a sports event or cause in an attempt to build a general corporate image that may lead to recognition and favourability with all of its stakeholder groups. In short, an organization can use multiple message styles simultaneously to communicate with different target audiences. At the same time, organizations often use the same message style to communicate about certain specific areas such as its products and services, its general corporate position, CSR or its financial performance. Philips, for example, has used the same preemptive message style around the core message of 'sense and simplicity' in all its corporate advertising and market-focused communication (advertising, sales promotions, direct marketing) to consistently communicate its commitment to developing technology for people.

Step 6: Develop a media strategy

The sixth step in the process involves identifying the media that can carry the message and its creative execution and can reach the target audience. In developing the media strategy, the overriding aim is to identify the most effective and efficient means of reaching the target audiences within the given budgetary constraints. Professionals need to consider criteria such as the reach and coverage of the target audience (to what extent does a particular medium reach subjects within the target audience so that they are at least once exposed to the message?), the creative match of the medium with the message (to what extent does the medium support a particular message style and creative format?), competitors' use of the media (to what extent do competitors use the same medium?), and the ability of media to enable dialogue and interaction with the audience (does the medium simply supply information or does it also allow interaction with the organization?).[16] Media selection needs to be 'zero-based';[17] meaning that the most appropriate medium in the light of these criteria is chosen rather than a pre-fixed and standard choice for a medium that may have worked in the past. In other words, professionals need to stay open to the wide range of media options available to them (e.g., free publicity, video-conferencing, promotions, meetings with stakeholders, sponsoring) rather than heading straight for, for example, (corporate) advertising. Professionals also need to decide upon the right mix of media for a particular communication pro-gramme or campaign. For example, when an organization launches a new product, it will need to use a range of media including mass media advertising to generate awareness, marketing public relations to generate excitement and interest in the product and sales promotions to stimulate people to try the product. Within the constraints of the budget, professionals will select multiple media and need to specify how these media complement each other in the achievement of the communication objectives, and when each medium is put to use within the time-frame of the programme or campaign.

Step 7: Prepare the budget

Finally, it is important to budget for the communication programme or campaign. Most of the budget for a communication programme or campaign will be spent on media buying, with the remaining amount going towards the production of the programme or campaign (including the hiring of communication consultants, advertising professionals and copy-editors) and the evaluation of results. Based upon the budget that is available for a particular programme or campaign, professionals may have to revise the previous steps and select a different mix of media and/or adjust their communication objectives.

Finally, when the entire programme or campaign is planned and executed, it will be evaluated for its results – specifically in terms of whether it has led to the achievement of the communication objectives. Effectiveness of the programme or campaign can be evaluated on the basis of process and communications effects. Process effects concern the quality of the communication programme or campaign (in terms of intelligence gathered, the detail that has gone into the planning, appropriateness of message content and organizational support) and whether the programme has been executed in a cost-effective manner. Communication effects include the range of cognitive and behavioral effects with targeted stakeholder audiences that the programme or campaign aimed to achieve. Here it is important to identify suitable impact measures (i.e. changes in awareness, attitude and reputation, or behaviour) rather than relying on interim measures of communication effects such as media coverage or simple exposure,[18] and to evaluate the effects achieved against the targets or benchmark set with the objectives of the communication programme or campaign.

The entire process of developing a communication strategy and of planning specific communication programmes is illustrated in the case study of Lucent.

CASE STUDY 5.1

DEVELOPING A COMMUNICATION STRATEGY FOR LUCENT*

Lucent Technologies Inc. (Lucent) was created as a result of a divesture in 1995 by AT&T. The company designs, builds and delivers a wide range of network systems (public networking systems and software for telecommunications providers and cable companies), business communication systems (advanced communication products and solutions for business customers), consumer telephone and network systems, and microelectronics components (high-performance integrated circuits, optoelectronic components, circuit boards and power systems for application in the telecommunications and computing industries). When Lucent was launched as an independent company in 1995, a cross-unit development team was set up to develop a communication strategy. At the time, this strategy consisted of identifying a new name and communication positioning platform together with a specific communication programme to launch the new company with employees, customers and the general public.

The search for a name and communication positioning platform

The 10-person cross-unit team brainstormed possible names for the new company. Several members of the team thought it would be a good idea to name the new company American Bell Laboratories to demonstrate its historical link with the world-renowned Bell Labs and to capitalize on the rich heritage and equity in the Bell Laboratories identity. However, there was some concern that other companies in the AT&T family would take issue with their rights to the Bell name. Because of these constraints, this option was not pursued. Another suggestion was to name the company AGB, an acronym for Alexander Graham Bell, who had invented the telephone more than a century before. This option seemed more realistic and was kept under consideration throughout the development stage. The cross-unit team recognized the complexity of finding a new name and drafted in the help of design experts Landor Associates.

When Landor Associates came in, they worked with the cross-unit team and senior management to identify what image the new name should convey. Before any naming or design work could commence, senior management and the cross-unit development team had to agree on what they most wanted to communicate through the name and logo about their new company. Landor asked everyone what equity from the past had to be kept, what of the old image should be left behind and, finally, what new attributes should be added to the desired corporate image. The answers to these questions were not immediately clear and Landor decided to conduct research with managers, employees, customers and dealers, and the general public. This research demonstrated that awareness of the Bell Laboratories was low to moderate with the general public. Bell Lab's image was generally positive but limited to telephony. Senior management wanted the company to be known for much more than telephony; thus they considered the name to be limiting. Among dealers, awareness and knowledge of what the company did were much higher. Although the company was thought of as smart and innovative, it was also perceived by a significant proportion of this group as being slow to respond and as being slow in getting products to market. High-end business customers equally had a very strong awareness of the company but considered the company not as fast to respond to their needs as they would like.

The result of this research and follow-up debate among the members of the cross-unit development team was an agreement to create what they called a 'communication positioning' platform that would retain the attributes of quality, reliability, technological innovation and stature. At the same time, they wanted to lose the perceptions of slowness, arrogance and inflexibility and to add the concepts of speed, energy and flexibility. In doing so, the cross-unit team formulated the strategic intent (step 1) for the communication strategy: to change the company's image with customers and the general public from being a slow technology giant to a market-driven, flexible, competitive and innovative provider of network solutions. When the CEO, Chief Operations Officer and Executive Vice-President for corporate operations agreed to the new positioning, the cross-unit team and Landor Associates continued with identifying the set of themed messages (step 2) that were to be communicated about the new company. These themed messages followed on from the strategic intent and included the company's leadership in innovation, the breadth and competitively priced nature of its product portfolio, the company's culture of innovation and reliability built on customer needs, and its heritage of Bell Labs and AT&T.

In parallel with the development of a positioning platform, a visual audit was conducted of all materials that would carry the new name and/or logo

Table 5.2 Desired image attributes

Keep	Lose	Add
Reliability	Slowness	Speed
Technology	Inflexibility	Energy
Stature	Arrogance	Flexibility
Integrity	High priced	Competitive
Service reputation	Hard to do business with	Value priced
Staying power		Customer focused
Experience/capability		Global
		Vision for the business
		Focus
		"can do"
		Innovative
		Enabling/user-friendly

(Continued)

(Continued)

of the company as well as competitors' materials. The audit of competitors showed that most companies used either blue or black as colours for their logos. Typography was typically all uppercase letter forms and with a few exceptions few symbols were used by prime competitors. To differentiate the new company from the competition, Landor also believed that it needed to avoid names that included conventional word segments like 'NET', 'TECH', 'SYS' or 'TEL', traditional colours and typographic styles and had to develop a symbol that was out of the ordinary. The goal was to stand out from the crowd in a cluttered environment and to communicate the new image attributes for which the company wanted to be known. After extensive work and research with business decision-makers and the general public, the name Lucent emerged as the team's first choice. Landor made the point that 'together with the qualities and imagery it evoked [Lucent stands for 'glowing with light' and 'marked by clarity'] Lucent expressed the energy, innovation, entrepreneurial spirit, and clear vision of the company's purpose, principles and future'. At the same time, both senior management and the cross-unit development team felt the need to leverage the past by somehow linking the new company to Bell Labs. The team therefore added the descriptive endorsement of 'Bell Labs Innovations' to the Lucent name; a tactic that would not be contested by other companies connected to AT&T.

Planning communication at the launch

When the cross-unit team had decided on the new name and the communication positioning platform, the next step was to work out the specific communication programmes for key internal and external stakeholder groups: employees, and customers and the general public. Based upon the strategic intent (step 1) of how the company wanted itself to be seen the team formulated specific objectives (step 2 – define communication objectives) for employees as one group and customers and the general public as another group (step 3 – identify and prioritize target audiences). Both these groups were prioritized as crucial stakeholders that needed to be communicated with at the launch of the 'new' company.

The team anticipated that employees would come to accept the new name and identity in time. However, because most were veteran AT&T employees, the sudden loss of the old identity was expected to cause serious emotional reactions from some. The new look and feel of the Lucent name and logo were also a clear break from the past logo. Initially, the objective towards employees was to raise awareness of the new name and identity and to communicate the themed messages about the new company's identity (step 4 – themed messages). An important message was to explain the new name and logo and its symbolic meaning in relation to the company's new purpose, principles and future. A symbolic association message style was adopted for this purpose (step 5 – message styles). This message was subsequently communicated (step 6 – media strategy) through a live internal video conference which was viewed by more than 100,000 employees. The team also set up remote two-way video in order to allow questioning from employees from different parts of the company. These events were followed up by meetings between (middle) managers and employees where again the new name and identity were explained to employees and incorporated into new initiatives and behaviours.

Communication with customers and the general public was all about raising awareness of the new name and about making a start with reshaping the image of the new company. Since the company needed to build its identity and image from scratch, the cross-unit team knew that it was important to 'establish a distinctive and memorable personality, along with very clear messages for the company'. The themed message that was highlighted in the communication campaign involved the company's longstanding leadership in developing innovative network and communication solutions (step 4 – themed messages). The key image attributes that the team wanted to be reflected in the campaign were quality and reliability, speed and responsiveness, customer focus and innovation. A rational message style was adopted in the campaign (step 5 – message styles); the company's claim that it 'makes things that make communications work' featured as a central promise and was backed up by supporting evidence about the awards that it has won and its link to AT&T and Bell Labs. The team subsequently decided to use mass media advertising (step 6 – media strategy) to announce the new name and identity and to make a start with changing the company's image.

After the divesture, Lucent operated quite successfully for a number of years until it merged in 2006 with Alcatel, one of the leading global suppliers of high-tech equipment for telecommunications networks. The merger is set to exploit the market opportunities for next-generation networks, services and applications by creating a global convergence leader. The combined company has the broadest range of product portfolio in the industry of advanced network solutions.

Questions for reflection

1. Describe the general communication strategy of Lucent and the specific programmes towards employees, customers and the general public. To what extent do you feel that the programmes are coherent with the overall strategy and are effectively planned and executed?
2. Lucent used a symbolic association message style in communication towards employees and a rational message style in advertising towards customers and the general public. Do you think that these message styles were wise choices? What other message styles would have been possible to communicate with these groups?

Note: ★This case study is based upon Philips, P.L. and Greyser, S.A. (1997), 'Creating a corporate identity for a $20 billion start-up: Lucent technologies', Design Management Institute, and on information retrieved from http://www.alcatel-lucent.com

5.5 Chapter summary

The chapter has described the process and content of corporate communication strategy. The process refers to the different parties (communication managers, the CEO and executive directors of other functional areas in the organization) that are involved in strategy formation and the way in which they work together to shape and formulate a communication strategy. The content refers to the themed messages within corporate communication and the message styles that are adopted to communicate those messages to different stakeholders. The final part of the chapter illustrated how communication professionals plan specific communication programmes or campaigns as part of a wider communication strategy.

A corporate communication strategy cuts across different hierarchical layers as well as different departments of the organization. Obviously, organizations need to organize their communication professionals in a way that allows them to interact and coordinate their work so that different communication programmes are consistent and planned in combination with one another. The following chapter picks up on this point and describes the various ways how theoretically and in practice communication is organized across different types of organizations (small businesses, multi-divisional and multinational corporations, public sector organizations and professional service organizations).

KEY TERMS

Budgeting	Preemptive message style
Communication effects	Process effects
Communication strategy	Rational message style
Corporate strategy	Strategic intent
Emotional message style	Symbolic association message style
Evaluation	Themed message
Generic message style	Vision
Planning	'Zero-based' media planning

Notes

1   *Financial Times*, 'Wal-Mart picks a shade of green', 7 February 2006.
2   Hamel, G. and Prahalad, C.K. (1989), 'Strategic intent', *Harvard Business Review*, May–June: 63–76, quote on p. 64.
3   See, for instance, Mintzberg, H. (1989), 'Strategy formation: schools of thought', in Frederickson, J. (ed.), *Perspectives on Strategic Management*. San Francisco, CA: Ballinger; Mintzberg, H., Ahlstrand, B. and Lampel, J. (1998), *Strategy Safari: The Complete Guide*

through the Wilds of Strategic Management. London: Prentice-Hall/Financial Times; or Elfring, T. and Volberda, H.W. (2001), 'Schools of thought in strategic management: fragmentation, integration or synthesis', in Volberda, H.W. and Elfring, T. (eds), *Rethinking Strategy*. London: Sage, pp. 1–25.

4 Steiner, G.A., Miner, J.B. and Gray, E.R. (1982), *Management Policy and Strategy*. New York: Macmillan, 2nd edn, p. 6.

5 Rumelt, R.P., Schendel, D.E. and Teece, D.J. (1994), 'Fundamental issues in strategy', in Rumelt, R.P., Schendel, D.E. and Teece, D.J. (eds), *Fundamental Issues in Strategy: A Research Agenda*. Boston, MA: HBS, p. 22.

6 Grunig, J.E. and Repper, F.C. (1992), 'Strategic management, publics and issues', in Grunig, J.E. (ed.), *Excellence in Public Relations and Communication Management*. Hillsdale, NJ: Lawrence Erlbaum Associates, pp. 122–123.

7 White, J. and Dozier, D.M. (1992), 'Public relations and management decision-making', in Grunig (1992), p. 92.

8 Moss, D. and Warnaby, G. (2000), 'Strategy and public relations', in Moss, D., Vercic, D. and Warnaby, G. (eds), *Perspectives on Public Relations Research*. London: Routledge, pp. 59–85.

9 Grunig and Repper (1992).

10 Webster, P.J. (1990), 'Strategic corporate public relations: what's the bottom line?', *Public Relations Journal*, 46 (2): 18–21, quote on p. 18.

11 Argenti, P., Howell, R.A. and Beck, K.A. (2005), 'The strategic communication imperative', *MIT Sloan Management Review*, Spring, 83–89, quote on pp. 86–87.

12 Ibid., p. 85.

13 Mintzberg, H. (1994), *The Rise and Fall of Strategic Planning*. New York: The Free Press; Whittington, R. (1993), *What is Strategy – and Does it Matter?* London: Routledge.

14 Based upon Shimp, T.A. (2003), *Advertising, Promotion and Supplemental Aspects of Integrated Marketing Communications*. Fort Worth, TX: Dryden Press. Thomson: and Rindova, V. (2007), 'Starbucks: constructing a multiplex identity in the specialty coffee industry', in Lerpold, L., Ravasi, D., Van Rekom, J. and Soenen, G. (eds), *Organizational Identity in Practice*. London: Routledge, pp. 157–173.

15 Rindova (2007), p. 167.

16 Jones, J.P. (1992), *How Much Is Enough?* New York: Lexington Books; Rossiter, J.R. and P.J. Danaher (1998), *Advanced Media Planning*. Boston: Kluwer.

17 See, for example, Deighton, J. (1996), 'Features of good integration: two cases and some generalizations', in Thorson, E. and Moore, J. (eds), *Integrated Communication: Synergy of Persuasive Voices*. Mahwah, NJ: Lawrence Erlbaum Associates, pp. 243–256; Deighton, J. (1999), 'Integrated marketing communications in practice', in Jones, J.P. (ed.), *The Advertising Business: Operations, Creativity, Media Planning, Integrated Communications*. London: Sage, pp. 339–355; Schultz, D.E. (1999), 'Integrated marketing communications and how it relates to traditional media advertising', in Jones, *The Advertising Business*, pp. 325–338.

18 Cutlip, S.M., Center, A.H. and Broom, G.H. (2000), *Effective Public Relations*, 7th edn. London: Prentice-Hall.

$\boxed{6}$

The Organization of Corporate Communication

CHAPTER OVERVIEW

The chapter outlines ways in which companies organize communication in order to strategically plan and coordinate the release of messages to different stakeholder groups. The basic concepts of vertical and horizontal structure are discussed and illustrated with case examples. The chapter demonstrates the importance of organizing communication in line with the general strategy and structure of the organization and in such a way that it facilitates the planning and coordination of communication programmes.

6.1 Introduction

How companies organize corporate communication is of crucial importance to the strategic planning and coordination of communication programmes towards different stakeholders. Organizations that have not adequately organized their communication often send out conflicting messages (see, for example, the Barclays case study in Chapter 2) and fail to make a consistent and strong impression on their stakeholders. In recent years, it has been emphasized that the most effective way of organizing communication consists of 'integrating' most if not all of an organization's communication disciplines and related activities such as media relations, issues management, advertising and direct marketing. The basic idea is that whereas communication had previously been organized and managed in a rather fragmented manner, a more effective organizational form is one that integrates or coordinates the work of various communication practitioners. At the same time, when communication practitioners are pulled together, the communication function as a whole is more likely to have an input into strategic decision-making at the highest corporate level of an organization.

This chapter sets out to discuss the subject of how communication is organized across different organizations, sourcing evidence from academic research as well as cases from practice. The general structure of the chapter is as follows. First, Section 6.2 discusses the different perspectives that have been brought to bear upon the subject of communication organization, its general importance to the corporate communication function and the organization as a whole, and the different elements of organizational structure that can be distinguished. Then the chapter moves on to discuss two of these structural elements in greater detail in the following two sections (6.3 and 6.4): the vertical structure; which includes the hierarchy of authority in which communication professionals are placed and the way in which they are organized into departments, and the horizontal structure, which encompasses cross-functional and lateral coordination mechanisms that exist over and beyond departmental structures to streamline and integrate work processes of those professionals. Then, in Section 6.5, the chapter explains how and why organizations differ in the way they have organized their communication (that is, differences in vertical and horizontal structures across organizations), and addresses the question of whether there is a best 'fit' between the type of organization (i.e. small businesses, multi-divisional and multinational corporations, public sector organizations and professional service organizations) and organizational form. In this way, the chapter aims to provide the reader not only with a clear overview of the various ways in which communication can be organized, but also with an understanding of which organizational form suits a particular organization best.

6.2 Perspectives on organizing communication

The subject of how communication is organized is important as it not only determines to a large extent whether the corporate communication function is enabled to provide strategic input into decision-making at the highest corporate level of an organization, but also whether the communication activities that are carried out at various places within the organization are streamlined and integrated in a cost-effective manner. In other words, the way in which corporate communication is organized carries important strategic and political dimensions and is crucial for the effective planning and management of communication programmes.

Despite its importance, historical evidence upon the subject is rather limited. The marketing historian Hollander, with his historical study of the market orientation of US firms, is one of the few exceptions. He observed that in the 1950s and 1960s the different marketing communication disciplines of advertising, promotions, selling, and publicity were functionally separate within the organization, but he suggested nonetheless that 'the indications are that advertising, sales, promotion and merchandising people in industry worked together more closely than is commonly thought'.[1] In the 1970s, there was equally fairly little systematic empirical research into how communication was organized, although there were some commentary pieces written by practitioners that again stressed the functional separation of communication disciplines, a feat that was generally seen as detrimental to the effective functioning of communication as a whole. Writing in 1973, Cook, one of these communication professionals, argued that companies should consolidate their entire communication function, bringing together various external communication disciplines, such as advertising, public relations, promotions and issues management, into a central organizational function, with the aim of increasing the organizational autonomy of communication within the organization.[2] Following in Cook's footsteps, many academics in the 1980s and 1990s similarly discussed the traditional division of communication responsibilities into separate disciplines. Don Schultz and his colleagues from Northwestern University, for instance, took issue with what they called the 'functional silos' of communication that had emerged within many organizations because of this division of communication into separate disciplines. They argued that in the 1970s and 1980s, because of an emphasis on functional specialism, there had been a trend towards dividing and splitting communication up into separate disciplines that were set up as independent units, which had led to each discipline protecting its financial and specialist 'turf' and to an ineffective use of communication as fragmented and conflicting messages were being sent out.[3]

In short, the views expressed on the subject in the 1980s and 1990s all voice a concern that dividing communication and organizing it in a functional manner by discipline or specialty leads to 'fragmentation', 'functional silos', 'stovepipes', and 'Chinese walls' between communication disciplines.[4] The suggestion was that organizations rather should move to other more 'integrated' forms of organizing communication that would enable communication practitioners from marketing communication, public relations and internal communication to work together and to coordinate their work. When corporate communication emerged within communication practice in the early 1990s, it equally suggested an alternative form of organizing communication to ensure the autonomy of the function and its strategic input into strategic decision-making and to enable practitioners from different disciplines to work together and to coordinate the timing and content of their communication to different stakeholder groups. Specifically, when corporate communication emerged, it suggested the following:[5]

- *Organizations should consolidate and centralize communication disciplines into a single department*: the general idea is to bring a range of communications disciplines together into a single department so that the knowledge and skills of practitioners can be shared, specialist expertise is enhanced, and the autonomy and visibility of the communication function within the organization are secured. Some communication disciplines might still be organized as separate units or devolved to other functional areas (e.g. finance, human resources), but the general idea here is to consolidate a sufficient number of communication disciplines into a single department so that communication can be strategically managed from a central corporate perspective.

- *Organizations should locate the communication department within the organizational hierarchy with easy access to decision-makers*: a second recommendation was to place this single communication department within easy reach of senior managers who are members of the decision-making team, so that the strategic input of communication into corporate strategy is secured. In practice, this often implies that the communication department is a staff function at corporate headquarters from where it can advise the senior decision-making team, and that the most senior communications practitioner has a direct reporting or advisory relationship to the Chief Executive Officer or even a seat on the executive board or senior management team.

- *Organizations need to implement cross-functional coordination mechanisms between the communication department and other departments across the organization*: it was also recognized that, while a range of communication disciplines may have been consolidated into a single department, further cross-functional 'integration' over and beyond departments (for instance, between the communication and marketing departments) was needed because most of the work related to communication cuts across different knowledge and skills domains and because in large organizations communication practitioners may be physically spread across different divisions and business units. The suggestion therefore was for companies to implement cross-functional coordination mechanisms such as teams and council meetings between practitioners working in different communication disciplines, departments and divisions which would lead to a sharing and cross-fertilization of expertise, a greater understanding on the part of practitioners of each other's knowledge and skills, and to the design of tonally and visually consistent communications programmes.

These three recommendations point to a particular way in which communication can, and perhaps should, be organized within contemporary organizations. These recommendations also suggest what the vertical and horizontal structuring of communication should look like. The *vertical structure* refers to the way in which tasks and activities (and the disciplines that they represent) are divided and arranged into departments (defined as the departmental arrangement) and located in the hierarchy of authority within an organization. The solid vertical lines that connect the boxes on an organization chart depict this vertical structure and the authority relationships involved (Figure 6.1). Within such vertical lines, the occupant of the higher position has the authority to direct and control the activities of the occupant of the lower position. A major role of the vertical lines of authority on the organization chart is thus to depict the way in which the work and output of specialized departments or units are coordinated *vertically*; that is by authority in reporting relationships.

The first two of the above-mentioned recommendations refer to the vertical structure. The third recommendation, on the other hand, refers to the *horizontal structure*: the structures that are laid over the vertical structure to coordinate and integrate functionally and physically separated tasks and activities. Vertical structure divides each organization's primary tasks into smaller tasks and activities, with each box on the organization chart representing a position assigned to undertake a unique, detailed portion of the organization's overall mission. Such vertical specialization, and the spreading out of tasks over different departments, however, require some coordination or integration of work processes. This coordination or integration is achieved through horizontal structure, which ensures that tasks and activities, while spread out over departments, are combined into the basic functions (i.e. human resources, finance, operations, marketing, and communication) that need to be fulfilled within the organization. Horizontal structure can take various forms including multi-disciplinary task or project teams, formal lines of communication, standardized work processes, council meetings, or the use of communication 'czars' (senior professionals working as integrators between departments), and is not normally displayed within an organization chart. Figure 6.1 illustrates this distinction between the vertical and

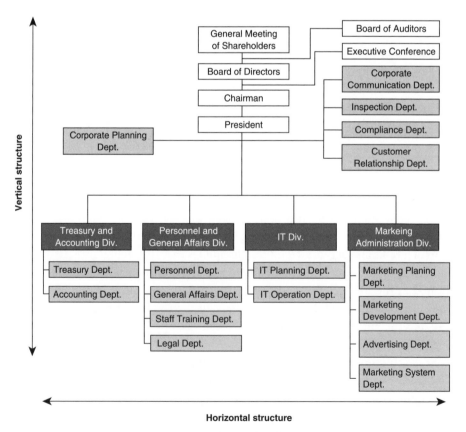

Figure 6.1   The vertical and horizontal structure in organizing communication

horizontal structure in relation to a mid-size Japanese corporation in the financial services industry. The vertical structure of this organization shows that corporate communication is placed quite high within the organization as an independent staff department advising the President (CEO) and Chairman of the corporation. The horizontal structure, which for this corporation is likely to involve formal collaborative ties connecting the corporate communication department with the advertising and general affairs departments, cannot as mentioned be read from the organization chart.

The above three recommendations also suggest that with a few exceptions (e.g. small businesses), organizations need to use both vertical and horizontal structures to organize communications. The obvious reasoning behind this is that although bringing communication practitioners together *vertically* into one or a few departments may lead to enhanced efficiency and to the ability to develop specialized, distinctive capabilities, it may not lead to coordination between communication disciplines and with other functional areas (e.g. marketing) outside those departments, and it risks 'turf wars', functional myopia, and over-specialization. A horizontal structure overlying the vertical structure is therefore needed in order to coordinate disparate communication tasks and activities, which also recognizes that communication with key stakeholders might emerge from various places within the organization[6] (Chapter 5).

Sections 6.3 and 6.4 discuss the vertical and horizontal structuring of communication across different types of organizations. Section 6.5 then elaborates on this in discussing what explains the choices that organizations make for a particular structure.

6.3 Vertical structure

To reiterate, organizing communication consists of a vertical and horizontal structure. The vertical structure refers to the way in which different communication disciplines are arranged into departments, and the formal reporting relationships that these departments abide by. The horizontal structure, which is discussed in Section 6.4, refers to the cross-functional mechanisms that are horizontally laid over departments and connect communication practitioners with one another and with professionals from across the organization.

In recent years there has been a lot of discussion on the departmental arrangement of communication and the reporting relationship of communication departments. Ultimately, the heart of this discussion is about the professional status of corporate communication (vis-à-vis other established functions such as human resources, marketing and finance) and its strategic involvement in decision-making at the highest corporate level of an organization. As mentioned, the argument is that different communication disciplines *should be consolidated* in a single department, and that the head of this department *should report directly to the CEO or the senior management team* (or be a member of this team) to bolster and secure the functional expertise as well as the strategic involvement of corporate communication in strategic decision-making. The communication scholars Broom and Dozier characterized this involvement in organizational decision-making as more important to communication practitioners than any other measure of professional growth.[7]

The following paragraphs discuss the actual departmental arrangement of communication and the reporting relationships involved across different types of organizations: (1) small businesses; (2) multi-divisional and multinational corporations; (3) public sector organizations; and (4) professional service organizations.

There are, in principle, many different ways in which organizations can arrange their communication disciplines, and the staff responsible for them, into departments. Depending on the range of communication disciplines (e.g. advertising, publicity, community relations, corporate advertising, crisis communications, internal communications, financial communications, government relations, investor relations, issues management, lobbying, promotions, sponsorship, public affairs) present in an organization, such disciplines can be brought together into one or two central communication departments, be devolved as stand-alone units (e.g. a governmental affairs unit), or be subordinated to other functions such as marketing, human resources or finance. Given these organizing options open to companies, much academic research has in recent years attempted to describe and explain how different communication disciplines are mapped onto organizational units or departments, and whether this mapping reveals tendencies towards consolidation or, alternatively, towards a dispersion of communication responsibilities.

The small business

Small businesses (organizations with less than 250 employees) operate in a single market or small number of markets with a limited range of products and services. The scope of the organization is therefore likely to be restricted to the primary operating processes, its products and services, and the market(s) that it serves. It is therefore unlikely that small businesses will have central service or staff departments such as communication to undertake complex analysis of the environment; rather, it may be senior managers themselves, perhaps even the founder of the firm, who has direct contact with the marketplace and other stakeholders (local government, community, etc.). In terms of organization structure, this means that many small businesses are likely to have a simple and lean 'functional' structure with the core functions of operations, marketing, finance and human resource, geared towards producing a single product and bringing it to market. Communication has often not evolved into various fully-fledged disciplines in small businesses (as there is less need for specific strategic expertise in, say, issues management), but promotional tactics are used and are added to the extant responsibilities of one or a few of the 'functional' managers, often the marketing manager.

The multi-divisional or multinational corporation

For multi-divisional or multinational corporations the key issues of organizing communication are substantially different from those facing the small business. Here the company is likely to be diverse in terms of both products and geographic markets. It may be that the company is in a range of different types of business in the form of subsidiary companies within a holding company structure, or divisions within a multidivisional structure. Therefore, issues of structure and control at the corporation, and relationships between businesses and the corporate centre, are usually a major strategic issue for multinational firms. One key structural consideration in organizing communications therefore, is as the management scholar Argenti suggests, to have 'all communications focused by centralizing the activity under one senior officer at a corporation's headquarters or to decentralize activities and allow individual business units to decide how best to handle communications'.[8] Centralization of all communication responsibilities by placing the majority of communication practitioners in a staff department at the corporate centre has advantages in terms of a greater corporate control and coordination of all communications programmes to stakeholders, ensuring consistency and achieving greater efficiency as research and communications materials can be shared. Decentralization, devolving communications responsibilities to departments within the separate business units, requires more personnel, but delivers advantages as communication can be attuned to the specifics of the business unit and the geographic market and stakeholders that it serves. Decisions on whether to centralize or decentralize communication are often also based on the identity structure of a company: centralization is likely to be greater in the case of a monolithic identity structure (where the company and its business units carry the same name), while decentralization is often chosen with endorsed and branded identity structures (where the business units profile their own distinct names) (see Chapter 4). The rationale behind this is that in branded and endorsed identity structures, greater leverage can be given to communication practitioners within the individual business units in their communication to markets and stakeholders.[9] A related issue in this regard is the extent to which the centre adds to or detracts from the value of its businesses. For the communication staff department at the corporate centre, this means that it must deliver value-added advice and assistance to communication practitioners in the individual business units, if it wants to secure a receptive environment for its involvement. This may require the staff department to move beyond a tactical or routine view of communication, where it is seen as part of organizational routine and overheads and just deals with programmed decisions such as using weekly news briefings and publishing the monthly employee newsletter. Practitioners within the corporate staff department rather need to provide expert and strategic advice and develop useful tools such as an overall communications strategy, so that the communications activities of the different parts of the company can be coordinated and so that 'individual' business units see their part in the 'overall' communications strategy.[10] Case Study 6.1 illustrates some of the challenges facing multinational companies.

CASE STUDY 6.1

SARA LEE/DE: ORGANIZING COMMUNICATION IN A MULTINATIONAL CORPORATION★

Sara Lee/DE, headquartered in Utrecht, the Netherlands, is a subsidiary of Chicago-based Sara Lee Corporation, and is a global group of branded consumer packaged goods companies. The DE part of the Sara Lee/DE name goes back to the Douwe Egberts (DE) brand, a Dutch coffee and tea producer that was taken over by Sara Lee in 1978. Initially, the situation for the organization that formerly traded under the DE name, changed little through the takeover. But, early in the 1980s, Sara Lee also acquired the Dutch company Intradel, a household and body care merchant, and decided to merge this newly acquired company with the existing DE organization. Having merged these two companies operating in very different sectors Sara Lee finally decided in 1989 to change the structure of the newly formed organization. A corporate holding was established carrying the name Sara Lee/DE with two divisions: Coffee and Tea, and Household and Body Care. Together, these divisions now encompass around hundred business units operating in more than forty countries. Within this holding structure, responsibilities are devolved to each of these business units so that local businesses can respond to and meet local market needs in the best possible way.

The restructuring in 1989 also entailed that communication responsibilities were split into a central corporate public relations department at the group level of Sara Lee/DE, and smaller communication departments and professionals being placed within the various business units.

The split seemed a logical division of tasks, and is typical for many multinational corporations, but almost immediately brought clear tensions with it about responsibilities and procedures concerning communication. Particularly in the area of media relations, managers and professionals from across the organization duly talked with the press on their own initiative, in the absence of clear procedures for media relations.

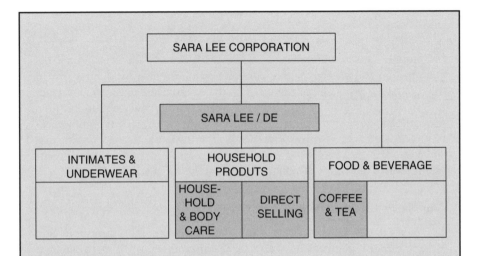

These tensions and debates on responsibilities and procedures have since led to the implementation of two formal initiatives that aim to ensure that the central corporate public relations department maintains its policy-making and coordinating role in an organization where communication responsibilities are largely decentralized to the level of the individual business units. The first initiative is that the corporate public relations department offers the general strategic framework for communication to business units. This basically means that the general corporate strategy of the Sara Lee/DE company is translated into a set of communication values and procedures by the corporate public relations department, which are then passed onto communication practitioners within the individual business units. These practitioners in turn develop their own communication plans, but need to adhere to these values and procedures. As the Chairman of the Executive Board once said: 'The corporate public relations department offers the frame, and professionals within the business units each deliver a picture for it.' The second formal initiative is that the corporate public relations department not only supports and counsels the executive board on organization-wide communication, but is also designated as an internal consultancy practice that the individual business units can turn to for advice and assistance. As an internal consultancy, the department operates on a project basis for communication practitioners in the business units, giving them value-added, expert communication advice and assisting and helping them to develop and execute communication plans. The corporate public relations department is for this purpose staffed with three expert consultants (each specializing in an area of communication) alongside the head of the department, an editor, a production manager and two personal assistants.

(Continued)

(Continued)

Through these two initiatives, Sara Lee/DE believes it is able to balance the coordination and management of communication issues at the central level, at the level of the whole organization, with its decentralized management structure in which individual business units manage their own communication plans. Individual business units are still responsible for their own communication plans, but these two initiatives are seen to ensure a greater coordination and collaboration across the organization, which leads to consistency of communication and a better profiling of the corporation as a whole.

Questions for reflection

1. To what extent are these tensions between a central communication department at group level and local communications practitioners at the level of individual business units typical of all multinational corporations? If not, which multinational corporations fall outside this characterization?
2. To what extent do you believe Sara Lee/DE has implemented suitable initiatives to deal with these tensions? What would you have done differently?

Note: *This case was based on Den Haan, J.J. (2002) 'De communicatie bij Sara Lee/DE: Corporate communicatie in een decentrale organisatie', *Communicatie Cases*, 11: 9–24, and corporate documents from the Sara Lee/DE website.

Academic research on multi-divisional and multinational corporations in the United States, the UK and continental Europe has found that communication disciplines are consolidated into a separate communication department, rather than arranged into various stand-alone units. A Conference Board study in 1996 showed that close to 80 per cent of the largest 'corporate affairs' or 'corporate communication' departments incorporated a whole range of communication disciplines including media relations, speechwriting, employee communication, corporate advertising and community relations. Similar results were obtained by a 1996 study sponsored by the US-based Public Affairs Council and a 2001 study sponsored by the Council of Public Relations Firms, which both indicated that a whole range of communication disciplines including community relations, issues management, employee communication and media relations are centralized in 'communication' departments. The results of these studies also indicated that disciplines such as consumer affairs and brand advertising were hardly if ever integrated into such a 'communication' department, suggesting that marketing activities and marketing communications are brought under a different department (and are thus not subservient or in a direct reporting relationship to corporate communication).[11] Surveying 75 of the 300 largest US corporations, Hunter equally found that, in 81 pert cent of these corporations, external communication disciplines have been arranged into separate corporate communication and marketing departments. Hunter's study also showed that both the communication and marketing departments operated at a similar level in these US corporations (as separate but equal management partners), and that there were no apparent moves towards a conversion of communication disciplines (e.g. marketing communications taken out of the marketing department and subsumed as the responsibility of the communication department) or towards increased structural alignment or even a consolidation of all communication disciplines into one overall communications or external relations department.[12] And Grunig and Grunig, reporting on the IABC Excellence study, corroborated these findings in their observation that communication is more effective when marketing communications does not dominate the communication function, as communications 'has its greatest value when that function and the marketing function are treated as equal partners in management'.[13] Figure 6.2 illustrates this greater consolidation of communication disciplines in Siemens, one of the world's largest electrical engineering and electronics companies. Figure 6.2 highlights the different disciplines within the central corporate communication department including media relations, corporate responsibility and employee communication. In addition, there are specific project teams for mergers and acquisitions (M&A) and crises incorporating staff from these different areas within corporate communication. Interestingly, Siemens has organized market communications as part of the wider corporate communication function rather than as a separate department. The explanation for this may be that Siemens is mainly a business-to-business organization and does not market itself to end-consumers or end-users of its technology.

In summary, all academic studies within the US, the UK and Europe indicate a greater consolidation of communication disciplines within companies than before, yet often they are still found in separate communication and marketing departments. Some of these studies have moved beyond this simple observation and have started to explain why across organizations and continents such consolidation exists. The following three sets of reasons figure most prominently as explanations:

1. *Staff versus line.* A traditional explanation for having a central communication department separate from marketing is that certain areas of communication fall outside the operational and more tactical remit of the marketing department.[14] Marketing is a so-called line function concerned with producing, distributing and promoting the company's products within selected markets; which includes marketing communication (advertising, promotions, publicity and selling). All other communication disciplines have a more general corporate (rather than product) focus, and are also more supportive and advisory in nature rather than being directly involved in the core business process of bringing products to markets. These other communication disciplines (e.g. issues

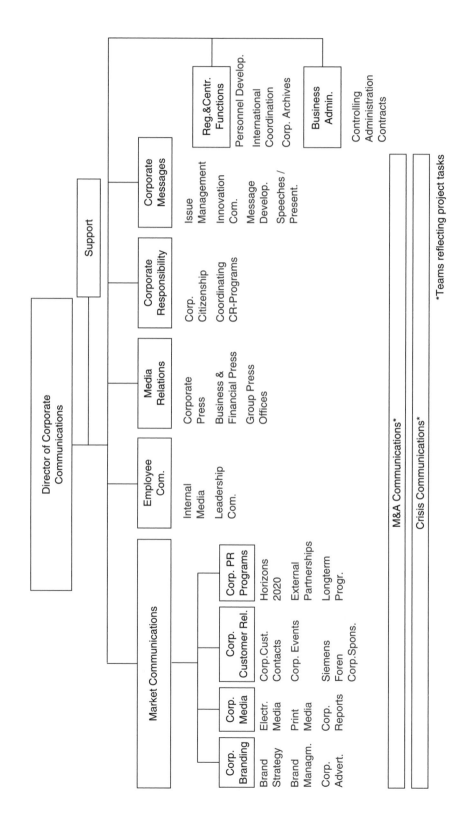

Figure 6.2 The departmental arrangement of communication in Siemens

management, investor relations, media relations, public affairs, government relations) have therefore been brought together into a separate staff department as a staff function. A *staff function* is a function where the manager has no direct executive power over the primary process or responsibility for it, but fulfils an advisory role, based on specific expertise, to all departments within the organization (see Figure 6.1 for an illustration). A *line function* such as marketing, in comparison, is concerned with the primary operating activities of the company. As a staff department, communication is enabled to advise the CEO and the senior management team and to support and assist line managers with strategic communication advice. In comparison, if communication had been organized as a line department (or incorporated into, for instance, marketing), it would be cast in the role of a tactical support function or production unit supporting the primary operating activities of the organization.

2. *Domain similarity and resource dependencies.* A second explanation for the grouping of communications disciplines into communication and marketing departments is that this reflects so-called domain similarities and task dependencies between certain disciplines. *Domain similarity* is defined as the degree to which two different individuals or disciplines share similar goals, skills or tasks. *Resource dependence* is the dependence of a practitioner in one communication discipline on obtaining resources (e.g. advice, assistance, communication products) from another discipline to accomplish his or her objectives. The explanation provided here is that separate communication and marketing departments, exist as practitioners and disciplines within each department share the same technical skills, knowledge, and a focus on either 'corporate' or 'marketing' stakeholders. The disciplines in each department are as a result highly dependent on each other's knowledge, skills and resources. In other words, the corporate communication and marketing domains in these departments, while showing some overlap, are sufficiently distinct (indicating significant differences in the skills of practitioners, the work performed by the unit, the operating goals of the unit, and the sources from which the departments obtain their funding) to warrant a departmental separation.[15] In this sense, in the words of the organization theorist Pfeffer, a departmental separation into communication and marketing is logical in that 'the process of grouping activities, roles, or positions in the organization [serves] to coordinate effectively the *interdependencies* that exist ... the implicit goal of the structuring process is achieving a more rationalized and coordinated system of activity'.[16]

3. *Economies of scale.* A third and final explanation is that there is a certain economic rationale behind bringing disciplines together into departments. The point here is that it is relatively expensive to have stand-alone units for different communication disciplines, as it raises the costs of coordinating tasks and responsibilities. In contrast, when disciplines are taken together into one or a few departments, it may not only enhance the functional expertise and skills base of communication professionals within those departments, but it may also ease coordination and minimize the necessity and cost associated with it of cross-department or cross-unit interaction. Because of these economies of scale, a discipline will normally only be separated off and organized as a separate unit when it is of critical and growing importance to a company, and comes to engross a critical mass of communication practitioners as a result. This

happened, for instance, with the discipline of investor relations in large US corporations, which, given the importance of informing shareholders (who can make or break a company) and the financial community, came to incorporate more staff, and was in many companies eventually split up and departmental- ized as a stand-alone unit. Research by Roa shows that of all the Fortune 500 industrial companies only 16 per cent (84 cases) had investor relations depart- ments in 1984, but that by the end of 1994, they had increased to 56 per cent (270 cases) of the sample.[17]

Different communication departments and units within multi-divisional and multinational corporations may in principle also have different reporting rela- tionships. The manager of a communication services unit in a particular divi- sion may, for instance, report to the head of the marketing department, whereas an investor relations unit may, for instance, have a dual reporting relationship to the finance and communication departments. Such reporting relationships are of course largely determined by the departmental arrangement of communi- cation; that is, where communication disciplines (as a separate department or unit, or as subordinated to another department) are placed within the organi- zation's hierarchy. Academic research in this area has been particularly con- cerned with identifying to whom the communication department reports: whether directly to the CEO and senior management team, or to another department at a lower level in the hierarchy.

The communication scholars White and Mazur have argued that a direct reporting relationship to the CEO and senior management team is important as it leads to 'excellent' communication management because senior manage- ment is advised on issues, and stakeholder and identity considerations may more easily be factored into the process of organizational decision-making.[18] The academic Wright argued that the credibility of communication executives may also be open to question unless they are seen to report directly to senior executive officers.[19]

The results from a number of studies indicate that in the large majority of cases, there is indeed such a direct reporting relationship between the staff cor- porate communication department and the CEO and executive team. Most multi-divisional and multinational corporations have a communication depart- ment linked to the CEO and executive team in an advisory capacity. In a recent study in the UK, Moss and his colleagues found that communication directors report directly to the CEO or chairperson of the senior management team but are not formal members of the senior management team responsible for deter- mining corporate strategy and strategic decision-making. In other words, all of the managers in the study indicated that 'they were often consulted on impor- tant issues likely to affect their organizations, [but] their involvement in key operational decision-making was often limited to advising on how best to pre- sent policies to the outside world or to internal stakeholders'.[20] This is not to say, of course, that the communication director should not have a seat on the executive board or executive team and should remain in this advisory capacity, but the UK study did show the current impediments to such a move. On the one hand, there is still a considerable lack of understanding and a lack of commitment to communication among the CEO and senior managers. On the other hand, many communication directors and senior communication practitioners often do not meet the needs of senior managers to provide communication advice and an input into corporate strategy in ways that contribute to the accomplishment of organizational objectives and that affect the bottom line (see also Chapter 7 for a more detailed look at the roles, knowledge and skills of communication practitioners). In other words, as the communication practitioner Osborne put it, strategic corporate communication stands or falls with highly qualified input from the communication director or practitioner at the decision-making table and only then will there be such a receptive environment for that contribution. The director or practitioner therefore will need to produce strategically focused recommendations for strategic corporate action by bringing to the attention of the CEO and top managers a broad understanding of the strategic management process and of those issues which may affect and impact upon an organization's reputation.[21]

Public sector organizations

An effective streamlining of communication activities is just as important to organizations in the public sector as in commercial organizations. The public sector involves many different types of organizations including nationalized companies (e.g. utilities), government agencies and departments (e.g. the Ministry of Defence), and public service organizations (e.g. hospitals and schools). The larger organizations in the public sector (as opposed to, for instance, small government agencies) traditionally have a strong presence close to senior management and the policy-making of 'public' communication disciplines (e.g. media relations, publicity) that are used to inform the general public, and traditionally little marketing communications. This is a result of the direct or indirect control or influence exercised from outside the organization by government in particular. With budgets being allocated by government and missions imposed, there was traditionally little incentive for public organizations to develop extensive marketing programmes, let alone think in marketing terms about the products and services that they deliver. Increasingly, however, organizations that once were in the public sector are being privatized or changes are carried through within them because government sees benefits in requiring public organizations to become more sharply focused on customer requirements and competitive pressures. Many public organizations have therefore developed marketing expertise in recent years, and have brought marketing communications professionals in-house. Often these professionals are incorporated into the staff communication department, from the viewpoint that marketing communications need to be aligned with the other communication systems of the organization that are aimed at informing and gaining acceptance among stakeholders for the public good that the organization delivers. Alternatively, the professionals in marketing communications may be departmentalized as a separate service unit and placed in the 'line' of the organization near the core operating units, or placed under marketing (when the organization has set up such a department).

Professional service organizations

Traditionally based values are often of particular importance in professional service organizations where professional advice has traditionally been seen as more important than revenue-earning capability. To a large extent this was the case in medicine, accountancy, law and other professions. Therefore, many of these organizations consisted of either a simple functional structure built on the expertise – and the products and services associated with it (often defined as 'practice areas') – of their professionals and a number of supporting departments (finance, human resource, and research and development), or loose network structures in the case of larger, geographically dispersed professional service organizations. The latter network structure is often the case in private sector professional service firms with global acumen and a partnership structure (i.e., partners managing and/or owning local branches) in place. Either way, the structure of professional service organizations is typically geared towards the development and nurture of specific professional expertise (whether in law, accountancy, medicine, or management consultancy) and the acquisition of clients through direct selling or referral, and therefore lacks separate, fully developed marketing or communication departments. As with the small business, communication and marketing responsibilities, if they do exist, are typically added to and integrated within existing responsibilities of professionals in each of the firm's 'practice areas'. Some professional service organizations have, however, in recent years, added a small communication unit to their supporting departments, usually charged with assisting in the acquisition of clients through the production of communication materials (website, brochures, etc.).

6.4 Horizontal structure

The horizontal structure involves a whole raft of coordination mechanisms that companies implement to integrate the work processes that are carried out in disparate parts of the organization. In the area of communication, horizontal mechanisms are important as these enable companies to respond fast and effectively to emergent issues or shifting priorities of stakeholder groups, and allow controlling and ensuring that consistent messages are being sent out through all the various communications channels to stakeholders. A final point stressing the importance of horizontal structure is that it may offset the potential disadvantages (functional silos, compartmentalization and 'turf wars') of the vertical structure as it allows cross-functional work processes, integration and sufficient flexibility. Academic research has identified a number of effective forms of horizontal structure such as teamwork, council meetings, and documentation of work processes.

Recruitment, training and job rotation

The horizontal integration of communication work processes often starts with the recruitment and training of communication practitioners within the organization. When practitioners who are recruited to an organization have a more general outlook and understanding of the communication profession, and know how work processes need to be integrated, they will look beyond their own departmental boundaries and start appreciating other communication disciplines and the professionals working with them. Recruitment is therefore important as companies can select practitioners who not only have the ability to work in teams, to appreciate different communication disciplines, and to fit into the company culture, but also have a 'generalist' focus (instead of a purely specialist focus on a particular communication discipline) that leads to strategic, integrated and holistic thinking.[22] Training is important as communication practitioners who receive ongoing skills training in different communication disciplines are generally found to be better able to integrate their work with people working in other communication disciplines. An additional mechanism to support integration among communication practitioners is job rotation. The benefits of rotating communication practitioners among different work tasks or among different business units of the company are increased appreciation for colleagues in other communication professions, increased personal networks within the company, and identification with the company rather than with occupational and technical specialization. The latter identification with the company is also important because it may lead to practitioners thinking more strategically about what communication can contribute to the company and to the achievement of corporate objectives.

Recruitment and training of practitioners are thus important for the horizontal integration of work, but, beyond this personal level of the communication professional, there are a number of further horizontal structures and processes of coordination within and across departments: teamwork, process documentation, open communication and networking platforms, council meetings, and communication guidelines.

Teamwork

Multi-functional teams are an important mechanism in the coordination and integration of work of different communication disciplines.[23] Teams can be further distinguished in terms of the natural work team, permanent teams that work together on an ongoing basis (e.g., a cross-company investor relations team), and the task force team, created on an ad hoc basis for specific projects (e.g., an internal communications team that guides a corporate restructuring). Task force teams are also assembled when an issue or crisis emerges in the company's environment (Chapter 10), and an adequate response needs to be formulated and communicated to key stakeholders. It is important for both the natural work teams and task force teams that team members with complementary skills are selected, that practitioners are trained in teamwork, that the whole team has authority to make decisions and implement suggestions, and that the team follows a step-by-step process in its work (from analysis and planning to action and evaluation).

Process documentation

Organizations can use various tools to document work processes across disciplines and departments in visual and comprehensive formats, such as flow charts, process maps, and checklists. Such process documentation creates a shared understanding among all communication practitioners about the processes of integration, institutionalizes processes of integration, thus making the organization less dependent on certain individuals, facilitates continuous improvements of the processes of integration, enables communication practitioners to benchmark their processes against other companies, and creates opportunities for cycle-time reduction. Traditionally, however, communication practitioners are unaccustomed to defining work tasks in terms of process steps. Many of them do not think the analytical and disciplined approach of documenting and standardizing processes is conducive to creativity. This was also the reaction of communications staff in Philips (see Case Study 6.2) when the company decided its process documentation exercise was to be carried out in all its functions and departments, including corporate communication. Senior managers argued that, even if the development of communication programmes is a unique creative process, there were some process steps that communication professionals always follow, and these steps can be identified, documented, and improved. Routine processes and repetitive steps in the company's communication processes have since been documented and standardized in flow-charts and worksheets, which the company believes has not stifled creativity, but has cut redundancies in the coordination process (e.g. too many meetings or approvals previously built in) and has made the horizontal organization of communications across the company more streamlined, more professional and, in light of the cost reductions received, more accountable.

Open communication and networking platforms

In addition to documented work processes that are explicit and formal, integration also often occurs through more informal channels. Much of the interaction among communication practitioners in fact takes place informally, in the e-mail system, over the phones, and in the hallways. Companies can facilitate such informal communications by placing communication professionals physically close to one another (in the same building), by reducing symbolic differences such as separate car parks and cafeterias, by establishing an infrastructure of e-mail, video-conferences, and other electronic communication channels, and by establishing open access to senior management. In large organizations, it is also important that communication practitioners from different disciplines (e.g. marketing communications, internal communications) frequently meet at internal conferences and meetings, where they can get to know one another, network, and share ideas.

Council meetings

Council meetings are often seen as critical to the coordination of communication practitioners from different departments and working in different business units.[24] A council meeting usually consists of representatives of different communication disciplines (e.g. media relations, internal communication, marketing communications), who meet to discuss the strategic issues concerning communication and review their past performance. Typically, ideas for improved coordination between communication disciplines bubble up at such council meetings, and the council appoints a subcommittee or team to carry them out. Most of the coordination of communication across many larger companies takes place in these council meetings and the subcommittees and teams that emerge from them. Generally, communication councils support coordination by providing opportunities for communicators worldwide to develop personal relationships, to coordinate communication projects, to share best practices, to learn from each other's mistakes, to learn about the company, to provide professional training, to improve the status of communication in the company, and to make communication professionals more committed to the organization as a whole. For all of this to happen, it is important that council meetings remain constructive and participative in their approach towards the coordination of communication (instead of becoming a control forum or review board that strictly evaluates communication campaigns), so that professionals can learn, debate and eventually decide on the strategic long-term view for communication that is in the interest of the organization as a whole.

Corporate vision and communication strategy

Processes of coordination and the integration of communication can also be supported by a strong vision and formulated strategy by senior communications practitioners. Senior communication practitioners need to meet CEOs and senior executives to help clarify the company's strategies and to reach agreement on how communication can strategically support them, and what performance measures their progress should be evaluated against. From this, a communication strategy (Chapter 5) can then be developed, which not only describes the strategic role of communication within the overall corporate and market strategies of the company, but also articulates the input, activities and performance expected of individual practitioners and communication disciplines from across the organization.

Communication guidelines

A final mechanism for horizontally integrating work processes of communication practitioners involves the use of communication guidelines. Such guidelines may range from agreed upon work procedures (whom to contact, formatting of messages, etc.) to more general design regulations on how to apply logotypes and which PMS colours to use. Often companies have a 'house style' book that includes such design regulations, but also specifies the core values of the corporate identity. For example, Ericsson, the mobile phone manufacturer, has a 'global brand book' that distills the corporation's identity in a number of core values that communication practitioners are expected to adhere to and incorporate in all of their messages to stakeholders. Ericsson also convenes a number of workshops with communication practitioners across the organization to familiarize these practitioners with the Ericsson identity, the brand book, and the general work procedures that come with their job.

The above-mentioned mechanisms apply to the coordination and integration of work among practitioners from different communication disciplines. But it is important to note that corporate communications and the management of stakeholders spiral to other functions as well. Horizontal procedures and arrangements for the coordination of work processes between communication practitioners and professionals in, for instance, human resources or finance therefore equally need to be put in place. This might take the form of simply a meeting between senior managers of communication, human resources and finance to sound out the issues, and align their strategies accordingly. FedEx fits this picture, where the director of communication meets once a year individually with all of the company's senior managers to discuss their communications needs. As he explains, 'We need to understand what the business priorities are, in order to align corporate communications with them.

Otherwise we will be relegated to a mouthpiece, a media impression generating machine'.[25]

It might, however, also be that there are more concrete interdependencies and work processes between communication and other management functions which requires more structural horizontal arrangements. The implementation of work teams connecting these functions might be an option in such cases, and it perhaps also requires that communication managers approach professionals from these other functions as their 'customers.' Hewlett Packard's corporate communication staff, for instance, has developed a database to profile its internal 'customers' to better meet their needs. Telefonica, the global telecommunications firm, equally has such an arrangement where the corporate reputation department advises other functions within the company (including finance, human resources, operations, and marketing) as 'clients' on stakeholder issues, and assists and supports each of these clients in the development of stakeholder engagement programmes.

Academic research on the use of horizontal coordination mechanisms across different companies has been scarce. There is very little systematic evidence from research that documents whether and how companies may be seen to use some of the horizontal mechanisms outlined above. Case studies and evidence from practice are equally limited, but the few existing case studies do indicate that generally not enough horizontal structures are put in place to assist communication practitioners in the carrying out and integration of their work. In small businesses, one might expect little formal horizontal structures such as teams and communication guidelines, as personnel can easily, and often informally, liaise with one another and solve the communications problem at hand. But large organizations in both the private and public sectors generally need more elaborate horizontal structures such as council meetings and teams. Particularly in multi-divisional firms operating across geographical borders, horizontal structures are not a luxury but an absolute necessity. Nonetheless, however, in many large organizations not enough attention is being paid to the use of horizontal structures, as there is often among managers and practitioners a preoccupation with the vertical structure of bringing disciplines together into departments. Gronstedt, author of an influential study into horizontal structures in eight best-practice US firms, challenges this preoccupation and suggests that there should be less focus on 'Who is in charge?' and 'Who belongs to what department?' and rather an emphasis on developing more knowledge about horizontal processes and structures of integration. He emphasizes the importance of horizontal structures: 'Integrated communication is not necessarily about putting public relations, marketing communications and other communications professionals into a single department, but about integrating their [work] processes.'[26] Gronstedt therefore suggests that each company should have a sufficient number of horizontal mechanisms in place, as this not only leads to a better coordination of the work of communication practitioners, but also to more job satisfaction, greater identification with the company, and generally more competent communication professionals.

Case Study 6.2 shows how communication is organized in a large multinational corporation. It shows the choices that were made within Philips regarding the vertical and horizontal structuring of communication and how these relate to changes in the corporation's corporate strategy, the company's culture and the geographical complexity of its operations.

CASE STUDY 6.2

ORGANIZING COMMUNICATION IN PHILIPS⋆

Philips, an international electronics firm, started off as a manufacturer of light bulbs and electrical equipment in the Netherlands. Since its founding in 1891, the company has been at the vanguard of technological innovation and is credited with several inventions such as the audiocassette, the CD and the DVD. However, despite its strength in technological innovation, the company's financial health deteriorated in the 1990s because of a lack of focus, as the company operated in too many industries and markets, and because it was lagging behind its competitors in terms of marketing its products. Through the 1990s, Philips initiated several restructuring exercises which included selling off several businesses. In 1992, a restructuring exercise called Operation Centurion (guided by C.K. Prahalad, a well-known management expert) involved reducing the workforce, effecting a change in the company's culture (which had become rather bureaucratic and resistant to change), and streamlining internal processes so that the time of bringing products to market could be reduced. In 1996, another intensive restructuring exercise included further job cuts, outsourcing component manufacturing, and selling off unprofitable as well as non-core businesses including the computer, defence electronics and semi-conductor businesses. In addition, the restructuring in 1996 meant that responsibilities and activities became heavily decentralized with each business unit having to work on its own to become profitable. In 2001, when Gerard Kleisterlee took over as CEO, he introduced a more cooperative approach through a programme termed 'Towards One Philips' (TOP). Kleisterlee's intention was to move away from promoting each division as a separate entity. In his view, Philips had over the years become rigidly compartmentalized with each division focusing on only on its own activities and on its own bottom line. The TOP programme set out to promote a more cooperative approach, with divisions working together across the company and streamlining their operations. In doing so, the company would be able to cut costs and to become more focused on its customers and other stakeholders. In the words of Kleisterlee; 'The customer doesn't want to deal with individual product divisions, with individual product lines. He wants to have one treatment from a company called Philips and experience a brand called Philips in one and the same way.' In 2003, Kleisterlee also redefined the company's business domains and product portfolio as restricted to healthcare, lifestyle and enabling technologies. The company now includes four major divisions: lighting, domestic appliances and personal care, medical systems and consumer electronics, with more focused business units within each division.

Brand positioning

The Philips brand itself also underwent change as a result of these changes in the company's strategic focus, product portfolio and internal structure. In 1995, Philips launched the 'Let's make things better' campaign which was meant to rejuvenate the Philips brand after a period of fragmented and ineffective product-led communication. The objective of the campaign was to project Philips as a company that delivers technology to improve people's lives. The campaign tried to convey that Philips technology, while improving people's lives, could also improve the world. In some ways, the campaign reflected the rich heritage of the company. This heritage goes back to the founders of Philips, Anton and Gerard Philips, who carried on a tradition begun by their father, Frederik, of providing housing, pension and free medical care, a sports centre (which led to the founding of PSV; the Philips sports association that is well known for its football team) and a foundation to finance the older children of Philips' employees through college. In true Dutch fashion, they even provided their early factories with full-time bicycle repair men. Anton and Gerard Philips set out to improve not just the lives of customers, through advanced technological products such as the light bulb, but also those of their employees and of community members. Their founding belief was that by daring to make choices that improve the lives of people both inside and outside the company, they would be successful. Though the 'Let's make things better' campaign was successful in profiling the company as a single brand, senior managers of the company felt that it failed to convey the design excellence and technical superiority of Philips' products. Therefore, in 2004, the 'Sense and simplicity' campaign was launched. The 'Sense and simplicity' brand positioning is rooted in Philips' traditional strengths of design and technology. In line with this positioning, the company set out to launch high-tech products that meet customers' needs but have simple designs and easy-to-use interfaces. By 'sense', Philips meant 'delivering meaningful and exciting benefits of technology that improve people's lives' while 'simplicity' referred to its ability to provide easy access to these benefits. Technological products had to be advanced but easy to operate and designed around the needs of the customer. In this way, the brand positioning is both a brand promise to customers as well as a potential differentiator from the company's competitors in the marketplace. While companies like Samsung and Apple are also working towards simplifying technology for customers, Philips is among the first to make it part of its brand positioning

(Continued)

(Continued)

and as core to its product design. The emphasis on simplicity not only related to marketing and the design of products, but was internally also linked to the TOP programme in that both initiatives shared the objective of making Philips itself a more simple, lean and internally aligned company.

Themed messaging and reputation management

Corporate communication within Philips incorporates the new brand positioning in communications towards customers and the market. The company has set itself the target of becoming recognized as a market-driven company known for the simplicity of its products, processes and communication. Besides more market-focused communication around the theme of 'sense and simplicity', senior corporate communication managers of the company have also identified a further set of messages that they feel need to be consistently communicated to the company's core stakeholder groups. These messages relate to its care and support for people inside and outside of the business, the company's leadership in innovation, the company's vision, leadership and strategy, its track record in social and environmental responsibilities, and the company's ability to communicate effectively and engage with different stakeholder groups. Across the company, corporate communicators embed these messages in their ongoing communication with different stakeholders; an approach that Philips has termed 'themed messaging'. In essence, the idea behind this approach is that it allows Philips to 'manage' the drivers that contribute to its corporate reputation with different stakeholder groups. By using this approach, corporate communicators aim to change public perception of the company from a traditional consumer electronics group into a healthcare, lifestyle and technology group with a more unified voice and more consistent image being directed towards its stakeholders. The company tracks its performance on seven drivers of its corporate reputation: leadership in innovation (the extent to which the company is seen to develop new and exciting products and is seen as a leader in innovation), performance management (the extent to which the company is seen as a financially strong company with strong leadership and management and a sound vision and strategy), care for its employees (the extent to which the company is seen to be trustworthy and supporting its employees), quality products and services (the extent to which the company is seen to develop reliable and high quality products and services), leadership in sustainability (the extent to which the company is seen as being environmentally and socially responsible in all of its business operations), market orientation (the extent to which the company is seen to be focused on customer needs), and strong communication (the extent to which the company is seen to be communicating effectively with its stakeholders). Based upon the feedback that corporate communicators receive from such reputation audits, the company revisits its communication campaigns and stakeholder engagement programmes in an attempt to ensure that its themed messages reach its core stakeholder groups.

Vertical and horizontal structures

The themed messaging approach and the continuous measurement of Philips corporate reputation reflect the company-wide importance that is now attributed to the company's reputation with different stakeholder groups. Reputation management is seen as wider than just the remit of corporate communication as it involves all of the business and many other functions (e.g., human resources, finance) that engage with stakeholders. The company has therefore formed a reputation committee with representatives from corporate communication and other key functions across the company and chaired by the CEO. The committee is responsible for overseeing the deployment of improvement actions in areas of the seven drivers of the company's reputation (leadership in innovation, performance management, care for employees, quality products and services, leadership in sustainability, market orientation and strong communication) in which action is thought to make sense. Corporate communication is organized as separate from marketing and is directed from the headquarters of the company in Amsterdam by Jules Prast, Global Director of Corporate Communication. Prast and his colleagues in the global corporate communication department are responsible for company-wide reputation issues, measurement and the formulation and planning of corporate communication and stakeholder engagement programmes. In the words of Prast, he and his colleagues had to 'select a communication model that fits and supports the culture, strategy and configuration' of Philips. The model that was adopted to organize communication involves an 'orchestration' model whereby individual 'businesses participate in a global communications management system'. In other words, the global corporate communication department sets the themed messages for all corporate communication and supports local corporate communication functions in different regions (Europe–Middle East–Africa, North America, Latin America, and Asia Pacific) with their local communication to stakeholders. As Prast put it, 'we organized our internal and external communications around themes that served as a common reference point' for communication with stakeholders across global and local levels of the company. Hence, like most multinational corporations, Philips has a combination of a centralized 'global' corporate communication department at the corporate centre and decentralized 'local' communication departments, teams and professionals in business units around the world. The themed messaging approach is one way in which the company tries to ensure consistency in its corporate communication across the organization. Besides themed messaging, Philips has also introduced so-called process survey tools which document and standardize work processes across functions within the organization and allow professionals to improve upon their performance. Similarly, central processes in corporate communication such as media relations, employee communication, editorial calendar management, crisis communication and speeches management have also been

(Continued)

(Continued)

documented and standardized. The decision to develop these process survey tools in corporate communication reflects the wider emphasis on standardization, optimization and measurement within the engineering culture of Philips. The result of having these tools is that certain key processes are documented and standardized in flow-charts and worksheets and specify a clear set of procedures and actions to professionals. For example, in media relations, the process survey tool tells a professional who else should be contacted in relation to a media inquiry and how to draft a press release. A further effect of these tools is that they allow professionals to adjust and optimize work processes and identify 'best practices' in corporate communication based upon their learning and feedback from stakeholders. In sum, these process survey tools have helped in making corporate communication processes more visible and consistent across the company and have strengthened the accountability of corporate communication in improving its performance and in delivering results.

Questions for reflection

1. Describe the vertical and horizontal structuring of corporate communication within Philips. What can you say about the effectiveness of these structures in the light of the company's repositioning around 'sense and simplicity' and its increased focus on managing its corporate reputation with different stakeholder groups?
2. To what extent do you think that process survey tools can be effectively used within corporate communication in other multinational corporations? Are these tools applicable to any type of multinational or instead does their effectiveness depend on characteristics of the corporation such as its size, strategy or culture?

Note: ★This case study is based upon Prast, J. (2005), 'The strategic importance of measuring corporate reputation: A Philips case study', *Critical Eye*, March–May, 4–9; documents from www.philips.com; and Cornelissen, J.P., Van Ruler, B. and and Bekkum, T. (2006), 'The practice of corporate communication: towards an extended and practice-based conceptualisation', *Corporate Reputation Review*, 9 (2): 114–133.

6.5 What explains structure?

Vertical and horizontal structures of communication organization may vary across organizations. Because of historical precedents, powerful coalitions, organizational size or environmental factors, companies might differ in how communication disciplines are arranged into departments, in terms of whether they have a central, independent communication department, and also in the degree and kind of coordination mechanisms that have been installed between communications disciplines and departments. The nature of these differences was documented in detail in Sections 6.3 and 6.4 which dealt with differences in vertical and horizontal structures across different types of companies. At this point it is worth mentioning that there is a lot of academic debate on why there are such differences in how communication is organized across organizations; on what factors seem to determine vertical and horizontal structures; and whether there is an 'optimal' or best way of organizing communication for different types of organizations (i.e. small business, manufacturing/service firm, public sector organization, professional service organization, multinational corporation).

The debate about what determines structure traditionally centred around two different schools of thought: contingency theory and power-control theory.[27] Both schools of thought offer an alternative framework for studying and explaining organizational structure. Contingency theory, first of all, is a so-called structural-functionalist theory of organizational structure which suggests that organizations are very dependent on the constellation of environmental factors affecting organizations at any point in time. This perspective was initially developed in the 1960s in the works of Chandler (1962) and Lawrence and Lorsch (1967) among others.[28] The situational factors affecting organizational structure such as environmental (in)stability, technology, size and strategy that they studied came to be called contingency factors, and the related body of work came to be called contingency theory. Here the basic principle is that of interdependency. Companies are seen to adapt their formal organizational structure to align it with factors in their environment.[29] A characteristic of contingency theory is that, as a theory, it assumes that such structural, deterministic relationships between contingency factors and structure can be found and that, as contingency factors broadly differ by classes of organizations, it therefore also accounts for differences across different types of organizations.

This latter point distinguishes contingency theory, which argues that variation in structures is thus dependent on mechanisms in the environment, from theories such as 'political choice' or 'power-control', which in contrast, argue against determinism and the existence of structural relationships between an organization and its environment.[30] These political frameworks challenged the determinism inherent in contingency theory, as they sought to replace contingency theory with approaches that focus often on individual perception, belief and choice, as well as conflict and power struggles between individuals or groups within the organization. A particular example of this stream of organization theory is the 'political choice' theory of organizational structure, which posits that individual managers exercise choice rather than necessarily bow to situational dictates. Hence, this theory rejects the notion that a functional structure will be chosen and suggests that organizational structure is often counter-productive and only serves the interests of certain organizational members (i.e. powerful coalitions). Similarly, another theory, 'power-control' theory, does not go as far as to deny any form of functionalism, but stresses the importance of managerial perceptions and actions mediating between the environment and the structures within an organization. This theory, initially framed by Child in 1972, now represents a separate and powerful school of thought in research on organizations. 'Power-control' theory states that organizational structures are partly determined by or related to conditions within a company's environment, but partly also result from managerial choices. Decisions on organizational structure are influenced by managerial perceptions, so that the preferences, interest and power of managers also affect which structure is chosen. Comparing these two perspectives suggests that contingency theory focuses for its explanation of organizational structure on material or 'objective' factors such as size and technology in the company's environment, rather than on 'subjective' or political factors such as ideas, perceptions, and norms, as 'power-control' theory does. In terms of managerial choice, contingency theory implies a relatively high level of determinism where managers are seen as having to adopt the organizational structure required by an organization's environmental conditions. The 'power-control' theory, in contrast, assumes a larger variance in structures and hence a tension between environment and structure possible because of the decisive influence and variable nature of managerial perceptions and actions.

The contingency perspective on organizing communication

The contingency perspective on organizing communication emerged with the work of Kotler and Mindak in 1978.[31] Observing increased dependencies and overlap between public relations and marketing, Kotler and Mindak argued for a more contingent view relating alternative relational concepts of public relations and marketing to such factors as organizational size and business sector. They, for instance, suggested that for some companies, particularly retail and manufacturing companies, it might be more effective to closely align marketing and public relations so as to reduce inter-departmental conflict and problems of coordination. Since Kotler and Mindak's groundbreaking work, a number of academic researchers have since followed the contingency path including Schneider, Van Leuven and Cornelissen.[32] Van Leuven, for instance, researched whether the structuring of the company and its communication department varies by and is contingent upon relationships between the company and its outside environment.

The power-control perspective on organizing communication

The power-control perspective is largely associated with the group of academic researchers of the IABC Excellence study into public relations. These researchers, including James Grunig, Larissa Grunig and Dozier, argued that earlier studies from a contingency perspective had produced little if any explanatory evidence of why communication is actually organized across organizations as it is. This group of academics critiqued Schneider's study in particular that had taken an environmental perspective towards explaining the structural variation of organizations but had provided only a minimal explanation for the structuring of the communication department.[33] Such weak and insignificant links between environment and organizational structure subsequently led these researchers to suggest the power-control perspective as a more viable theoretical framework to research and explain structural variations of communication across organizations. Larissa Grunig argued, 'Organizations do what they do because the people with the most power in the organization – the dominant coalition – decide to do it that way.'[34] The rationale here, from the power-control perspective, is that the lack of contingent relations between environment and structure indicates the considerable latitude of choice among the dominant coalition of senior managers, permitting them to devise structures and organizational responses that in the light of environmental needs 'satisfice' rather than 'optimize'.[35] The idea is thus that perceptions and choices of senior managers within the company, which are influenced by intra-organizational power and the forming of coalitions, are the main determinants of the structuring of communication. In other words, as research within the power-control paradigm suggests, the structuring of communication is dependent upon the intra-organizational power of the communication function in terms of the valuable resources and knowledge that it holds (that other departments are dependent upon) and its perceived value by the dominant coalition within an organization.

In summary, both the contingency and power-control perspectives offer alternative theoretical frameworks for studying and explaining the way in which communication is vertically and horizontally structured within companies. Both have been supported by some empirical data in research; and both go some way towards explaining the variance in structures discussed in Sections 6.3 and 6.4. The *size of the organization*, for one, clearly explains some of the variance in vertical structures across companies. Small businesses generally have communication responsibilities located with one or a few managers in other functional areas (marketing, human resources) within the organization. When organizations grow larger, however, and adopt a multi-divisional structure (with each division catering for a certain product–market combination), the proportion of communication personnel it contains equally increases, and communication disciplines will be taken together into departments or separate units. This is particularly evident in the consistent findings that in large manufacturing and service companies communication disciplines are arranged into separate communication and marketing departments. Also the *domain similarities and resource dependencies* between disciplines, as discussed above, may be seen to account for the departmental arrangement of communications; in terms of whether communication disciplines are taken together or rather split up into separate departments. All these elements – size, and domain similarities and resource dependencies – are factors in a company's internal and external environment, and thus point to a contingency explanation of communication structure. At the same time, however, the location of communication departments in the *hierarchy of the organization* seems to be associated with managerial discretion. When senior managers value communication for its input into decision-making, the senior communication manager may be promoted to a seat on the executive board or management team, or, alternatively, may be working in a close reporting relationship with senior managers. In other words, the reporting relationship, and particularly the question of whether the senior communication manager just reports to the CEO and executive team or whether he is really a member of that dominant coalition, can be more aptly explained by power-control theory.

6.6 Chapter summary

How communication is organized within companies is crucial to the effective planning and coordination of communication to different stakeholder groups. An effective set of vertical and horizontal structures not only determines whether communication activities that are carried out at various places within the organization are coordinated in a cost-effective manner, but also whether communication is enabled to provide strategic input into corporate decision-making. In fact, the fullest strategic use of corporate communications in many ways stands or falls with an effective structuring of communication in the form of a consolidated communication department with ready access to the decision-making coalition and with horizontal mechanisms that align the work and communications products (campaigns and messages) of practitioners from different departments. Fortunately, as this chapter has suggested, many companies have such consolidated departments placed in a high position in the organization's hierarchy. This high position, however, often consists of a direct reporting relationship of the senior communication manager to the CEO or executive team rather than this manager actually having a seat on the executive board. The reason for this, as mentioned, is the still considerable lack of understanding of and lack of commitment to communication among many senior managers as well as the inability of many communication practitioners to meet the needs of senior managers in ways that contribute to the accomplishment of organizational objectives. The next chapter takes a closer look at the roles, competencies and skills of communication practitioners.

KEY TERMS

Centralization	Line function
Contingency	Power-control
Coordination mechanism	Procedures and guidelines
Council meeting	Process documentation
Departmental arrangement	Reporting relationship
Domain similarity	Resource dependence
Dominant coalition	Staff function
Economies of scale	Team
Horizontal structure	Vertical structure

Notes

1 Hollander, S.C. (1986), 'The marketing concept: a déjà vu', in Fisk, G. (ed.), *Marketing Management Technology as a Social Process*. New York: Praeger, pp. 3–29.

2 Cook, J. (1973), 'Consolidating the communications function', *Public Relations Journal*, 29 (6–8): 28.

3 Schultz, D.E., Tannenbaum, S.I. and Lauterborn, R.F. (1993), *The New Marketing Paradigm: Integrated Marketing Communications*. Lincolnwood: NTC Publishing; Schultz, D.E. (1996), 'The inevitability of integrated communications', *Journal of Business Research*, 37: 139–146.

4 See, for instance, Gronstedt, A. (1996), 'Integrated communications at America's leading total quality management corporations', *Public Relations Review*, 22 (1): 25–42; Prensky, D., McCarty, J.A. and Lucas, J. (1996), 'Integrated marketing communication: an organizational perspective', in Thorson, E. and J. Moore (eds), *Integrated Communication: Synergy of Persuasive Voices*. Mahwah, NJ: Lawrence Erlbaum Associates, pp. 167–183.

5 See, for instance, Argenti, P.A. (1998), *Corporate Communication*, 2nd edn. Boston: McGraw-Hill; Dozier, D.M. and Grunig, L.A. (1992), 'The organization of the public relations function', in Grunig, J.E. (ed.), *Excellence in Public Relations and Communication Management*. Hillsdale, NJ: Lawrence Erlbaum Associates, pp. 395–417; Moss, D., Warnaby, G. and Newman, A.J. (2000), 'Public relations practitioner role enactment at the senior management level within UK companies', *Journal of Public Relations Research*, 12: 277–307; Stewart, D.W. (1996), 'Market-back approach to the design of integrated communications programs: a change in paradigm and a focus on determinants of success', *Journal of Business Research*, 37: 147–153; Schultz, D.E. et al. (1993).

6 Heath, R.L. (1994), *Management of Corporate Communication: From Interpersonal Contacts to External Affairs*. Hillsdale, NJ: Lawrence Erlbaum Associates; Gronstedt, A. (1996), 'Integrating marketing communication and public relations: a stakeholder relations model', in Thorson, E. and Moore, J. (1996), pp. 287–304.

7 Broom, G.M. and Dozier, D.M. (1986), 'Advancement for public relations role models', *Public Relations Review*, 12: 37–56.

8 Argenti, (1998), p. 50.

9 Körver, F. and Van Ruler, B. (2003), 'The relationship between corporate identity structures and communication structures', *Journal of Communication Management*, 7 (3): 197–208.

10 Van Riel, C.B.M. (1995), *Principles of Corporate Communication*. London: Prentice Hall, pp. 144–146.

11 Post, J.E. and Griffin, J.J. (1997), 'Corporate reputation and external affairs', *Corporate Reputation Review*, 1 (1): 165–171; Hutton, J.G., Goodman, M.B., Alexander, J.B. and Genest, C.M. (2001), 'Reputation management: the new face of corporate public relations?', *Public Relations Review*, 27: 247–261.

12 Hunter, T. (1997), 'The relationship of public relations and marketing against the background of integrated communications: a theoretical analysis and empirical study at US American corporations', Master's thesis (unpublished), University of Salzburg, Austria.

13 Grunig, J.E. and Grunig, L.A. (1998), 'The relationship between public relations and marketing in excellent organizations: evidence from the IABC study', *Journal of Marketing Communications*, 4 (3): 141–162, quote on p. 154.

14 Kitchen, P.J. and Moss, D.A. (1995), 'Marketing and public relations: the relationship revisited', *Journal of Marketing Communications*, 1 (2): 105–119; Van Riel (1995).

15 Cornelissen, J. and Thorpe, (2001), 'The organisation of external communication disciplines in UK companies: a conceptual and empirical analysis of dimensions and determinants', *Journal of Business Communication*, 38 (4): 413–438.

16 Pfeffer, J. (1978), *Organizational Design*. Arlington Heights, VA: Harlan Davidson, p. 25.

17 Rao, H. (1997), 'The rise of investor relations departments in the Fortune 500 industrials', *Corporate Reputation Review*, 1 (1/2): 172–177; Rao, H. and Sivakumar, K. (1999), 'Institutional sources of boundary-spanning structures: the establishment of investor relations departments in the Fortune 500 industrials', *Organization Science*, 10: 27–42.

18 White, J. and Mazur, L. (1995), *Strategic Communications Management: Making Public Relations Work*. Wokingham: Addison-Wesley.

19 Wright, D.K. (1995), 'The role of public relations executives in the future of employee communications', *Public Relations Review*, Fall: 181–198.

20 Moss, D., Warnaby, G. and Newman, A.J. (2000), 'Public relations practitioner role enactment at the senior management level within UK companies', *Journal of Public Relations Research*, 12 (4): 277–307, quote on p. 299.

21 Osborne, J. (1994), 'Getting full value from public relations', *Public Relations Journal*, October/November: 64.

22 Stewart, D.W. (1996), 'Market-back approach to the design of integrated communications programs: a change in paradigm and a focus on determinants of success', *Journal of Business Research*, 37: 147–153.

23 See, for instance, Duncan, T. and Moriarty, S.E. (1998), 'A communication-based marketing model for managing relationships', *Journal of Marketing*, 62 (April): 1–13.

24 Van Riel (1995), Dolphin, R. (1999), *The Fundamentals of Corporate Communications*. Oxford: Butterworth-Heinemann, p. 73.

25 Gronstedt, A. (2000), *The Customer Century: Lessons from World-class Companies in Integrated Marketing and Communications*. London: Routledge, 180.

26 Gronstedt (1996), p. 40.

27 Cornelissen, J.P. and Lock, A.R. (2000), 'The organizational relationship between marketing and public relations: exploring paradigmatic viewpoints', *Journal of Marketing Communications*, 6 (4): 231–245.

28 Chandler, A.P. (1962), *Strategy and Structure*. Cambridge, MA: MIT Press; Lawrence, P.R. and Lorsch, J.W. (1967), *Organization and Environment: Managing Differentiation and Integration*. Boston: Division of Research, Graduate School of Business Administration, Harvard University.

29 Burrell, G. and Morgan, G. (1979), *Sociological Paradigms and Organizational Analysis: Elements of the Sociology of Corporate Life*. London: Heinemann Educational Books;

Donaldson, L. (1996), *For Positivist Organization Theory: Proofing the Hard Core*. London: Sage; Donaldson, L. (1999), 'The normal science of structural contingency theory', in Clegg, S. and Hardy, C. (eds), *Studying Organization: Theory and Method*. London: Sage, pp. 51–70.

30 Child, J. (1972), 'Organizational structure, environment and performance: the role of strategic choice', *Sociology*, 6 (1): 2–22; Child, J. (1997), 'Strategic choice in the analysis of action, structure, organizations and environment: retrospect and prospect', *Organization Studies*, 18 (1): 43–76; Silverman, D. (1970), *The Theory of Organizations: A Sociological Framework*. London: Heinemann; Weick, K.E. (1979), *The Social Psychology of Organizing*, 2nd edn. Reading, MA: Addison-Wesley.

31 Kotler, P. and Mindak, W. (1978), 'Marketing and public relations, should they be partners or rivals?', *Journal of Marketing*, 42 (10): 13–20.

32 Schneider, (aka Grunig), L.A. (1985), 'The role of public relations in four organizational types', *Journalism Quarterly*, 62 (3): 567–576; Van Leuven, J. (1991), 'Corporate organizing strategies and the scope of public relations departments', *Public Relations Review*, 17 (3): 279–291; Cornelissen, J.P., Lock, A.R. and Gardner, H. (2001), 'The organisation of external communication disciplines: an integrative framework of dimensions and determinants', *International Journal of Advertising*, 20 (1): 67–88; Cornelissen and Thorpe (2001); Cornelissen, J.P. and Harris, P. (2003), 'The management of corporate and marketing communications in UK companies: interdependencies between marketing and public relations as correlates of communication organisation', *Journal of Marketing Management*, 17 (1/2): 49–71.

33 Grunig, J.E. and Grunig, L.A. (1989), 'Toward a theory of the public relations behavior of organizations: review of a programme of research', in Grunig, J.E. and Grunig, L.A. (eds), *Public Relations Research Annual*, Vol. 1. Mahwah, NJ: Lawrence Erlbaum Associates, pp. 27–63; Grunig, L.A. (1992), 'How public relations/communication departments should adapt to the structure and environment of an organization … and what they actually do', in Grunig, J.E. (ed.), *Excellence in Public Relations and Communication Management*. Hillsdale, NJ: Lawrence Erlbaum Associates, pp. 467–481.

34 Grunig, L.A. (1992), 'Power in the public relations department', in Grunig (1992), p. 483.

35 Dozier, D.M. and Grunig, L.A. (1992), 'The organization of the public relations function', in Grunig (1992), pp. 395–417.

7

Communication Practitioners: Roles and Professional Development

CHAPTER OVERVIEW

The chapter presents an overview of the roles and activities that communication practitioners carry out on a daily basis. Based upon what practitioners do, they can be categorized as either communication 'technicians' or 'managers'. Both roles require a different set of competencies and skills and the chapter outlines how practitioners can professionally develop in both roles. The chapter ends with a discussion of the status and development of corporate communication as a recognized profession.

7.1 Introduction

Chapters 5 and 6 have discussed the importance of the strategic use of communication within an organization and what this requires in terms of the *process* of strategy-making as well as the way in which communication staff and their tasks are *structured* and *organized*. This chapter examines another critical element within the management of corporate communication: the *people* working in communication. What people bring to the communication job in terms of expertise, competencies and skills is a crucial element in the effective functioning of corporate communication and influences how corporate communication is being seen by managers from other functions within the organization.

This chapter provides a detailed look at the practice of communications and the people working within it. It starts with an overview of the roles and activities carried out by practitioners in Section 7.2. Based on these roles and activities, practitioners have often been characterized as either 'technicians' or 'managers'. This distinction between technicians and managers is important as it not only captures the nature of the work and the views that these practitioners themselves have of it, but also explains and suggests how the communication function is regarded by others (i.e. as a strategic management function or as a lower-level technical support function) and whether it has any involvement in corporate decision-making.

From this overview of roles and activities performed by practitioners, Section 7.3 then moves on to discuss issues around the professional development of communication practitioners. The issues addressed involve the development of competencies and skills in both technician and manager roles and the career transition from a technician to a more managerial role. Finally, Section 7.4 discusses the general state of the professional occupation of corporate communication at the start of the twenty-first century and attempts to answer whether it can be characterized as a true profession (similar to the professions of, for example, medicine, law and accounting). Although the jury is still out on this, this section suggests that communication has not yet evolved into a full-blown profession because it still lacks a comprehensive body of knowledge and standards of expertise and skills that not only are unique to communication, but are also valued within organizations and accredited by peer groups such as other managers, government and practitioners from established professions.

Taken together, the chapter should provide the reader not only with an overview of the roles and various activities performed by practitioners, but also with an understanding of ways in which communication practitioners can develop their professional competence and skills.

7.2 The roles of communication practitioners

On a day-to-day basis, practitioners working in communication are engaged in a broad variety of activities ranging from, for instance, editorial work, internal counselling, handling of inquiries, gathering information, looking at data from research, talking to press contacts, drafting communication plans, delivering presentations, producing communication materials (brochures, visuals, etc.), and administrative tasks within the department. The job of communication practitioners, at various levels of seniority, thus consists of a broad range of activities that in their scope and variety not only vary with the tasks that have been assigned to a communication department (i.e. whether the department is a service unit or is involved in advice and decision-making at the senior management level), but also with the range of issues and inquiries from stakeholders that are directed at communication practitioners. In companies where stakeholder groups indeed make many claims upon the organization and raise issues that require a response, practitioners often work at an unrelenting pace to advise management, draft resolutions and policy documents, and respond to and communicate with those outside stakeholder groups.

As in many other organizational jobs, practitioners thus often work, at a hectic pace and under pressure, upon a whole range of different tasks and activities.[1] While these activities may be characterized by variety and brevity, and thus differ from practitioner to practitioner, academic research has established that despite this variety practitioners can generally be cast in two broad role types: managers and technicians. These general roles are based upon the outlook of a practitioner upon the job and the *general* range of activities that he or she performs.

In 1978 Katz and Khan initially identified the importance of the role concept in organizations. They defined organizations as role systems and 'role behaviour' as 'recurring actions of an individual interrelated with the actions of others so as to yield a predictable outcome'.[2] An organizational role is, of course, an abstraction. It is a conceptual order imposed on the many activities performed by individuals in organizations to make sense of organizational behaviour and to explain its causal factors and its consequences. Working with the role concept, Glen Broom pioneered roles research in communication to explain the pattern of activities performed by practitioners. Using a battery of 24 self-reporting measures of roles activities, Broom conceptualized four dominant theoretical roles, which he argued captured the main patterns of activities that communication practitioners perform.[3] These four theoretical practitioner roles comprised:

1. *The Communication Technician Role*: in this role, the practitioner provides the specialized skills needed to carry out communication programmes. Rather than being part of the management team, technicians are concerned with preparing and producing communication materials.
2. *The Expert Prescriber Role*: in this role, the practitioner operates as the authority on both communication problems and their solutions. The client or management is often content to leave communications in the hands of the 'expert' and to assume a relatively passive role.
3. *The Communication Facilitator Role*: this role casts the practitioner as a sensitive 'go-between' or information broker. The practitioner serves as a liaison, interpreter and mediator between the organization and its stakeholders.
4. *The Problem-Solving Process Facilitator Role*: in this role, practitioners collaborate with other managers to define and solve communication and stakeholder problems for the organization. Unlike the expert prescriber role, here practitioners work with management and are more likely to play an active part in strategic decision-making.

Reflecting on these four role types, Broom also observed that the expert prescriber, communication facilitator and problem-solving process facilitator roles were closely correlated, but quite distinct from the communication technician role. The academic Dozier equally suggested that these four practitioner roles could be reduced to more general 'technician' and 'manager' roles because the expert prescriber, the communication facilitator, and the problem-solving process facilitator roles all represented a broader managerial role. Reworking Broom's data, Dozier identified two *major* conceptual roles: communication technician and communication manager.

1. *Communication technician*: communication practitioners are characterized as technicians if their work focuses on activities such as writing communication materials, editing and/or rewriting for grammar and spelling, handling the technical aspects, producing brochures or pamphlets, doing photography and graphics, and maintaining media contacts and placing press releases. Dozier and Broom define a technician as 'a creator and disseminator of messages, intimately involved in production, [and] operating independent of management decision making, strategic planning, issues management, environmental scanning and programme evaluation'.[4] In other words, a technician thus tactically implements decisions made by others and is generally not involved in management decision-making and strategic decisions concerning communication strategy and programmes.

2. *Communication manager*: practitioners enacting the manager role predominantly make strategy or policy decisions and are held accountable for programme success or failure. These practitioners are primarily concerned with externally oriented, long-term decisions, rather than solving short-term, technical problems. Activities within the manager role include advising management at all levels in the organization with regard to policy decisions, courses of action and communications taking into account their public ramifications and the organization's social or citizenship responsibilities, making communication programme decisions, evaluating programme results, supervising the work of others, planning and managing budgets, planning communications programmes, and meeting other executives. Communication managers also typically use research to monitor the organization's environment and opinions of key stakeholders. And because they possess needed intelligence gained from research, managers are more likely to participate in the organization's decision-making and strategic planning.

While the manager and technician roles are very distinct in terms of the activities performed within them, it is important to note that these two general roles are conceptual abstractions. In other words, manager and technician role activities are different, but neither mutually exclusive nor in opposition to each other. As Dozier and Broom point out: 'All practitioners enact elements of both the manager and technician roles which are themselves simply useful abstractions for studying the wide range of activities that practitioners perform in their daily work.'[5] As such, senior communication managers, for instance, do not exclusively occupy themselves with managerial tasks as they are often still engaged in handling routine technical communications tasks (media relations, publicity, the production of in-house newspapers, etc.).[6] Nonetheless, the concept of *predominant role types* has proved useful in thinking about and studying roles in communication practice. If a practitioner enacts activities of the manager role set with greater frequency than the activities of the technician role set, then this practitioner can be categorized as a manager. Such categorization is helpful not only in understanding the tasks and activities carried out by practitioners, but also in explaining practitioner involvement in decision-making and in thinking about the further professional development of communication practitioners.

First of all, the concept of two dominant role types – technicians and managers – is helpful *in capturing and explaining daily behavioural patterns of individual practitioners*. The two roles are important theoretical concepts because they explain how people behave in carrying out their job responsibilities and predict the likely results of their actions. Academic research on roles in communication practice[7] has, for instance, examined how the roles communication personnel played related to variables such as environmental uncertainty, size of the department, gender and length of professional service. Environmental uncertainty, for instance, implies that when decisions about organizational responses to the environment become more novel and non-programmed, practitioner roles change from technician to manager. Practitioners working in organizations faced with such uncertain environments then change activities from generating communications to making strategic decisions – or helping management to do so. A second factor involves the size of the communication department. For practitioners to focus on managerial tasks, they usually require a support team to release them from technical tasks. Hence, manager roles tend to be found more often in larger communication departments (i.e., more than 5-6 people). A third factor, and the one often igniting the most response, is that gender determines role enactment. In various studies it has been observed that women were more likely than men to perform the technician role. According to some, this merely reflects the widespread influx of women into the communication profession today (who start their careers working in technician roles), although for others it indicates a 'glass ceiling' for women who are disadvantaged in terms of career advancement (as they are hindered from progressing to manager roles). And, finally, also the length of professional service of the practitioner explains the adoption of either the manager or technician role by practitioners. Generally, practitioners tend to enter the profession by performing technician roles. And it is only as practitioners become more experienced and move up the hierarchy in organizations that they are typically able to adopt manager roles.

Thinking about manager and technician role types is not only helpful in capturing what activities practitioners are engaged in and explaining why they do so, but is also important as it suggests what the *consequences of role enactment* are. In particular, predominant manager role enactment is positively related to participation in management decision-making. The enactment of management and technician roles thus also indicates whether, as a consequence of role enactment, communication departments participate in strategic decision-making of the dominant coalition or simply execute decisions made by others. In a management-oriented communication department, one or a few senior communication managers oversee a range of management and decision-making oriented activities, including analysis and research, the formulation of communication objectives for the organization, the design of short-term and long-term organizational philosophies, and advising senior management. In contrast, practitioners enacting the technician role are predominantly located in a peripheral department. Technicians do not participate in management decision-making but only make programme decisions necessary to the internal functioning of their department. These practitioners are concerned with day-to-day operational matters (providing services such as writing, editing, photography, media contracts, and production of publications), and they carry out the lower-level communication mechanics necessary for implementing decisions made by others. In other words, *the enactment of the manager role is crucial for communication to be involved in management decision-making concerning the overall strategic direction of the organization.* When communication practitioners are involved at the decision-making table, information about relations with priority stakeholders gets factored into the process of organizational decision-making and into strategies and actions.[8] This would mean, among other things, that senior communication practitioners are actively consulted concerning the effects of certain business actions (e.g. staff lay-offs, divestiture) on a company's reputation with stakeholders, and even have a say in the decision-making on it, instead of being called in afterwards, after the decision has been made, to draft a press release and deal with communication issues emerging from it.

7.3 Competencies, skills and professional development

Both the technician and manager role require different sets of competencies and skills. A competence is defined as a domain of knowledge or specific expertise that an individual needs to possess to properly perform a specific job. When a practitioner possesses the competence relevant to the technician or manager role, he or she is adequately or well qualified and thus has the relevant knowledge to effectively perform the role. A skill is defined as the task-specific ability of a communication practitioner to effectively perform a certain task. A skill may draw upon the competence or knowledge of a practitioner but is conceptually distinct from it in that it often involves knowledge-in-action and a practical ability to complete a certain task or activity. Table 7.1 provides an overview of relevant competencies and skills in communication in relation to four different types of communication practitioners representing different levels of seniority.[9] The four types of practitioners are: (1) a novice practitioner ('novice technician'), who has just started in the role of a communication technician; (2) a communication technician with at least three years of experience ('experienced technician'); (3) a communication manager who oversees a specific area of corporate communication such as internal communication or media

Table 7.1   Levels of competence and skills

Novice technician	Experienced technician	Communication manager	Communication director
		PROFESSIONAL COMPETENCE	
		Concepts of stakeholder, identity and reputation	
→ has heard of these concepts; has a basic understanding of what they mean	→ has a basic understanding of what these concepts mean; knows the theoretical background to these concepts and their practical relevance to specific areas such as media relations, internal communication, marketing communication	→ has an advanced understanding of these concepts; knows the theoretical background to these concepts and their practical relevance to specific areas such as media relations, internal communication, marketing communication; knows how they can be operationalized and used as reference points for a specific communication program or campaign	→ has an advanced understanding of these concepts; knows the theoretical background to these concepts and their practical relevance to specific areas such as media relations, internal communication, marketing communication; knows how to incorporate these concepts into a communication strategy and in the development of company-wide communication programs and campaigns
		Theories of communication and organization	
→ knows about the standard models and theories of communication, including corporate communication	→ knows about the standard models and theories of communication, including corporate communication; knows about models of organizing communication within the organization	→ knows the history of corporate communication and developments in theory; has an understanding of how communication and organization theories relate to practical situations and contexts; knows how to translate theories into practical applications	→ knows the history of corporate communication and developments in theory; has an understanding of how communication and organization theories relate to complex practical situations and contexts; knows how to translate theories into practical applications; knows what roles communication can play in the development of strategy at the level of the entire organization
		SKILLS	
		Research and environmental scanning	
→ knows the basics of communication research and its relevance to the practice of corporate communication	→ knows how to apply the basic methods of communication research including quantitative and qualitative methods	→ has an intimate understanding of different research methods; knows what method is most appropriate to a particular communication problem or question; is familiar with software packages for the analysis of research data; knows how to analyse and present the results of research	→ has an intimate understanding of different research methods; knows what method is most appropriate to a particular communication problem or question; is familiar with software packages for the analysis of research data; knows how to analyse and present the results of research; knows how to develop a programme of research for the entire corporate communication function; knows how to translate results from research into actions for corporate communication and for other areas within the organization

Table 7.1 (Continued)

Novice technician	Experienced technician	Communication manager	Communication director
		Producing communication materials	
→ knows the characteristics of standard media including digital media and knows how to produce and edit content for them	→ knows the characteristics of face-to-face, written, electronic, digital and audio-visual media; is familiar with the media landscape at the regional and national level; knows about the production, editing, design and dissemination of content; knows about the appropriate media for specific areas such as media relations, internal communication, marketing communication	→ is up to date on media and on the production, design and dissemination of content through various media; has a deep knowledge of characteristics and applications of different media; has an intimate knowledge of the media landscape at the regional and national level including (legal) procedures associated with each medium	→ has a thorough understanding of the effective use of classic and modern media; knows, in relation to the overall communication strategy, the practical implications of the regional, national and international media including (legal) procedures associated with each medium
		Leadership, advice and counselling	
	→ has the ability to direct others who are involved in the execution	→ has the ability to lead and direct others in a particular area of corporate communication; has the ability to foster collaboration in a project- or task-team; has the ability to monitor progress; has the skill to understand others and knows how to motivate and incentivize them; has the ability to take decisions in relation to complex or ambiguous situations	→ has the ability to lead a multi-disciplinary group of communication practitioners; has authority in taking decisions; has the ability to delegate responsibilities and tasks in a clear way; has the ability to create a good work atmosphere; has the skill to understand others and knows how to motivate and incentivize them; has the ability to take decisions in relation to complex or ambiguous situations
		Developing communication strategy, programmes and plans	
→ knows how in the context of a communication program a plan for a particular activity can be developed	→ has the ability to develop a specific communication plan for a non-complex issue or area of activity; including	→ has the ability to develop communication plans for comprehensive programmes (e.g., media relations, internal communication) that are	→ has the ability to develop a comprehensive corporate communication strategy; develops communication plans as part of a long-term communication strategy; has

(Continued)

Table 7.1 (Continued)

Novice technician	Experienced technician	Communication manager	Communication director
	objective setting, segmentation of audiences, identification of tactics, timing, budgeting and evaluation	part of the corporate communication strategy; develops plans and budgets on an annual basis; has the ability to evaluate communication plans of others	the ability to evaluate communication programmes and plans of communication managers
		Financial management	
→ knows the basics of financial budgeting	→ knows the basics of financial budgeting; knows the basics of corporate finance in relation to the annual report	→ has a detailed understanding of corporate finance including financial measures and ratios, bookkeeping and financial reporting	→ has a detailed understanding of corporate finance including financial measures and ratios, bookkeeping and financial reporting; has an ability to understand financial consequences of corporate decisions in relation to the organization's stakeholders and its corporate reputation

relations ('communication manager'); and (4) a senior communication manager ('communication director') who directs corporate communication for the entire organization and oversees a whole department of practitioners. Each of these categories, and the roles that they suggest, represent particular stages in the professional development of a communication practitioner. In other words, following Table 7.1 from left to right, the development of a practitioner from a novice technician to a senior communication manager requires a step-change in the level of competence and skills expected of a practitioner.

Most practitioners will start their careers as technicians or communication assistants ('novice technician') with a certain level of competence and skill expected of them. When practitioners subsequently progress through the ranks they are expected not only to become more knowledgeable and skilled but also to adopt a wider managerial perspective upon corporate communication in the context of their organization.

In particular, the career transition from technician ('novice technician' and 'experienced technician' in Table 7.1) to 'manager' and possibly 'director' of corporate communication requires a step-change in expertise and abilities. The transition to a manager role requires that practitioners are able to formulate the importance and use of communication in the context of general organizational issues and objectives. In the words of a recent US study: 'effective communicators are those who speak the same language as senior executives and have a deep understanding of the business and its strategy'.[10] In other words, practitioners need to have knowledge of the industry or sector in which the organization operates and of the nature of the strategy-making process, as well as a strategic view of how communication can contribute to corporate and market strategies and to different functional areas within the company[11] (Chapter 5). In other words, instead of a 'craft' approach to communication that is skills-based and focuses on the production of communications materials, manager role enactment requires that a practitioner is able:

> to bring thoughtfully conceived agendas to the senior management table that address the strategic issues of business planning, resource allocation, priorities and direction of the firm. Instead of asking what events to sponsor and at what cost, [practitioners] should be asking which customer segments to invest in and at what projected returns … instead of asking how to improve the number of hits to the website, [practitioners] should be asking who their key stakeholders are and how to get more interactive with them.[12]

Manager role enactment depends on the willingness of practitioners to enact a manager role and the professional support in terms of training or mentoring that they receive to make the transition from technician to manager. As for their willingness, some practitioners have little aspiration to enact the manager role as they have built their careers around technical specializations and skills and exhibit high levels of job satisfaction in the stability of technician role enactment over time. A number of surveys of communication practitioners have found that many communicators are often happiest performing the 'down and dirty' tasks, such as writing, editing and the production of news releases and publications.[13]

Practitioners also need to be supported in their transition from technician to manager. There are various ways in which organizations can help and facilitate such transitions. For example, organizations may provide training and education to practitioners. Such training and formal education may be provided through in-company programmes (Case Study 7.1) or by universities and training companies outside of the organization. Practitioners themselves can also facilitate the transition by building an informal network of contacts within the organization and by getting involved in every aspect of the business. When Lynn Tysen, Dell's vice-president of investor relations and corporate communication, first joined the company, she attended operations and other functional meetings so that she could learn about Dell inside and out.[14] In addition, James and Larissa Grunig's study into 'excellent' practitioners shows that 'excellent' practitioners are the ones who increasingly have enjoyed some education, but also continually read, study and learn – through books, scholarly journals and professional publications. When practitioners think and approach their work in this way, it may indeed be easier for them to learn the values, skills and repertoires of action that come with the manager role.[15] Finally, the transition from technician to manager can also be facilitated through job rotation and a mentoring system within corporate communication. When communication practitioners are rotated among different work tasks or among different business units of the company, they can gain a better understanding of different disciplines within corporate communication which in turn may enable them to think more strategically about what communication can contribute to the organization and to the achievement of corporate objectives. When communication technicians are mentored by more senior communication managers, they obtain new insights, are exposed to examples of good practice and gain advice as they advance in their jobs. Within Philips, for example, mentoring is used to groom up-and-coming practitioners deemed to have the potential to move up into manager or leadership roles. Practitioners are paired with a senior level leader (or leaders) for a series of career-coaching interactions and are rotated across areas of communication within the organization to learn the organization's structure, culture, and methods of working across different disciplines of communication.

Practitioners who are expected to enact the manager role, however, do not always meet these requirements for competencies and skills associated with the manager role. This may be partly the result of a lack of career development opportunities and professional support within their organizations. Many communication practitioners in particular lack knowledge and skills in financial management, the strategy-making process, and the use of communication in organizational development and change. As a result, these practitioners and the communication disciplines that they represent may be sidelined by companies and treated as a peripheral management discipline – one viewed as unimportant to the overall functioning of the corporation. Pincus and his colleagues refer in this regard to a belief commonly held among some parts of senior management that communication adds little to corporate performance[16] as it is a 'fluffy' discipline that is insufficiently focused on the practicalities and demands of the business. A similar sentiment was expressed by CEOs in a recent survey in the UK. CEOs of leading UK corporations felt that corporate communication as an area of practice 'will be more valued when advice is offered by practitioners who have the background, knowledge and standing that will enable them to contribute to decision-making at the highest levels'. CEOs felt that 'barriers to entry to the practice are, at the present time, too low and the practice fails to attract the most able candidates' as most CEOs 'felt there were too few high-calibre practitioners and too few quality people coming into the industry'.[17] Practitioners in senior positions who are expected to enact the manager role are thus under pressure to show and communicate the value of communication in terms of what it contributes to the organization:

> There is a lot of bemoaning in the hallways of marketing and communications offices of how CEOs 'don't understand communications', when the real problem is that marketing and communications professionals do not understand the intricacies of business management well enough to become part of the governing coalition'.[18]

In summary, the professional development of practitioners from technicians to managers is crucial to the status that is accorded to communication and its input into management decision-making. To make this developmental shift, practitioners, particularly those who come from a communication technician background, need to be trained and educated to become fully knowledgeable and skilled as communication managers. In this sense, thinking in technician and manager roles and knowing what competencies and skills are needed in each capacity suggest a trajectory of professional development in terms of what is needed of practitioners within organizations if they want to progress from technician to manager roles (Table 7.1). The professional development from technicians to managers is important at the level of individual organizations (Case Study 7.1) but is also central to the development of the practice and occupation of corporate communication as a whole, in terms of whether this occupation acquires professional status. The final section of this chapter picks up on this particular point and suggests ways in which the occupation can be further developed.

CASE STUDY 7.1

TRAINING AND PROFESSIONAL DEVELOPMENT PROGRAMMES IN ASTRAZENECA★

AstraZeneca, one of the largest pharmaceutical companies in the world, emerged as the result of a merger between the Swedish Astra and British Zeneca Plc in 1999. The company specializes in prescription medicines for the treatment of high cholesterol, cancer, asthma, heart disease, neurological disorders and stomach ulcers. The company has in recent years placed a stakeholder orientation at the core of all its business operations. AstraZeneca works, for example, closely with stakeholders such as patients, physicians, employees and investors to gain insights into how the company can continue to make a valued contribution to patients and healthcare. In the words of David Brennan, CEO of AstraZeneca:

'Understanding the needs of our stakeholders is essential for effective leadership of our business. We have increased our emphasis on stakeholder dialogue and are making it a more permanent feature of how we operate in AstraZeneca. Stakeholder engagement is also important in identifying our corporate responsibility priorities and, during 2006, we published internally a new guideline on how to engage stakeholders in corporate responsibility-specific dialogues as an important step in local priority action planning'.

Besides external stakeholders, the company also tracks the views of employees through a bi-annual global employee survey.

(Continued)

(Continued)

This stakeholder orientation has also led to the realization that corporate communication is of strategic importance to the organization. The company has set up a training and professional development programme to create a 'best in industry' corporate communication function across offices over the world. The programme entitled CER360 (CER refers to Communication and External Relations) consists of a set of in-house training courses that provide CER practitioners with applied learning, skills and competences to 'successfully function in a generalist role but with specialty skills as required'. The courses are taught by subject matter experts from communication consultancy Edelman as well as other external experts who are paired with in-house experts within AstraZeneca. The CER360 programme as a whole is part of AstraZeneca's corporate university system of training and professional development programmes.

The CER360 programme consists of core fundamental courses, core group-specific courses and electives. The core fundamental courses cover essential areas that each professional within CER must have knowledge of in line with the core competences defined by Human Resources for all CER employees. These courses are requirements for all CER professionals at all levels unless an exemption is granted by an executive director. In exceptional circumstances it is possible for an employee to replace a core fundamental course with a similar course offered by a university or professional association. Core group-specific courses cover area-specific information required for members of the four departments within CER: Brand Public Relations, External Relations, Internal Communication, and Health and Community Alliances. These courses enable professionals from each of these areas to gain deeper knowledge, perspectives and best practices in their specialty. The relevant group-specific courses are also obligatory for members of that department. In addition to the core courses, the programme also offers elective courses on a periodic basis to allow CER employees to explore a variety of subjects that may be of interest. There are no elective requirements, but professionals are encouraged to take appropriate ones based on the outcomes of their self-assessment and discussion with their managers.

Core fundamental courses included (in 2005–2006) 'clear and effective business writing', 'agency relationship fundamentals', 'issues management fundamentals', 'managing projects and internal clients fundamentals', 'managing corporate reputation fundamentals', 'strategic thinking and planning fundamentals' and 'government and regulatory affairs fundamentals'. In the same year, core group-specific courses included 'PR and the media', 'employee communication' and 'ally development and community relations'. Elective courses in the same year included an additional 'interpreting and publicising medical data' course as well as any of the group-specific courses that can be attended by people outside of the relevant department (and providing there is still space available on the course). Professionals are recommended to take at least six work days worth of training within one year, which should include all fundamental courses, the relevant core group-specific course as well as ideally an elective course. Professionals are also expected to assess and record their progress over the year and discuss this on an annual basis with their relevant manager. The overall aim of the programme is to equip managers with a broad set of competencies, skills and industry-specific insights so that they can successfully function as generalists with the flexibility to rapidly respond to business needs and to move into other areas of CER if needed.

Question for reflection

1. Reflect upon the design and delivery of the CER360 programme of training and professional development from the perspective of a communication professional. What are the potential advantages of such a programme? What other areas of training and professional development (e.g., mentoring), if any, would be useful in becoming a generalist communication professional and specifically in making the transition from a communication technician to communication manager role?

Note: * This case study is based upon interviews with communication professionals at AstraZeneca UK and on information sourced from www. astrazeneca.com

7.4 Corporate communication as a vocation or profession

Virtually all organizations, with the exception of small businesses, employ one or more communication practitioners. These practitioners, as we have seen, carry out various tasks and activities, and in the general patterns of activities that they undertake can be characterized as technicians or managers. In other words, the practice or occupation of communication thus simply *exists* as an inevitable part of organizations, with thousands of practitioners being employed in communication roles in organizations across the world. This observation, of course, just simply asserts that communications is practised in large measure across organizations, which furthermore begs the more qualitative question of whether the current way in which it is practised can be characterized as a true and full-grown profession.

To answer this question, one of course first needs to have a clear picture of what a profession actually entails. Wylie suggests that interdisciplinary guidelines for a 'profession' as opposed to a mere occupation generally include requirements for: (1) a well-defined body of scholarly knowledge; (2) completion of some standardized and prescribed course of study; (3) examination and certification by a state as an authoritative body; and (4) oversight by a state agency which has disciplinary powers over practitioners' behaviours.[19] Reflecting upon professionalism in the context of communication, Nelson added that professionalism is furthermore characterized in: (1) practitioners being guided by professional values in their work; (2) membership of a professional organization; (3) professional norms that regulate the practice; (4) an intellectual tradition underpinning it; and (5) a constant development of technical skills.[20] Other criteria that have been mentioned by writers and commentators on professionalism in communication include intellectualism, a code of ethics, a comprehensive self-governing professional body, greater emphasis on public service than self-interest such as profits, and performance of a 'unique and essential service based on a substantial body of knowledge'.[21] Judged by these different writings, there is evidently no mutually shared understanding or strict definition of standards of professional performance in communication management. While there is some overlap and consensus regarding criteria – the familiar troika of (1) existence of a body of knowledge; (2) a code of ethics to guide the practice; and (3) certification of the practice being most often mentioned as the defining characteristics of a profession – there is still, as far as academic writings on the subject go, no strict set of criteria by which to judge the occupation of communication management and its professional acumen.

Nonetheless, as with other professions (e.g., medicine, law and accountancy), it is reasonable to suggest that an occupation is seen and judged as a profession when it is socially valued and recognized as such. This generally happens when practitioners in an occupation address a need or solve a problem through their specific competencies and skills that are: (1) critical (to individuals, organizations, society at large) and therefore valued; (2) difficult to substitute or emulate; and (3) recognized, and possibly protected (by codes of practice, or through certification by the occupation's governing body, state agencies or companies themselves), as such.[22] In other words, professionalism is not just about solving problems and executing solutions in a way that others (outside the occupation) cannot, but also about 'convincing others about the legitimacy of these solutions and the practitioners' right to deal with the problem in the first place'.[23] As such, a fully-fledged and mature profession is characterized by:

1. the articulation of a domain of expertise;
2. the establishment of monopoly in the market for a service based on that expertise;
3. the ability to limit entry to the field;
4. the attainment of social status and recognition; and
5. systematic ways of testing competence and regulating standards.

Against the background of these five criteria, the occupation of corporate communication is indeed acquiring some of the attributes of a profession: its

Table 7.2   Practitioners' views on the qualities needed in communications

Personality is important … you are flitting daily from one thing [or] another, so you need your wits about you.

One has to have lateral thinking like Edward de Bono.

Common sense [is important]. You need to be reasonably practical … You need to be able to communicate.

Critical ability [is important, as are] … [being] persuasive in writing and verbally …, integrity …, personal courage …, [and] a sense of humour … it doesn't matter if they can write a press release.

[Practitioners should be] ideas men who … wish to change things, and that's what I mean by being creative.

People [who] speak up, who dress nicely, who've got something intelligent to say [can be successful] … The old slap-dash approach is just not good enough … Personality and good interpersonal skills [are important].

Credibility [is important] … People who can operate at a senior level on very sensitive topics [can be successful] …, so the ability to have those relationships is more important, in a way, than technical training … There is a personality requirement … Salesmanship is a crucial skill for the top people in consultancy … In the noncommercial area, the key skill is persuasiveness.

More character than anything else [is important] …, getting along with clients, … being relatively intelligent, a streetwise intelligence, … [and] a sense of humor … [to be able to] come up with ideas and think at a bit of a tangent [is important].

domain of expertise is gradually being circumscribed, and practitioners have acquired expert skill sets in a number of different communication specialties and techniques. In fact, many practitioners have now grown into full masters of communication techniques, as they have become skilful in how to secure media coverage, prepare press releases, write speeches, write and design brochures, produce video news releases, lobby representatives in government, stage a special event, or prepare annual reports. The body of knowledge of communication management is, however, far less developed, primarily as theory and formal education are lagging behind, and as practitioners, perhaps because of historical precedent, continue to regard communication as a craft or vocation. Table 7.2 presents some practitioners' views on their occupation, and illustrates that the job of the communicator is often vocationally defined in terms of personal characteristics (including elements such as 'courage', 'discretion', 'empathy', 'handling people', 'creative', 'up to speed', 'energetic', 'attitude of mind') that are often seen as subjective and intuitive, as well as by technical skills (writing, editing, etc.) that can be learnt.[24]

Figure 7.1 overleaf displays a similar set of views of practitioners on their occupation. Figure 7.1 is based upon results of a recent survey in the UK with practitioners across the private and public sectors and incorporates both in-house practitioners and communication consultants.[25] When practitioners were asked to list the characteristics that are most important in the job of a communicator, they ranked communication skills (verbal communication, writing and editing

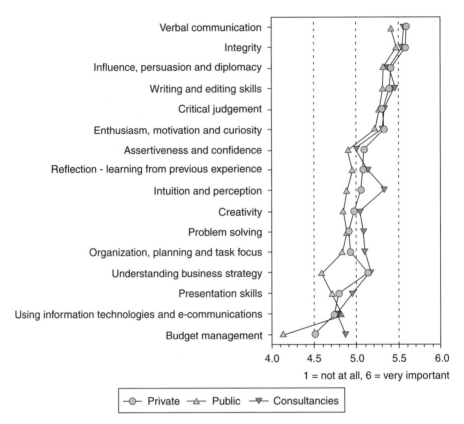

Figure 7.1   Practitioners' views of important competencies and skills in corporate communication

skills) and personal characteristics (integrity, influence, persuasion and diplomacy, critical judgement) at the top of their list.

Practitioners themselves appear to define their practice as built on personal characteristics and skills, but not on a specific domain of knowledge or expert competence. In other words, they themselves define the job as one of gifted craftsmanship but not as a profession that is based upon a distinct domain of expertise or set of competencies.

In recent years, many academics and industry commentators have agreed that in the process of professionalization, the field of communication is developing and has shown considerable progress as it now possesses its own professional associations (such as the International Association of Business Communicators and the Chartered Institute of Public Relations), ethical codes of conduct and professional guidelines, as well as skills training and educational courses.[26] But these commentators have also agreed that the field still lacks a well-grounded and distinct domain of expertise that is difficult to emulate and thus raises barriers for entry to novices and practitioners from other functions. James Grunig has suggested that professional knowledge requirements increase with the development into a profession. In his view, the development of a distinct body of professional knowledge has been lagging behind in communication and means that we cannot yet consider corporate communication as a fully-fledged profession. A body of knowledge is a stepping-stone towards a mindful and more managerial approach to the practice of communication[27] and may also lead to a recognition of the profession in the eyes of others. In the words of Jacquie L'Etang: 'The development of a body of knowledge not only increases the ability of the practice to base decisions on sound knowledge but also provides external vitality that is essential in the post-industrial world'.[28] The development of a body of knowledge is thus the crucial plank in the quest for professional status. It is the body of knowledge that can provide the cognitive core to the occupation, bolster practitioners' expertise and competencies and help define their field of jurisdiction. Such knowledge can be developed by practitioners themselves when they reflect upon their practice and attempt to develop models, concepts and principles that they have successfully applied in their own organizations. Professional associations also play an important role in that they can provide practitioners with learning and networking opportunities, with an understanding of best practices, and with professional norms and values. Universities and other higher education institutions equally have a role to play by stimulating scholarly research on corporate communication and by developing curricula and programmes that are built on the development of competencies and skills of practitioners.

Together, these different parties may increase and solidify the body of knowledge of corporate communication, and in doing so may advance what is now still seen by many as an occupation into a full profession. Professional development is also associated with the more widespread enactment of the manager role across organizations. Several studies have indicated that enactment of the managerial role is associated with multiple benefits: enhanced expertise, greater status within the organization, lower possibility of encroachment (i.e. taken over by another function or department), and a powerful indicator of an expert and strategic approach to communications management.[29] Such a link between manager role enactment and professional development does not devalue the role of skilled 'technicians' but nonetheless suggests that technician activities need to be embedded within a larger domain of expertise of how communication can be put to use in and for organizations.

A greater enactment of the manager role would also suggest that considerably more emphasis is placed on competencies (i.e. knowledge that is difficult to emulate) than just simply skills as has been the focus in the past. This, in turn, would not only provide a cognitive base in the form of expert knowledge to the field of communication, and an associated increase in status and legitimacy (i.e. acceptance of the function and acknowledgement of its standards of practice), but would also provide greater barriers to entering the practice of communication. In the past, the focus on skills created relatively low barriers for entry, as these could be relatively quickly learned. As a result, people with very different backgrounds and with little formal education were often found within communication. Adding a set of competencies as expected and required of practitioners would greatly raise the barrier for entry, comparable to other, more established professions, as it would stipulate the need for more baggage (acquired through formal education, training or 'on the job' experience) before one qualifies as a full professional and is also seen by others as such.

7.5 Chapter summary

Although the practice of communication has already come a long way in its development towards a profession, it still fails to receive the recognition and status afforded to other management disciplines. In many organizations, communication is still regarded as an afterthought, a duty for delegation, or as a peripheral management discipline. A central reason for this is the stage of professional development of numerous practitioners. Many practitioners operate largely as technicians and are located in a peripheral department that may support but does not directly participate in management decision-making. The chapter therefore discussed the importance of manager role enactment in terms of what it entails and in terms of its importance to professional development.

KEY TERMS

Body of knowledge	Occupation
Certification	Practitioner roles
Code of ethics	Problem-solving process facilitator
Communication facilitator	Profession
Competence	Professional association
Environmental scanning	Professional standards
Expert prescriber	Reflective practitioners
Issues management	Skills
Licensing	Technician
Manager	Vocation

Notes

1 Mintzberg, H. (1994), 'Rounding out the manager's job', *Sloan Management Review*, 36 (1): 11–25.

2 Katz, D. and Kahn, R.L. (1978), *The Social Psychology of Organizations*, 2nd edn. New York: Wiley.

3 Broom, G.M. (1982), 'A comparison of sex roles in public relations', *Public Relations Review*, 8 (3): 17–22.

4 Dozier, D.M. and Broom, G.M. (1995), 'Evolution of the manager role in public relations practice', *Journal of Public Relations Research*, 7: 3–26, quote on p. 22.

5 Ibid., pp. 5–6.

6 See, for example, Moss, D., Newman, A. and DeSanto, B. (2005), 'What do communication managers do? Defining and refining the core elements of management in a public relations/corporate communication context', *Journalism and Mass Communication Quarterly*, 82: 873–890.

7 Toth, E.L., Serini, S.A., Wright, D.K. and Emig, A.G. (1998), 'Trends in public relations roles: 1990–1995', *Public Relations Review*, 24(2): 145–163; Moss, D., Warnaby, G. and Newman, A.J. (2000), 'Public relations practitioner role enactment at the senior management level within UK companies', *Journal of Public Relations Research*, 12: 277–307; Wrigley, B.J. (2002), 'Glass ceiling? What glass ceiling? A qualitative study of how women view the glass ceiling in public relations and communications management', *Journal of Public Relations Research*, 14 (1): 27–55; Dozier, D.M. (1992), 'The organizational roles of communications and public relations practitioners', in Grunig, J.E. (ed.), *Excellence in Public Relations and Communication Management*. Hillsdale, NJ: Lawrence Erlbaum Associates, pp. 327–355.

8 Lauzen, M.M. (1995), 'Public relations manager involvement in strategic issue diagnosis', *Public Relations Review*, 21: 287–304.

9 This overview of competencies and skills is informed by a publication from the Beroepsvereniging voor Communicatie (Dutch professional association for communicators) entitled *Beroepsniveauprofielen* (July 2002).

10 Argenti, P., Howell, R.A. and Beck, K.A. (2005), 'The strategic communication imperative', *MIT Sloan Management Review*, Spring, 83–89, quote on p. 89.

11 Moss et al. (2000); Cropp, F. and Pincus, D.J. (2001), 'The mystery of public relations: unraveling its past, unmasking its future', in Heath, R.L. (ed.), *Handbook of Public Relations*. Thousand Oaks, CA: Sage, pp. 189–204.

12 Gronstedt, A. (2000), *The Customer Century: Lessons from World-class Companies in Integrated Marketing and Communications*. London: Routledge, p. 203.

13 See, for example, McGoon, C. (1993), 'Life's a beach for communicators', *Communication World*, 10 (1): 12–15; CIPR/DTI (2003), *Unlocking the Value of Public Relations*. London: CIPR.

14 Argenti et al. (2005), p. 89.

15 Grunig, J.E. and Grunig, L.A. (2002), 'Implications of the IABC Excellence Study for PR education', *Journal of Communication Management*, 7 (1): 34–42, quote on p. 41.

16 Pincus, J.D. et al. (1994), *Public relations education in MBA programmes: challenges and opportunities*, *Public Relations Review*, 2045: 52–68.

17 Murray, K. and White, J. (2004), 'A report on the value of public relations, as perceived by organizational leaders' (http://www.chime.plc.uk/downloads/reputationkm.pdf).

18 Gronstedt (2000), p. 204.

19 Wylie, F. (1994), 'Commentary: public relations is not yet a profession', *Public Relations Review*, 20: 1–3.
20 Nelson, R.A. (1994), 'The professional dilemma', *PR Update*, November, 1.
21 Sallot, L.M., Cameron, G.T. and Weaver Lariscy, R.A. (1998), 'Pluralistic ignorance and professional standards: underestimating professionalism of our peers in public relations', *Public Relations Review*, 24 (1): 1–19, quote on p. 3, see also Cameron, G.T., Sallot, L.M. and Weaver-Larsicy, R. (1996), 'Developing standards of professional performance in public relations', *Public Relations Review*, 22 (1): 43–61.
22 L'Etang, J. (1999), 'Public relations education in Britain: an historical review in the context of professionalization', *Public Relations Review*, 25 (3): 261–289.
23 Pieczka, M. and L'Etang, J. (2000), 'Public relations and the question of professionalism', in Heath (2000), pp. 223–235.
24 These practioner quotes were taken from ibid., p. 235.
25 CIPR/DTI (2003).
26 Pieczka and L'Etang (2000).
27 Grunig, J.E. (2001), 'The role of public relations in management and its contribution to organizational and societal effectiveness', speech delivered in Taipei, Taiwan, 12 May 2001.
28 L'Etang, J. (2002), 'Public relations education in Britain: a review at the outset of the millennium and thoughts for a different research agenda', *Journal of Communication Management*, 7 (1): 43–53.
29 Dozier and Broom (1995).

Part 4

SPECIALIST AREAS IN CORPORATE COMMUNICATION

Corporate communication involves a number of specialist areas of activity including media relations, issue and crisis management, public affairs and government relations, investor relations, and internal communication to employees. Each of these areas involves specialist knowledge, tools and techniques around communicating to particular stakeholder groups such as journalists and media organizations, investors and shareholders, activist groups and NGOs and an organization's managers and employees.

Part 4 explores three of the most important specialist areas in corporate communication: media relations, internal communication and change communication, and issue and crisis management. These three areas involve stakeholder groups (the media, employees and the general public) whose goodwill is important to an organization and its corporate reputation.

After reading Part 4 of the book, the reader should be familiar with effective approaches to media relations, internal communication and change communication, and issue and crisis management. The reader will also gain knowledge on how best to communicate with the media, employees and with the general public during an organizational change, issue or crisis

8

Media Relations

CHAPTER OVERVIEW

Communicating with the media is a central area of activity in corporate communication. Drawing on theories from mass communication, the chapter outlines how journalists and media organizations work and how news content may have an impact on corporate reputation. The chapter also explores the use and effectiveness of particular tools and techniques within media relations such as media monitoring services, press releases and press briefings.

8.1 Introduction

Working with the media is what most people associate with corporate communication. Media relations involve managing communication and relationships with the media; all the writers, editors and producers who contribute and control what appears in the print, broadcast and online news media. From a corporate communication standpoint, these news media are important as channels for generating publicity (Chapter 2) and because their coverage of business news may influence many important stakeholders such as (prospective) investors, customers and employees. Many corporate communication professionals therefore see the news media as a 'conduit' for reaching their stakeholders, rather than as a stakeholder or audience themselves.

This chapter explores how journalists and news organizations operate and how corporate communication professionals can best liaise and communicate with them. The aims of the chapter are, first of all, to provide an overview of the roles and values of news journalists and news media organizations (Section 8.2) and to discuss their importance in terms of the impact of news coverage on corporate reputation (Section 8.3). Based on this overview, the chapter continues by exploring the relationship between corporate communication professionals and journalists (Section 8.4) and sets out to discuss various tools and techniques such as media research and press releases that communication professionals can use to manage this relationship (Section 8.5).

8.2 Journalists and media organizations

The news media involve a variety of organizations with as core operational process the production and dissemination of news content through various media (newspapers, radio, TV and the internet). The production of news content typically involves two levels: (1) journalists who on an individual basis consult sources and write news stories; and (2) other parties within the news organization (e.g., copy editors) who, based upon their news routines, edit stories before they make it into print.[1] This distinction between journalists and news routines is important for corporate communication professionals because it illustrates the variety of influences on the production of news content and points to the limited degree of control that journalists producing stories about organizations actually have on the whole process, including the final printed words that make up the news story.

Journalists may talk to sources, cover a beat, and write a story, but at the same time not even recognize their own story when the story goes to print. This is because, at the level of *news routines*, there are many other people involved in the writing process who affect the story, such as the fact checker who verifies that the names of people, organizations and places mentioned are all spelled correctly. Copy editors may check that quotes are appropriately attributed to sources in a way that minimizes conflict and controversy. Layout and design specialists may be involved and check that news stories do not go over a certain word limit and that the story is designed within the format of the outlet and probably with an idea of how to attract readers. Moreover, the newspaper editor may decide that what was once a business news story should be a front page article for a much broader audience. In such a case, the lead paragraphs would need to be re-written from a business or strict financial perspective into a public interest perspective attracting a much wider reading audience typical of the front page. When there is a strong set of news routines within a news organization, it means that the journalist is to an extent writing for the needs of the editorial desk to which they are assigned: a national news desk, a local news desk, the financial/business news desk, or perhaps even an international news desk or the arts. On the other hand, when news routines are absent or less strong, there may be more flexibility for a journalist to write the story from a preferred angle and in a way in which he or she would like to write it. For example, an internet blog written by an individual journalist is subject to less rigorous scrutiny and further editing than an article published in a daily newspaper.

For journalists, writing for the needs of the desk is their way of ensuring that their story makes it into print. While no journalist ever writes a story without the intent of it getting picked up, whether the story is published or not is not their call. Moreover, journalists do not have a say on the final printed story, what the headline of the story is, or which photographs will be included (if any) with their story. Those decisions lie with their editors, including the front page editor, national editors, business/financial editors, and arts/community editors, among others. For journalists themselves, the pressure of writing for a news desk is sometimes experienced as a hindrance in their work and produces conflict with their professional ideals of objectivity, fairness and impartiality. Many journalists share a set of values based on seeking information and maintaining a measure of independence from all organizations including their own.[2]

News routines within a media organization may also reflect a certain ideology (a set of principles and values) or political orientation that is shared by journalists and editors of that organization. For example, *The New York Times* has been characterized as 'the editor's paper' and *The Washington Post* as the 'reporter's paper' referring to the levels of bureaucracy that exist between them. Similarly, articles in the *Guardian* newspaper are generally in sympathy with the middle-ground liberal to left-wing end of the political spectrum. This ideology may have a direct bearing upon the way in which news about organizations is reported. For example, a recent study commissioned by the BBC trust found that programmes on the BBC (e.g., *The Money Programme*, *Radio Five Live* and the *10 O'Clock News*) failed to represent shareholders' and employees' perspectives on corporate stories in favour of a consumer perspective. The study criticized the BBC business editors' negative and narrow views on business and made three recommendations: (1) the BBC should address the lack of knowledge of business issues among editorial staff; (2) it should widen 'the range of editorial ideas and programming about business'; and (3) 'ensure compliance in business coverage with standards of impartiality'.[3] Hence, ideology matters in terms of how organizations are covered in the news media and whether this will largely consist of 'good' or 'bad' news coverage.

8.3 Impact of news coverage on corporate reputation

In general, media coverage of an organization can have a strong influence on the corporate reputation of that organization. Ranging from reports on annual results to investigations of corporate issues, media coverage often has an 'amplifying' effect on a company's reputation when 'good' or 'bad' news is reported. While media coverage does not strictly determine a company's reputation or the way in which stakeholders think about an organization, it does have an impact in terms of highlighting an issue or increasing the already held positive or negative view of an organization.[4]

This amplifying effect has often been studied through the lens of agenda-setting theory. This theory traditionally was developed in mass communication and public opinion research but has recently been extended to the domain of corporate reputation. The agenda-setting hypothesis underlying the theory is that the frequency with which the media report on an issue determines that issue's salience in the minds of the general public.[5] In other words, 'The press may not be successful much of the time in telling people what to think, but it is stunningly successful in telling its readers what to think about'.[6]

The basic idea behind agenda-setting theory is that news media communicate a wealth of information when they report on organizations, politics, the economy or issues of social and human concern. In doing so, they also signal to their viewers, readers or audience what issues are salient about these topics. Over time, and through repeated mention of the same issues, such issues may become lodged in the public's mind. The public, in other words, will use the input from the media to decide which issues are important. The news media 'set' the public agenda.

Agenda-setting theory distinguishes two levels of agenda setting. The first level of agenda setting relates to the salience of an organization, whereas the second level of agenda setting deals with the attributes or associations related to that organization. First-level agenda setting occurs when Shell, for example, comes first to mind for members of the general public when Shell receives more media attention than other petroleum companies. The media report on certain organizations and in doing so prime awareness of an organization and certain content about that organization. Second-level agenda setting is apparent when the public associates Shell primarily with a particular issue (e.g., renewable energy) that has received much attention in the news during a particular period. Craig Carroll, a mass communication scholar, tested both levels of agenda setting in relation to US corporations.[7] Carroll content analyzed coverage of those corporations in *The New York Times*, which he used as a proxy for all reporting on those companies in the US. He then correlated the findings of news content with data on the public's awareness of those corporations and their associations with those corporations. Positive results were found for both levels of agenda setting: results revealed that news coverage influences which corporations were salient in the public's mind and the amount of media coverage devoted to certain corporate issues or attributes of the organization (e.g., workplace environment) were roughly in line with public associations regarding those corporations. A further study by May-May Meijer confirmed the same agenda-setting effects of media coverage. She also extended these results by testing the hypothesis that the higher the salience of an issue associated with a company in media coverage, the better the reputation of the company that is seen to 'own' that issue. For example, news coverage on environmental issues in the petroleum sector may benefit the reputation of BP as this organization is seen to take a leadership role in recognizing the ecological impact of business and in reducing carbon emissions.[8]

The second level of agenda-setting also suggests that news coverage not only reports facts and neutral observations, but also conveys feelings through its stance and tone on the issue. This affective dimension has been talked about in terms of media favourability – 'the overall evaluation of a firm presented in the media ... resulting from the stream of stories about the firm'.[9] Reputation expert David Deephouse used this term to suggest that the media not only convey information, they actually make and represent reputational assessments to their audiences. Deephouse referred to 'favourable' news coverage when an organization was praised for its actions or was associated with activities that should raise its reputation, while 'unfavourable' coverage referred to reporting in which an organization was criticized for its actions or associated with actions that should decrease its reputation. A 'neutral' rating identified a story that was the 'declarative reporting of role performance without evaluative modifiers'.[10] Deephouse found evidence suggesting that the higher the level of media favourability, the higher the level of an organization's performance. While the media does not directly impact upon an organization's performance (the media are an intermediary between organizations and stakeholder opinions and actions), this finding has one central implication for corporate communication professionals: they should seek to cultivate positive evaluations by the media through releasing well-placed stories that report on organizational actions (e.g., charitable giving, CSR initiatives) or significant newsworthy events.

Agenda-setting theory may also explain why certain companies are higher on reputation rankings (e.g., the *Fortune* or *Financial Times* rankings) than others. Companies making these rankings are prominent on the media agenda and are more likely to be prominent on the public agenda, while those companies that are outside of these rankings are far less likely to be prominent in the public's mind.[11] The news media often also rely upon large and well-known organizations for information subsidies, and there is evidence to support the claim that only companies with significant corporate reputations – whether good or bad – are used as information sources.[12] Organizations that are not well known are often ignored because of their low levels of newsworthiness, or simply because the media are not familiar with them. This has of course significant implications for the media's role as a watchdog when only certain organizations are monitored and covered in the news and other organizations are simply ignored and stay outside the public eye.

Agenda setting thus points to a powerful paradox for news organizations: on the one hand, their watchdog role means that they have to systematically report on news across the economy and across all types of organizations ranging from small and medium-sized enterprises to multinational corporations and public sector organizations. On the other hand, news organizations cannot wholly perform this role because of a lack of information on smaller companies and the lack of visibility of these organizations – which makes them less interesting to the general public.

8.4 Framing news stories

The relationship between communication professionals and journalists has often been described as adversarial. Journalists often have a negative opinion about communication professionals, in part because they feel that there is a clear divide between their interests: according to journalists, communication professionals think about the needs of their companies first and less about what journalists need. Past research has also found that journalists felt that professionals withheld information, were not always objective and certainly not focused on issues of public interest.[13] On the other hand, communication professionals are less negative about journalists and are often eager to work with them. However, professionals also realize that journalists have their own agenda and may frame news about the company in line their news routines and the ideology of the news organization that they work for (Section 8.2). While both professionals and journalists have different agendas and thus different angles on news related to a company, they do realize that they are interdependent: journalists need and often use information provided by professionals, and, equally, professionals and the companies that they work for often need the media as a conduit to generate coverage on the company and to reach important stakeholders such as the financial community, customers, prospective employees, government and the general public. According to some reports, as much as 80 per cent of news reports about companies is prompted and delivered by communication professionals.[14] The realization of this interdependence has led to a further specialization of media or press relations within corporate communication: many large companies have a dedicated press office or media team dealing with the general media which subsumes or is separate from investor relations professionals who deal with financial media such as *The Wall Street Journal* and *The Financial Times*.

When corporate communication professionals propose a particular story (in the form of, for example, a press release) to a journalist, they engage in two separate but related processes. The first is to solicit interest in the story topic itself. The second is to make sure that the story is framed in a way that is consistent with the organization's preferred framing (i.e., how the organization would like to have its story told). Exchanges between professionals are essentially *negotiations* about how news is *framed*.[15] Framing theory is a theoretically rich approach that has been used to understand and investigate communication and related behaviours in a wide range of disciplines including psychology, speech communication, organizational decision-making, economics, health communication, mass communication and political communication. Framing theory focuses on how messages are created in such a way that they connect with the underlying psychological processes of how people digest information and make judgements. Because people cannot possibly attend to every little detail about the world around them, framing in communication is important because it helps shape the perspectives through which people see the world. The notion of framing is best understood metaphorically as a window or portrait frame drawn around information that delimits the subject matter and, thus, focuses attention on key elements within it. Hence, framing involves processes of *inclusion* and *exclusion* of information in a message as well as *emphasis*. The communication scholar Entman summarized the essence of framing as follows:

> Framing essentially involves selection and salience. To frame is to select some aspects of perceived reality and make them more salient in the communicating text, in such a way as to promote a particular problem definition, causal interpretation, moral evaluation and/or treatment recommendation for the item described.[16]

In the context of corporate communication, framing theory suggests that communication professionals *frame* a particular corporate decision, issue or event in such a way that it furthers and promotes the interests of the organization. This frame which features in a press release, in corporate reports on the company's website, in speeches of spokespersons and the CEO is labelled the *corporate frame* that is provided to the media and to the general public. Journalists and editors, on the other hand, may interpret and represent the same decision, issue or event in a different way. *News framing* refers to the way in which news is selectively portrayed by the media in an effort to explain news or ideas about organizations in familiar terms for a broader audience. How a news item is framed also largely depends on the political views and ideology of journalists and their news organizations. Much research in mass communication has documented how journalists use dominant frames on politics, society and corporations to construct an understanding for their audience. Journalists often use such frames unconsciously as they relate to deeply ingrained assumptions about the social world.[17]

Because of their different interests, communication professionals and journalists may frame the same decision, issue or event in completely different ways. For example, when the industrial gases corporation BOC (now part of Linde) released its first quarter earnings in February 2006, the company framed the news in terms of 'record first quarter earnings' which the company said indicated that BOC was 'well positioned for growth' as an independent company. The news media, including *The Financial Times* and *The Guardian*, however, framed the earnings as increasing the likelihood that the company would be taken over by one of its competitors. In other words, journalists from these newspapers selected some elements of the press release (the actual recorded earnings) but reinterpreted them in the light of BOC as a take-over target, which was the frame that was made salient in their news coverage.

Skilful communication professionals play on journalists' knowledge and views to propose stories that follow dominant news frames, fit certain categories of content and resonate with a journalist's notion of expectations of their audience. Publicists such as Max Clifford are often very skilful in aligning a story proposal (corporate frame) with a story expectation (news frame) which leads to a greater probability of the story being placed and reported. The skill in media relations, in other words, is often in spotting the stories or the angles that can turn corporate news into media news or bring a corporate story into a global news story. This process is referred to as the *alignment* of frames between professionals and journalists.

Because not all journalists are necessarily going to frame a story in the same way, communication professionals often find themselves engaged in *frame contests* with journalists. Market models of journalism suggest that journalists will deliberately strive to frame stories in ways that resonate with what journalists perceive to be the largest segment of their audience. For example, in July 2006, a trader with Citigroup committed suicide by jumping from the 16th floor of the bank's Canary Wharf offices after climbing over a barrier. Despite evidence that the trader had committed suicide because of mental depression, many newspapers (including the *Telegraph*) framed the suicide in inverted commas (i.e., as 'suicide') and openly suggested a link to work pressures in the investment banking industry. Journalists from these newspapers chose to frame the news in what turned out to be a biased and inaccurate way because of a link with reader expectations and despite any evidence of trading irregularities or substantial losses.

How, then, can professionals avoid such frame conflicts? Alignment of frames is more likely when the substance of the corporate frame relates to common norms and expectations about business and society. For example, the Body Shop's (see Case Study 8.1) long-standing focus on social equality and fair trade aligns with some journalists' expectations of the role of business in society. Frame alignment is also more likely when professionals and journalists openly discuss an issue, decision or event so that a journalist is more likely to understand the other side. The opportunity for such an open discussion presupposes of course that communication professionals have developed a relationship with journalists in which both parties respect each other.

8.5 Tools and techniques in media relations

Communication professionals can use a wide range of tools and techniques to obtain news coverage and to monitor reporting on their organization over time. These include press releases, press conferences, interviews, and media monitoring and media research:

1. **Press release**. Press releases are a typical form of communication with the news media. The aim is to transfer news to journalists so that it can be made public. Press releases are more likely to be used and placed in a news medium when they refer to newsworthy events or items that are current and have a human

interest or appeal, when the release is written in a factual (as opposed to judgemental) manner and with a clear heading and lead (first paragraph) into the topic. When writing a press release, communication professionals should keep the expectations, preferred frames and deadlines of the different media in mind. Different media organizations and media forms (TV, print, internet) involve different reporting styles, timetables and deadlines. The print journalist, for example, will employ a pyramid scheme where the most important information is shared first in the article, and as the article increases in length, the information appearing further down in the news article will be deemed less important. In contrast, the radio journalist will try to share all of the information early on. Moreover, a reporter who is assigned to a business or financial desk will be concerned about angles from the perspective of business audiences and the implications for financial performance and financial markets. The public affairs reporter will be more concerned about the public angle. A feature writer will be more concerned about the human interest angle. As mentioned, it is important that professionals are sensitive to the dominant frames and interests of journalists and their news organizations so that there is a greater likelihood of frame alignment. Another point to be made when writing press releases is the time frame of different news media. Television and the internet are 'fast' media in the sense that a topic or article when it is finished is published directly whereas newspapers are slower in that they wait with publication until the next deadline. Magazines even have longer deadlines. This timeframe, which is short for internet and television, is of importance to corporate communication professionals, because the chance of incorrect reporting is greater for these fast media.

2. *Press conference.* Another typical tool of disseminating information to the news media involves inviting journalists to a press conference. Press conferences are normally organized around fixed periods in the calendar when organizations release financial results or share corporate information at the annual general meeting with shareholders. Incidentally, there may also be ad hoc press conferences around an issue or crisis (e.g., product defects, accidents) (see Chapter 10) in order to provide journalists with up-to-date information. An important element of the press conference is that it allows journalists to ask questions from the company executives gathered at the event. This 'interactive' feature distinguishes a press conference from a press release. A press conference is therefore more applicable when information cannot be conveyed in a standardized, written form or when the information involves a controversial or sensitive issue (see Chapter 3). In preparation for a press conference, professionals need to draw up a list of journalists and editors whom they would like to invite to the conference and brief them about the conference in time.

3. *Interviews.* Journalists often request an interview with official spokespersons or with the CEO or other senior executives of the organization. For this purpose, communication professionals need to offer executives advice and training on news angles in relation to corporate themes and on specific guidelines regarding the interview format. Such guidelines may consist of advising staff to keep 'control' of the interview by asking the journalist to call or come at a prearranged time, to brief them about the interview topics in advance, and to supply them with a copy of the interview transcript and final article so that facts,

opinions and attributions can be checked. In addition, CEOs and other exec-utives who are likely to be interviewed by journalists over the telephone, face-to-face or in front of a camera need to be trained to be skilled communicators. Many organizations therefore instruct their CEO and senior executives in media training so that they stay on message, synchronize their body language with their verbal messages, and can anticipate questions from journalists. When a CEO becomes an effective communicator, that can translate into admiration, respect and trust and a stronger overall corporate reputation.[18]

4.   *Media monitoring and research*. The most common type of media research consists of monitoring media relations efforts. Two of the most commonly used monitoring techniques are gatekeeping research and output analysis. In addi-tion, many corporations also use syndicated media monitoring services such as Carma International and Media Tenor:

   (a)   *Gatekeeping research*. A gatekeeping study analyses the characteristics of a press release or video news release that allow them to 'pass through the gate' and appear in a news medium. Both content and style variables are typi-cally examined. For example, previous research has found that press releases dealing with financial matters (e.g., annual results) are more likely to be used than those dealing with other topics. Press releases that are aimed at the specific interests of the newspaper to which they are sent are also more likely to be published than general releases. Editors furthermore typically shorten news releases and rewrite them to make them easier to read before publication.[19]

   (b)   *Output analysis*. The objective of output analysis is to measure the amount of exposure or attention that the organization receives as a result of media relations. Several techniques can be used in output analysis. One way is to simply measure the total amount of news coverage (i.e. total number of sto-ries or articles) that appears in selected mass media. In addition, it is also pos-sible to examine the tone (positive or negative) of stories or articles. Many communication professionals systematically collect press clippings (copies of stories or articles in the press) and record the degree of exposure in terms of column inches in print media, the number of minutes of air time in the elec-tronic media or the number of cites on the web. An often used measure for exposure is the 'advertising value equivalent' (AVE), which consists of count-ing the column inches of press publicity and seconds of air time gained and then multiplying the total by the advertising rate of the media in which the coverage appeared. It is not uncommon, using this measure, for communica-tion campaigns and well-placed press releases to bring in many hundreds of thousands of pounds, euros or dollars of advertising. However, AVE does not incorporate an evaluation of the tone of the stories or articles or the expo-sure of the organization compared to competitors. Another form of output analysis is to calculate the reach and frequency of media reporting on an organization. Reach is usually based on the total audited circulation of a newspaper or the estimated viewing or listening audience of TV or radio, while frequency refers to the number of times a story or article about an organization is carried in the same medium.

(c) **Syndicated media monitoring services**. Countering the shortcomings of output analysis, a number of media research agencies (e.g., Carma, Media Tenor) have developed sophisticated media monitoring packages. These packages focus on measuring the total circulation or audience reached; the tone of the news stories or articles on the organization; the extent to which key messages (for example, in a press release) were picked up and communicated; and the share-of-voice compared to competitors or other comparable organizations. Philips, for example, uses the Carma media monitoring tool to monitor news coverage on the firm compared to competing consumer electronics firms (e.g., Samsung, Sony) and other relevant firms (e.g., Shell which is similarly a Dutch corporation). The advantages of these tools involve the focus on outcome (share of voice and tone) as opposed to mere exposure or output, the automated analysis of mass media around the world and easy-to-use web portals which allow a communication professional to view real-time developments in media coverage.

CASE STUDY 8.1

L'ORÉAL'S TAKE-OVER OF THE BODY SHOP*

On 17 March 2006, the Body Shop International Plc (the Body Shop), a retailer of natural-based and ethically sourced beauty products, announced that it had agreed to be acquired by the beauty giant L'Oréal in a cash deal worth £652 million. The Body Shop had been put up for sale two years prior to the take-over by L'Oréal. Although there were a few interested parties at the time, no formal offer was made.

The Body Shop

The Body Shop, a cosmetics retailer which promotes itself based on ethics, fair trade and environmental campaigning, was founded in 1976 by Dame Anita Roddick. Roddick had copied the business model for the Body Shop from a Californian outfit with the same name that she had visited in 1970. Roddick modelled the look of her shops, the colour scheme, the products, her brochures and catalogues upon the Californian chain. In 1987, when Roddick's the Body Shop entered the US market, the company offered the Californian owners $3.5 million as compensation for use of the name. They also agreed to change the name of their six shops in California to Body Time.

Roddick started her first Body Shop in 1976 in Brighton in the UK. The store sold around 15 lines of homemade cosmetics made with natural ingredients such as jojoba oil and rhassoul mud. From its early days, the Body Shop was associated with the social activism of Roddick. The windows of the early Body Shop outlets, for example, featured posters of local charity and community

(Continued)

(Continued)

events. Roddick was from the start also very critical of the environmental insensitivity of big business and called for a change in corporate values.

Profits-with-a-principle

The Body Shop's core brand identity is its 'profits-with-a-principle' philosophy and the brand was closely marketed in combination with a social justice agenda. This was a revolutionary idea at the time and the Body Shop developed a loyal customer base. By the late 1970s, the company had grown into a number of franchise stores around the UK. Growing at a rate of 50 per cent annually, the Body Shop was getting a lot of media attention in the 1980s. Roddick hired a PR firm at the time to handle the media attention.

The Body Shop became fully listed on the London Stock Exchange in 1986. At the same time, the company formed an alliance with Greenpeace for the 'save the whales' campaign. Following some disagreements with Greenpeace, Roddick discontinued the relationship and formed instead an alliance with Friends of the Earth in 1990. The Body Shop also teamed up with Amnesty International and from the 1990s onwards became very vocal in its support for international human rights.

The company had its fair share of critics during the 1980s and 1990s who accused the company of hypocrisy as they felt that it was making profits under the guise of endorsing social equality. At the same time, some shareholders complained that instead of maximizing profits, the company was diverting money into 'social work' projects. For example, Jon Entine an award-winning journalist published a damning critique of the Body Shop in an article in 1994. Entine reported that the Charity Commission records in the UK did not show any charitable contributions from the company in its first 11 years of operation and only a less than average contribution (1.5 per cent of pre-tax profits) in subsequent years. He also said that the company made false claims that its products were natural, as chemicals were still used in the production of many of the Body Shop's products at the time. In 1998, McSpotlight and Greenpeace put forward similar criticisms that Body Shop exploited the public by championing a social agenda. They said that the Body Shop's products were not completely free from chemicals and although the company claimed that it was against animal testing, its products contained ingredients that had been tested on animals by other companies.

Throughout the 1990s, the company continued to grow in size, although its market value declined. The Board of the Body Shop had also got tired of Roddick's radicalism, her combative stance on globalization and her vocal criticism of anti-wrinkle cream. In 1998, Roddick was forced to step down as the CEO. In 2000, Roddick announced that she would quit the Board in two years but that she would continue to carry out media functions for the Body Shop and would keep travelling around the world in search of new product ideas. Anita Roddick became a Dame in 2003 in recognition of her social campaigning and passed away on 10 September 2007.

The take-over by L'Oréal

L'Oréal is one of the largest and most successful cosmetics companies in the world with 17 global brands in its portfolio. By 2004, L'Oréal had achieved 19 years of consecutive double digit growth. The company had successfully strengthened its market dominance by promoting its major brands such as L'Oréal Paris and Lancôme and by acquiring and internationalizing popular local brands such as Ralph Lauren, Redken, Maybelline and Garnier. Advertising was focused on the superior quality of the company's products and endorsements by successful career women and celebrities. L'Oréal became interested in the acquisition of the Body Shop as the take-over would provide the company with a new perspective on retailing (speciality stores, direct-sales business), a brand capable of generating publicity in developing markets (China, Russia, India), an entry into the 'masstige' market (premium mass cosmetics), a foothold in the fair trade movement, as well as additional revenues. At the same time, L'Oréal realized that it had not been previously associated with ethics or fair trade and had been criticized in the past for its use of animal testing in the production of cosmetics. Therefore, a take-over of the Body Shop would present L'Oréal with some communication challenges.

When the deal was finalized between the two companies, both L'Oréal and the Body Shop came out with press releases and video clips to announce and rationalize the deal and to communicate the advantages to both parties. L'Oréal's chairman and CEO Lindsay Owen-Jones issued a written statement. Adrian Bellamy (Chairman of the Body Shop), Peter Saunders (CEO of the Body Shop) and Anita Roddick (Non-executive Director) all issued pre-recorded video clips with answers to questions about the take-over. The transcripts of these video releases were also made available as press releases. Adrian Bellamy said: 'I'm extremely positive about the deal. We'll be stronger as part of the L'Oréal group than by sailing our own boat. We'll be able to share its global platform and experience:' Similarly, L'Oréal's chairman and CEO Owen-Jones said: 'We have always had great respect for the Body Shop's success and for the strong identity and values created by its outstanding founder, Anita Roddick'. He also added:

> A partnership between our two companies makes perfect sense. Combining L'Oréal's expertise and knowledge of international markets with the Body Shop's distinct culture and values will benefit both companies. We are delighted that the Body Shop has agreed to unanimously recommend our offer to the company's shareholders. We look forward to working together with the Body Shop management, employees and franchisees to fulfil the Body Shop's independent potential as part of the L'Oréal family.

L'Oréal also said that the management team at the Body Shop would be retained and that the company would continue to operate as a separate company to preserve its own identity.

(Continued)

(Continued)

In her own press release, Roddick justified the deal by saying that L'Oréal wanted to learn from the Body Shop's value-based management. She denied that she had sold out and maintained that the Body Shop's values and focus on social development would not change. As she stated in the press release: 'I do not believe that L'Oréal will compromise the ethics of the Body Shop. That is after all what they are paying for and they are too intelligent to mess with our DNA ... I want to make things happen, to spread human values wide in business if I possibly can. And this sale gives us the chance to do so'. She added:

> The campaigning, the being maverick, changing the rules of business – it's all there, protected. And it's not going to change. That's part of our DNA. But having L'Oréal come in and say we like you, we like your ethics, we want to be a part of you, we want you to teach us things, it's a gift. I'm ecstatic about it. I don't see it as selling out.

Roddick also mentioned that she hoped that the Body Shop values would rub off on the way in which L'Oréal does business. 'But with L'Oréal now, the biggest cosmetics company in the world, for them to partner with us on our projects in 35 countries in the world, I think it's amazing, amazing. They could work with our Nicaraguan farmers who sell us 70 tons of sesame oil. How many tons could they use? A thousand? I mean it's mind-blowing in terms of poverty eradication'.

Media reporting

The media reported the take-over on the same day (17 March 2006) that the deal was finalized and announced. Initially, news coverage consisted of reports on the details of the take-over with quotes from the press releases of L'Oréal's Owen-Jones and of Anita Roddick. The BBC, for example quoted from Roddick's press release in which she said that 'this [the takeover] is the best 30th anniversary gift the Body Shop could have received'. *The Guardian* published the same quote from Roddick along with another demonstrating the complementary link that Roddick mentioned in her press release: 'L'Oréal has displayed visionary leadership in wanting to be an authentic advocate and supporter of our values'. However, later that afternoon, the *Guardian* on-line edition published an article on a call by animal welfare activists to boycott the Body Shop. A coalition of activist groups including Naturewatch opposed L'Oréal's policy on the testing of cosmetics ingredients on animals. None of the other newspapers reported the same or a similar story on the same day.

Editorial pieces in subsequent weeks now and again picked up on the nature of the relationship between the two companies. For example, an article in *The Economist* on 25 March 2006 questioned the complementary but independent link between the two companies. The article suggested that it would be difficult for L'Oréal not to adopt any cross-selling practices across Body Shop outlets. Rhetorically the article asked; 'Will L'Oréal really be able to resist slipping its ethically challenged wrinkle cream onto the shelves next to the bracing and naturally inspired body scrubs offered by the Body Shop?' However, by and large, the news media and the general public accepted the claim from Roddick and Owen-Jones that the Body Shop would remain an independent entity with the upshot that its value-based practices and social change campaigns could have a wider impact with the support from L'Oréal. Part of this news framing may be attributed to the strong media presence of Roddick, who with her frank style of communicating convinced many journalists of the rationale of the deal. While early indications showed that the brand of the Body Shop had dropped somewhat in brand indices such as YouGov BrandIndex, the Body Shop's image is making a comeback and on its own terms.

Questions for reflection

1. Discuss the framing of the take-over of the Body Shop by L'Oréal in terms of the concepts of frame alignment and frame contests. Why do you think that some media reported frames and quotes from corporate press releases while others published alternative frames about the take-over?
2. When the take-over was announced, the Body Shop issued pre-recorded interviews to journalists. In your view, should the Body Shop have done anything else (e.g., face-to-face interviews, press conference) to influence the news coverage and framing of the take-over?

Note: ⋆ This case study is based upon www.thebodyshopinternational.com; 'The Body Beautiful', *The Economist* (www.economist.com), 25 March 2006 and articles downloaded from www.jonentine.com

8.6 Chapter summary

This chapter started with an overview of journalists and news organizations and of the production of news content. Given the importance of the news media for a company's reputation, the chapter continued by discussing ways in which professionals can frame news items in such a way that they are picked up by the press. Finally, the chapter outlined various practical tools and techniques that communication professionals use to obtain media coverage, build relationships with journalists and monitor reporting on their organization over time.

KEY TERMS

Agenda setting	Journalist
Corporate frame	Media favourability
Frame alignment	Media monitoring
Frame conflict	News desk
Frame contest	News frame
Frame negotiation	News routines
Gatekeeping research	Output analysis
Ideology	Press conference
Interviews	Press release

Notes

1   Deephouse, D.L. and Carroll, C.E. (2007) 'What makes news fit to print: a five-level framework predicting media visibility and favourability of organizations', Working paper, Alberta School of Business.

2   See, for example, Lorimer, R. (1994), *Mass Communications*. Manchester: Manchester University Press.

3   Conlan, T. (2007), 'BBC business news failing impartiality test, says report', *The Guardian*, 26 May, p. 18.

4   Fombrun, C.J. and Shanley, M. (1990), 'What's in a name? Reputation building and corporate strategy', *Academy of Management Journal*, 33: 233–258.

5   McCombs, M. and Shaw, D. (1972), 'The agenda-setting function of mass media', *Public Opinion Quarterly*, 36: 176–187.

6   Cohen, B.C. (1963), *The press and foreign policy*. Princeton, NJ: Princeton University Press, p. 120.

7   Carroll, C. (2004), 'How the mass media influence perceptions of corporate reputation: agenda-setting effects within business news coverage', unpublished doctoral dissertation, the University of Texas at Austin. TX, USA.

8   Meijer, M. and Kleinnijenhuis, J. (2006), 'Issue news and corporate reputation: applying the theories of agenda setting and issue ownership in the field of business communication', *Journal of Communication*, 56: 543–559.

9   Deephouse, D.L. (2000), 'Media reputation as a strategic resource: an integration of mass communication and resource-based theories', *Journal of Management*, 26: 1091–1112, quote on p. 1097.

10 Ibid., p. 1101.

11 Carroll, C.E. and McCombs, M. (2003), 'Agenda-setting effects of business news on the public's images and opinions about major corporations', *Corporate Reputation Review*, 6: 36–46.

12 Carroll (2004), p. 2.

13 See, for example, Belz, A.D. Talbott and Starck, K. (1989), 'Using role theory to study cross perceptions of journalists and public relations practitioners', *Public Relations Research Annual*, 1: 125–139; Neijens, P.C., and Smit, E.G. (2006), 'Dutch public

relations practitioners and journalists: antagonists no more', *Public Relations Review*, 32 (3): 232–240.

14 Merten, K. (2004), 'A constructivist approach to public relations', in van Ruler, B. and Vercic, D. (eds), *Public Relations and Communication Management in Europe*. Berlin: Mouton de Gruyter, pp. 45–54; Elving, W.J.L. and Ruler, A.A. Van (2006), *Trendonderzoek communicatiemanagement* [Trend research communication management]. Amsterdam: University of Amsterdam.

15 See, for example, Hallahan, K. (1999), 'Seven models of framing: implications for public relations', *Journal of Public Relations Research*, 11: 205–242.

16 Entman, R.M. (1993), 'Framing: toward clarification of a fractured paradigm', *Journal of Communication*, 43 (4): 51–8, quote on p. 55.

17 See, for example, Hallahan (1999) and Entman (1993).

18 See, for example, Gaines-Ross, L. (2003), *CEO Capital: A Guide to Building CEO Reputation and Company Success*. Hoboken, NJ: Wiley; Hayward, M.L., Rindova, V.P. and Pollock, T.G. (2004), 'Believing one's own press: the antecedents and consequences of CEO celebrity', *Strategic Management Journal*, 25: 637–653.

19 Morton, L. and Ramsey, S. (1994), 'A benchmark study of the PR news wire', *Public Relations Review*, 20: 155–170; Morton, L. and Warren, J. (1992), 'Proximity: localization versus distance in PR news releases', *Journalism Quarterly*, 69: 1023–1028; Walters, T., Walters, L. and Starr, D. (1994), 'After the highwayman: syntax and successful placement of press releases in newspapers', *Public Relations Review*, 20: 345–356.

9

Internal Communication and Change Communication

CHAPTER OVERVIEW

Employees are a crucial stakeholder group in the survival of organizations. Organizations need to communicate with their employees to strengthen employee morale and their identification with the organization and to ensure that employees know how to accomplish their own, specialized tasks. The chapter discusses strategies for communicating to employees within the organization. These strategies range from communication that makes employees feel comfortable speaking up and providing feedback to managers to communication during and after the implementation and routinization of an organizational change.

9.1 Introduction

Organizations require employees to cooperate with one another to achieve the company's goals. Most organizations have divided complex activities up into more specialized tasks for individual employees. While efficient, the pay-off of such specialization depends almost wholly on coordinating tasks and activities across employees. Organizations also need to control their employees' interpersonal relationships, both in terms of who they form relationships with and how they communicate with their colleagues. For example, Intel Corporation forbids dating between managers and their subordinate employees and enforces the rule by transferring offenders to different departments. Organizations of course vary in how tightly they control their employees' actions and relationships, but in essence all organizations must exercise some level of control if they are to survive.

These two sets of needs – those of the organization and those of its individual employees – must be balanced. If an organization controls its members through top-down command and delegation, the individual needs of employees for autonomy, creativity and sociability may be frustrated. But if the organization fails to control its employees, it loses the ability to coordinate its employees' activities, and will ultimately fail. Hence, organizations must find ways to meet their employees' individual needs while persuading them to act in ways that meet the organization's needs. Organizations do so by adopting various communication strategies with employees. Section 9.2 defines the strategies and processes of internal communication. Section 9.3 discusses the importance of internal communication in employees' identification with their organization. The degree to which managers communicate to employees and involve them in decision-making also has an impact on employee morale and their commitment to the organization. Section 9.4 discusses the importance of supporting employees to speak up and not withhold valuable information from management. Finally, Section 9.5 outlines various communication strategies during and after major organizational changes (e.g., organizational restructuring, lay-off of staff) within organizations to reduce employee resistance and to facilitate the implementation and routinization of such changes.

9.2 Defining internal communication

Contemporary organizations realize that their employees need to be communicated with. The terms that have often been used to label this area of corporate communication are 'employee communication', 'staff communication' and 'internal communication'. Traditionally, internal communication, which is the term used in this chapter, was defined as communication with employees internally within the organization. Internal communication was distinguished from forms of external communication wtih stakeholders such as customers and investors. However, the advent of new technologies (e.g., internet blogs, e-mails) has meant that messages to employees do not always remain 'inside' the organization. These new technologies have blurred the boundaries between 'internal' and 'external' communication. Employees can nowadays distribute their own information about an organization electronically to outside stakeholders, sometimes without any gate-keeping or control from corporate communication professionals. On an internet blog, for example, employees can share their views and publish their grievances as well as organize and demand action from the organization. Indeed, with access to e-mail, blogs, and social networking sites for sharing corporate information, many employees become somewhat like corporate communication professionals themselves. Robert Scoble, a former employee of Microsoft, wrote a daily blog on technology which often promoted Microsoft products like Tablet PCs and Windows Vista, but also frequently criticized his own employer and praised its competitors. His blog was read by many independent software developers around the world and built a more humane image of Microsoft. In February 2005, Scoble became the first person to earn the newly coined term of 'spokesblogger'. A spokesblogger is an official spokesperson for an organization who, while publishing an independent blog, often does not speak only for himself, but also on behalf of their employer or the organization that he represents.[1]

Clearly, communication technologies have led to many changes in the workplace. Computer technologies have made it easier to produce, multiple, distribute and store written documents; to exchange messages over long distances and to work together and to execute meetings relatively independent of time and space. Employees are now often connected to each other by electronic means rather than by close physical proximity. E-mails, the intranet, videoconferencing and podcasting are used by managers to communicate with employees and by employees themselves to stay informed of company news. IBM, for example, offers more than 5,000 podcast 'episodes' to employees, who can download these files and watch them at a convenient time. IBM feels that these podcasts are a useful way to disseminate corporate information in an efficient and engaging way.

If we look at the use of communication technologies within organizations, we can distinguish two central areas of internal communication: (1) management communication; and (2) corporate information and communication systems. Management communication refers to communication between a manager and his or her subordinate employees. Communication in this setting is often directly related to specific tasks and activities of individual employees as well as to their morale and well-being. Research on what managers do has demonstrated that managers spend most of their time communicating, and much of that time is spent in verbal, face-to-face communication.[2] Besides face-to-face communication, managers also increasingly use e-mail, videoconferencing and enterprise software to communicate to their employees. While the responsibility for management communication lies with managers themselves and not with the corporate communication department, communication professionals often advise and support managers in their communication to staff. Communication professionals in AstraZeneca, for example, have developed training material for senior and middle managers to help them become better communicators.

Corporate information and communication systems (CICS) has a broader focus than the manager–employee dyad. CICS refers to the broadcasting of corporate decisions and developments to all employees across the organization. The emphasis is on disseminating information about the organization to employees in all ranks and functions within the organization in order to keep them informed about corporate matters. CICS is often the preserve of the communication department who are charged with releasing information to employees through the intranet, e-mails and so-called 'town hall' meetings (i.e. large employee meetings where senior managers announce and explain key corporate decisions or developments). Corporate TV such as the digital FedEx

Television Network or Nokia's digital broadcasting systems are also used as communication channels for reaching employees around the world.

Whereas management communication is often restricted to the specific inter-personal work setting of a manager and employee, CICS may not differentiate content between employees and typically relates to more general organizational developments rather than specific areas of work. Although different, both areas of internal communication complement each other in ensuring that information flows vertically, horizontally and laterally across the organization. Without both forms of internal communication, a company's overall communication effort will be ineffective and its employees demotivated. The complementary nature of both can best be understood through the concepts of downward and upward communication. Downward communication consists of electronic and verbal methods of informing employees about their organization, its performance, and their own performance in terms they can comprehend. In other words, downward communication involves 'information flowing from the top of the organizational management hierarchy and telling people in the organization what is important (mission) and what is valued (policies)'.[3] Both management communication and CICS are central to downward communication; together, they provide employees with general information from the top of the organization (CICS) as well as with more specific information from their managers (management communication). Upward communication, on the other hand, involves information from employees that is sent upwards towards managers within the organization. It often involves information about the employee him/herself, information about co-workers, information about organizational practices and policies, and information about what needs to be done and how it can be done. Allowing employees to communicate upwards is important because employees' ideas, responses to their working environment, or critiques of the plans and ideas announced by managers may be used to find ways to improve an organization's overall performance and profitability. Upward communication is typically facilitated within the inter-personal setting of management communication. Managers can stimulate employees to voice concerns and to provide them with feedback on practices, procedures and new organizational changes. At the same time, CICS may include communication systems such as message boards on an intranet and 'town hall' meetings, allowing employees to ask questions of senior managers and to ask for further information on corporate decisions or organizational developments.

9.3 Internal communication and organizational identification

When employees strongly identify with the organization that they work for, they are more satisfied in their work, they will be more cooperative and they will also demonstrate behaviour that is helpful to the organization.[4] Organizational identification, in other words, plays a significant role in many organizations. Organizational identification can be defined as: 'the perception of oneness with or belongingness to an organization, where the individual defines him or herself in terms of the organization(s) of which he or she is a member'.[5] Research has shown that organizational identification increases as a result of the perceived external prestige of the organization[6] and as a result of the degree of overlap between the personal identity of the employees and the identity of the organization. When employees perceive their organization to be associated with a strong reputation and prestige in the eyes of outsiders, they often feel proud to belong to that organization and may feel inclined to bask in its reflected glory. Employees identify with an organization partly to enhance their own self-esteem: the more prestigious an individual employee perceives his or her organization to be, the greater the potential boost to self-esteem through identification. Employees also identify more strongly with their organization to the degree that the corporate values and attributes of the organization (organizational identity) correspond with one's own personal values. In other words, the higher the perceived fit between the values of an individual employee and the corresponding organization, the stronger the degree to which that employee identifies with his or her organization.

   Internal communication also has a significant impact on organizational identification. Two recent studies demonstrate that downward communication enhances organizational identification when the information transmitted is perceived as adequate and reliable.[7] Adequate information involves receiving useful and sufficient information about what is expected of employees in their work and regarding their contributions. The more adequate or specific the information to the employee involved, the higher the level of identification with that organization. Reliable information involves the perception that managers release information that is trustworthy and instrumental to the accomplishments of tasks. When information coming from management is perceived as reliable, employees are more likely to identify with their organization.[8] A further factor that has a significant impact on organizational identification involves the degree to which employees feel that they are listened to and are involved by managers when decisions are made. When employees feel that they participate in decision-making and are able to exert some control over their working life, they identify more strongly with their organization and are also generally more committed. Good internal communication, therefore, combines upward and downward communication in such a way that employees are well informed about the future directions of the organization (in particular the organization's strategies and policies), are allowed to interact with management about their policies, and where this interaction has an impact on managerial decisions. In other words, internal communication is most productive in the sense of eliciting employee commitment and organizational identification if it is a two-way process of communication, rather than a one-way flow of feedback and instructions. The role of corporate communication professionals and managers is therefore to use management communication and ICIS in such a way that internal communication provides 'each employee with adequate information and the opportunities to speak out, get involved, be listened to, and [to] actively participate' in the organization.

9.4 Voice, silence and employee participation

Voice and silence and employee participation are terms used to refer to the degree to which employees speak up, are listened to and participate in organizational decision-making. Employee participation involves organizational structures and processes designed to empower and enable employees to identify with organizational goals and to exert power over decision-making. Unionization of the workforce, for example, is one way in which the interests of workers are represented and communicated to senior managers. In some organizations, participation is also anchored in the identity and corporate governance of the organization. Cooperative organizations, for example, are jointly owned and democratically controlled by all those who work for the organization. John Lewis, a successful cooperative chain of department stores in the UK, attributes much of its success to employee co-ownership which the company feels has led to 'sky-high' levels of employee engagement.[9]

Whilst most organizations are not based on a form of employee co-ownership like John Lewis, employee participation has been an issue of concern as long as organizations have existed. Employees want a say in shaping their work lives, and organizations equally often feel that participation is desirable for a number of reasons including genuine concern for the welfare of employees to a desire for the productivity benefits that can follow from employees engaging with the organization. However, even though participation is desirable, enabling employee participation is by no means straightforward.

The management scholars Morrison and Milliken have argued that there are often powerful forces in many organizations that prevent employees from participation and that force them to withhold information about potential problems or issues.[10] They refer to such withholding of information as organizational silence. When employees share a perception that speaking up is unwise or without any consequence, they remain silent. Such silence in turn may mean that vital upward information is not passed on to managers. Morrison and Milliken pointed to two factors that often systematically cause employees to feel that their opinions are not valued and that thereby discourage them from speaking up. The first factor relates to managers' fear of receiving negative feedback from employees. There is evidence to suggest that senior and middle managers often feel threatened by negative feedback, whether this information is about them personally or about a decision or a course of action with which they identify. Managers often feel a strong need to avoid embarrassment, threat, and feelings of vulnerability or incompetence. Therefore, they are likely to avoid any negative information and negative feedback coming from subordinates. The second factor that may influence organizational silence involves a set of managerial beliefs which suggest that managers know best about organizational matters. The basic assumption underlying such beliefs of managers is that, because of information asymmetries, employees will not have a broad enough understanding of the organization. The information that employees therefore provide about organizational matters is seen as not relevant or up-to-date compared to the knowledge that managers already have. This particular belief is quite strong in managers who view their role as one of directing and controlling, with employees assuming the role of unquestioning followers.

If the dominant belief of managers in an organization is that employees are not sufficiently knowledgeable about what is best for the organization, then it is reasonable for managers not to involve them in decision-making processes. Decentralized or consensus forms of decision-making will be seen by managers as not worth the time and effort they require. Excluding employees from decision-making is also a way to avoid dissent and negative feedback and, thus, will also stem from fear of negative feedback. In many organizations, although there may be the appearance of some forms of participative decision-making (e.g., task forces, committees), managers still often attempt to hold on to their decision-making authority. When managers fear negative feedback from employees, they are unlikely to engage in seeking much informal feedback from subordinates. Instead, managers may be more inclined to seek feedback from those who are likely to share their perspective and who are, thus, unlikely to provide negative feedback.

The fear of negative feedback and the belief that upward information is often of little value will also be associated with a lack of mechanisms for soliciting employee feedback after decisions are made. Using procedures such as employee surveys or 360-degree feedback will be unlikely, because there will be a tendency to believe that little of value will be learned from them and because negative upward feedback will be seen as a challenge to management's control. It is important to realize that these various managerial beliefs and practices contributing to silence may operate at multiple levels of an organization. For example, middle managers and work supervisors may hold these beliefs and exhibit the day-to-day practices that impede upward communication, while corporate communication professionals and senior executives feel that employee feedback and involvement is a key performance indicator.

Organizational silence can damage the organization in that it blocks negative feedback and, hence, an organization's ability to detect and correct errors. Without negative feedback, errors within an organization may persist and may even intensify, because corrective actions are not taken when needed. The quality of decision-making may also be affected by organizational silence. Potentially useful viewpoints and alternatives from the perspective of employees are not considered. The effectiveness of organizational decision-making will be compromised because of the restricted information available to managers. The tendency of managers to discourage employee opinions and feedback is also likely to elicit negative reactions from employees. Employees may come to feel that they are not valued and that they lack any control in their work. When employees feel that they are not valued, they will also be less likely to identify with the organization.

The concept of organizational silence is closely related to the concept of communication climate. Communication climate is defined as the internal environment of information exchange between managers and employees through an organization's formal and informal networks.[11] A communication climate is characterized as 'open' when information flows freely between individuals, groups and departments and it is characterized as 'closed' when information is blocked. Organizational silence corresponds to a 'closed' communication climate because it involves a shared and widespread feeling among employees that speaking up is of little use, leading them to withhold potentially valuable information. In an 'open' communication climate, in contrast, employees feel free to express opinions, voice complaints, and offer suggestions to their superiors. In such a climate, information also passes without distortion upward, downward, and horizontally throughout the organization. Employees feel that they have enough support from their managers that they can give information to them without hesitation, confident that superiors will readily accept it, whether good or bad, favourable or unfavourable. In an 'open' communication climate, employees also know that their information will be seen as valuable, and hence sending communication upward will have an effect.

9.5 Change communication

An important area of internal communication involves communicating to employees during and after a change. Large organizations are prone to initiate and implement many organizational changes ranging from, for example, a restructuring, a new performance initiative, the adoption of new technology or new way of working, or the laying off of parts of the workforce. All of these changes affect employees in one way or another and their successful implementation often crucially depends on communication. Poorly managed change communication may result in rumours and resistance to change. Communication and change are related in a number of different ways. Communication is central to how a change is formulated, announced and explained to employees and also contributes to a successful implementation and institutionalization of the change. Kurt Lewin highlighted the importance of communication in his simple model of the change process.[12] Lewin likened the change process to a process of water freezing. When snow melts as a result of heat from the sun and then refreezes again when the temperature drops again it takes on a different texture (e.g., it becomes more icy). Lewin argued that change in an organization is a very similar process involving an alteration of the organization (water) in terms of its structure or function (in the form of snow or ice) over time. Based on this metaphor, he argued that change involves four phases: (1) recognizing the need for change (unfreezing); (2) development of a change plan (vision); (3) implementation of the new change (moving); and (4) routinization of the change (refreezing). All of these phases (identification of the need for change, formulation of a change initiative, implementation of the change, and institutionalization of the change) require communication between managers and employees.

Organizational changes have often been classified in terms of degrees of change. For example, change can be major or radical (e.g., a complete restructuring of an organization) or more minor and convergent (e.g., an adjustment of customer service guidelines as a result of customer feedback). Radical change involves a complete re-orientation of an organization, whereas convergent change consists of fine-tuning the existing orientation and ways of working. Change can also be defined in terms of its time-frame: evolutionary changes occur slowly and gradually whereas revolutionary changes happen swiftly and affect virtually all of the organization.[13] Organizational changes can of course also be classified in terms of the primary focus of the change. Changes may involve the adoption of novel or updated *technology* to accomplish work; a *restructuring* and change in *policies* and routine *ways of working*; a change in the *products* and *services* of an organization; or a change in the *organizational identity* and *culture* of the organization.

Depending on the degree and focus of the change, an organization will have to identify an effective way of communicating the change to employees. Obviously, when a change is radical and involves the entire organization, managers would have to engage in a lot of conversations with employees across all levels of the organization, to initiate the desired overhaul in thinking. Alternatively, when the change involves an updating of technology (e.g., the introduction of a new intranet system), communication may consist of informing employees about the new technology and training them in their use of it. The management scholar Clampitt and his colleagues observed five different communication strategies that managers use to communicate a change to employees[14].

1. *'Spray and pray'*. The first strategy, labelled 'spray and pray', involves managers showering ('spray') employees with all kinds of information about the change. The idea with this strategy is that information is simply passed onto employees who, it is hoped ('pray'), will then themselves sort out the significant from insignificant details and work out what the change means for their day-to-day

job. While this strategy may seem admirable, it is rarely effective. More information does not necessarily equate to better communication when it is not sufficiently focused and tailored to the needs of employees.

2. *'Tell and sell'*. A second strategy, labelled 'tell and sell', involves managers communicating a more limited set of messages that they believe address the core issues about the change. In this strategy, managers first tell employees about the key issues and then try to sell employees a particular approach. The strategy is a top-down strategy; employees are not engaged in a dialogue, but simply informed of a change. The danger with this strategy is that employees feel that they are not listened to and become sceptical, if not cynical, about the change.

3. *'Underscore and explore'*. The third strategy is labelled 'underscore and explore' because it involves managers focusing on several fundamental issues most clearly linked to the organizational change, while allowing employees the creative freedom to explore the implications of the change in a disciplined way. When managers use this strategy, they often assume that communication is not complete and effective until they know how employees react to the core ideas behind the change. In other words, managers are concerned not only with developing a few core messages but also with listening to employees in order to identify potential misunderstandings and unrecognized obstacles to the change.

4. *'Identify and reply'*. The fourth strategy, labelled 'identify and reply', is different from the first three because it starts with the concerns of employees. The strategy involves employees setting the agenda to which managers reply. The assumption behind the strategy is that employees are in the best position to know the critical issues and the feasibility of a change. However, the danger is that employees do not have the wider picture of the entire organization and that managers use this strategy as a defensive posture in which they are seen to attend to employee concerns without actually using that feedback.

5. *'Withhold and uphold'*. The fifth and final strategy labelled 'withhold and uphold' consists of managers withholding information until they can no longer do so because of rumours or employee revolt. When confronted by rumours or revolt, managers simply uphold the party line. Managers who use this strategy often assume that information is power, that employees are not sophisticated enough to grasp the big picture or simply do not need to know the rationale for a change.

Managers may use other strategies or a combination of these five strategies. The underlying differences between these strategies involve the degree to which employees are provided with relevant information, are given guidance on the change, and feel involved and consulted in the change process. As demonstrated in Figure 9.1, the communication strategies towards the middle of the figure tend to offer employees more guidance by prioritizing communication and by providing relevant and focused information on the change. These strategies are also more sensitive to employee concerns and needs, although of course they make different assumptions about the importance and nature of those concerns and needs. The 'underscore and explore' strategy in particular maximizes the likelihood of effective change by creatively synthesizing managers' change initiatives and employee concerns.

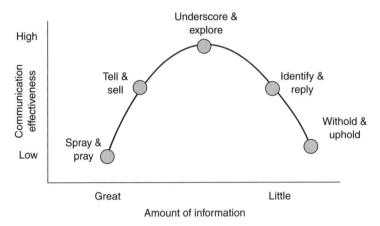

Figure 9.1   Change communication strategies

The 'underscore and explore' strategy is in line with what other research on organizational change has supported: organizational change is more successful when employees in non-management positions are able to exert influence over the change process by providing feedback on the change and its implementation. Managers may be tempted to impose changes on employees. However, joint involvement and collaboration between managers and employees in identifying the need for change and in formulating and implementing change programmes lead to greater employee commitment to a change. In a general sense, then, bottom-up involvement in change is generally more effective than a top-down or programmed implementation of change. At the same time, many organizations do not or cannot always involve all of their employees in the formative stages of a change. Particularly in large, multinational corporations, top-down approaches are still common for practical reasons because it will be impossible to involve all if not most of their employees in the development of a change initiative. British Airways (see Case Study 9.1), for example, has often opted for top-down implementation of changes using a combination of 'tell and sell' and 'identify and reply' strategies. Issues in customer service, for example, have been 'sold' to all front-line staff through training programmes after they had been 'identified' by employees.

The choice of either a top-down or bottom-up approach to communicating change is coupled with the use of certain media.[15] When organizations opt for a top-down approach, they may involve employees only to a limited extent in the routinization of the change. Managers will not consult employees in the identification of the need for change and the formulation of a change initiative; instead they will meet each other in management meetings and will consult external sources (e.g., management consultants), periodicals and formal documents. Once a change initiative is formulated, it will then be rolled out to employees through organization-wide media such as the intranet, announcement meetings and one-way audio or video messages. On the other hand, in a bottom-up approach, employees are involved to a greater degree in the entire change process. Managers speak to employees face-to-face and through e-mails and over the phone in the identification stage, will meet them in meetings and electronic conferences in the formulation stage and will engage with all employees through interactive meetings and technologies (video conference, e-mail) during the implementation and routinization stage.

The communication consultants Larkin and Larkin argue that for top-down change initiatives to be successful, they need to be communicated to employees in plain English and largely through face-to-face communication.[16] They argue that managers should only communicate the facts and essential information to employees, and not refer to management speak. Face-to-face communication is also more successful, they argue, than videos and newsletters because of the involvement of the employee and because it allows employees to ask questions and talk back (see Chapter 3). Ideally, employees prefer the news about the change to be given to them by their direct supervisors rather than more senior managers. Employees are more likely to trust their immediate supervisors, increasing the likelihood of the change being understood and accepted and decreasing the likelihood of resistance.[17] Face-to-face communication is also associated with an 'open' communication climate. Communication climate refers to the possibilities within an organization for employees to respond and to ask questions about the change. A more 'open' climate influences employees' trust, commitment and the willingness to change.[18]

Managing change thus involves encouraging participation from as many employees as possible; addressing their concerns in the change programme and ensuring that managers act as role models for the changes.[19] However, as mentioned, managers cannot always involve all employees in the entire change process from formulation to routinization. In some change initiatives, the need for communication efficiency is higher than in others. Communication efficiency is defined as the accomplishment of change communication with a minimum expenditure of time, effort and resources.[20] The need for communication efficiency is high in organizations where (1) it is physically impossible to communicate in a face-to-face or interactive manner with all employees; (2) when resources devoted to change communication are scarce; and (3) when there is an urgent need to progress through the change process and, thus, little time for interaction about it. Besides deciding how efficient the communication process should be, managers also need to decide how important a consensus with employees is for the success of the change. Consensus-building is defined as the effort in change communication to achieve commitment to a course of action as a result of joint decision-making. The need for consensus-building is high in organizations (1) when changes are perceived to be radical and/or controversial; (2) when there is a history of resistance to similar change; (3) when critical resources (e.g., expertise, approval) are controlled by employees; and

High need for communication efficiency	Need to know strategy	Quid pro quo strategy
Low need for communication efficiency	Equal dissemination strategy	Equal participation strategy
	Low need for consensus building	High need for consensus building

Figure 9.2   Factors affecting the choice of communication strategies

(4) when ongoing support and cooperation are needed to maintain the change. When these two dimensions of the change situation are combined, managers are provided with four different communication strategies. These communication strategies provide an element of depth to the 'underscore and explore' strategy discussed above by highlighting the differential treatment of different groups of employees and the practical considerations of communication efficiency and consensus-building that will go into the decision for a change communication strategy. Figure 9.2 shows the matrix of factors affecting the choice of communication strategies.

1. **Need to know strategy**. With this strategy, managers keep quiet about planned change except to those employees who really need to know or who explicitly express a desire for the information. This is done in part out of an efficiency motivation, in part to avoid giving rise to potential objections from some employees and in part to avoid overburdening employees with large amounts of information for which they have little time or use. The strategy's exclusive focus on a select group of employees may be useful when the change is more convergent than radical and when employees of the organization are themselves selective about which of the organization's activities are of interest to them.

2. **Quid pro quo strategy**. In this strategy, as the name implies, managers give more communicative attention to those employees who have something valuable (e.g., expertise, approval power, resources) for the change process. A franchise organization, for example, may only communicate to its franchisees and not to other hired staff about a change in governance. These employees are crucial to the change and thus need to be consulted and communicated with. The strategy combines a focus on consensus-building with efficiency as only certain groups of employees are communicated with. Because of cost considerations, managers focus their time and energy on the employees who are most crucial to the change's success. However, the risk of using this strategy is that they may anger other employees who feel left out of the change process.

3. **Equal dissemination strategy**. This strategy focuses on disseminating information to employees across the entire organization, early, often and, most importantly, on an equal basis. The strategy is one of blanket dissemination of information through newsletters, general meetings, listserve postings, individual meetings, phone calls, posters and banners. The purpose of this strategy is

not to involve all employees in the change but simply to give everyone fair notice of the change and to keep them informed of goings-on in the organization. The strategy is also often used to prevent the complaint by employees unfriendly to the proposed change that they were not told early enough or given enough details. The strategy is common in large organizations where communication channels are abundant and where extensive information dissemination thus adds little further costs.

4. **Equal participation strategy**. This final strategy involves two-way communication (i.e., both disseminating information and soliciting input) between managers and employees. This participative strategy is used when employees are crucial to the success of the change. However, the strategy is quite costly and may become overly political when opinions, support and advice from all sectors of the workforce are sought. This strategy is common in small and public sector organizations that embrace participative and democratic values and that have sufficient time, resources and communication channels available.

Organizational changes often present challenges to employees. Employees usually do not resist the change itself, but rather the uncertainty associated with the change: uncertainty about job security, the fear of losing status and power within the organization, and the uncertainty about whether they will fit in with the changed organization.[21] Uncertainty and fear may lead to stress, to a lack of trust between employees and managers and to low levels of commitment. It may even encourage people to leave the organization.[22] Effective change communication recognizes these uncertainties and as far as is possible (based on the need for communication efficiency) tries to inform employees of the change and tries to engage with them to facilitate the implementation and routinization of the change.

CASE STUDY 9.1

BRITISH AIRWAYS: EMPLOYEE MORALE AT THE WORLD'S FAVOURITE AIRLINE*

British Airways (BA) was privatized in 1987. Over the years, BA has been one of the world's most profitable airlines. Strategically, BA has made concerted efforts to become not just a global player, but effectively a global company – senior executives of BA took the view that the airline industry was undergoing consolidation, and that the future industry would consist of a very small number of very large international airlines. Emphasis was therefore placed on globalizing the business; primarily through establishing alliances and partnerships in the US, Australia and Europe, to overcome gaps in BA's coverage of routes as well as to access the lucrative but highly protected US domestic

(Continued)

(Continued)

Table 9.1   IATA rankings for 2006 (scheduled services)

	Passengers (in thousands)		Passenger kilometres (in millions)		Seat kilometres (in millions)	
1	Lufthansa	38,236	Air France	112,689	British Airways	145,531
2	Air France	30,417	British Airways	111,336	Air France	139,580
3	British Airways	29,496	Lufthansa	109,384	Lufthansa	137,922
4	KLM	22,322	Singapore Airlines	87,646	Singapore Airlines	112,052
5	American Airlines	21,228	American Airlines	81,129	American Airlines	105,413
6	Singapore Airlines	18,022	United Airlines	74,578	Emirates	97,588
7	Emirates	16,748	Emirates	73,903	United Airlines	90,190
8	Cathay Pacific	16,667	KLM	71,761	Cathay Pacific	89,507
9	SAS	13,926	Cathay Pacific	71,124	KLM	85,682
10	Air Berlin	13,890	Japan Airlines	59,913	Japan Airlines	83,235

Source: Lufthansa *Facts & Figures*

market. Indeed, as Table 9.1 indicates, BA has become a truly 'international' airline in the routes that it covers and the passengers it serves.

Coupled with the effort to globalize the company's operations, BA has also constantly tried to upgrade its product by improving flights and services at an internationally competitive rate (through, for instance the provision of 'beds' in first class, improved seating, interactive media on board, as well as innovations in check-in arrangements to reduce queuing time and 'hassle' for the passenger, etc.). BA also felt that in order to become a truly global airline it had to adapt its corporate identity.

Corporate identity

The current corporate identity of BA follows form the company's vision: 'to become the undisputed leader in world travel by ensuring that BA is the customer's first choice through the delivery of an unbeatable travel experience'. The identity of the BA brand is based on a blend of Britishness, cosmopolitanism, innovation and service. The strap-line or motto associated with this identity is the well-known 'the world's favourite airline' which is carried through in all of the design, livery, and communication of BA.

To give this corporate identity shape, BA unveiled a striking new visual identity in June 1997. Fifty ethnic designs were commissioned from artists around the world to adorn the tailfins of BA's entire fleet, as well as ticket jackets, cabin crew scarves and business cards. Over the next three years, the new look would gradually replace the sober blue and red livery and crest along with the motto 'to fly, to serve' which dated back to 1984. The decision to change was based on market research in the early 1990s which suggested that passengers viewed the airline as 'staid' and 'stuffy' (see Chapter 4). The colourful designs attracted tremendous free publicity, but they also generated more controversy than anticipated. The backlash was disappointing, but CEO Robert Ayling anticipated that these emotionally charged reactions from the more conservative-minded sections of the British public would soon wear out. In any case, the £60 million identity change was not to be judged in isolation but as part of the airline's new corporate vision, formally announced in June 1997: 'to become the undisputed leader in world travel'.

The launch of the new corporate identity coincided with two trade union ballots on possible strike action, which promoted criticism from the unions that the airline should attend to its employees rather than its image. One dispute over the sale of the company's catering division was quickly resolved with management proposing a new deal. The other dispute concerned the cabin crews and turned out to be more delicate. One cabin staff union, BASSA, felt that some of its staff would lose out under the proposed new salary scheme. BA accepted that a minority of staff might lose money, but guaranteed that existing cabin crew would not suffer financially and offered loyalty bonuses and employee travel entitlements. Unsatisfied with this response, the largely female cabin staff voted for a 72-hour strike. When the strike deadline approached and talks broke down, BA warned those considering to take part in the strike that they risked being sacked or even sued for damages. BA argued that the strike ballot was procedurally flawed making the strike illegal. Only a small fraction of staff eventually went on strike but 1,500 called in sick disrupting BA's schedule for days. BA followed a tough approach in asking staff who reported sick to produce a doctor's note. This approach was widely criticized by the British press and by ten Labour MPs who criticized the tactics of intimidation pursued by the airline.

Looking after employees

In September 1997, BA issued a press release in which the company announced the settlement of the cabin crew dispute that had provoked the strike. BASSA had agreed to the pay package on the table and BA lifted sanctions against the 300 cabin crew who had gone on strike. As Ayling commented at the time: 'Today's agreement signals a genuinely new beginning for relations and a spirit of co-operation within the company. It safeguards our plans for growth and will help the airline at the forefront of what is now a ferociously competitive global industry, in the interests of all our customers, employees and shareholders.'

Building on the settlement, BA started an intensive programme of activities to lift staff morale under the heading of winning 'hearts and minds'. Those cabin staff who had called in sick at the time of the strike were interviewed to try to understand what had motivated them to action. Ayling also pledged to staff that he would be more 'caring'. He said that people were back at the top of his agenda and that the company would try to re-engage with everyone inside the business.

BA set up a task force (entitled the *Way Forward*) which was designed to learn lessons from the dispute and to produce a new spirit of co-operation. The mandate of the task force was to look at how morale and motivation could be rebuilt, find ways to improve customer relationships and repair the damage to

(Continued)

(Continued)

BA's reputation. The task force specifically focused on significant declines in morale in some areas of the business and on improving communication between management and employees. Informed by the findings of the task force, BA launched a series of initiatives such as a *Good People Management* framework which was based on interviews with 100 employees about what good managers actually do. The framework set down some simple guidelines on management communication and was also used to simplify the performance management system by introducing more observable behavioural criteria as well as certain mandatory tasks including two proper performance reviews per year and at least one career development discussion. Another initiative called *In Touch* involved placing employees who were normally not in direct contact with customers for one day in the front-line to experience how it felt.

Cutting costs and employee morale

While employee morale improved somewhat as a result of these initiatives, it was quickly under pressure again as a result of the company having to cut costs and make staff redundant. In 1999, BA suffered as a result of the economic crisis in Asia and reported significant losses. The company initiated cost reduction and efficiency programmes, which had an impact on staff morale. An internal survey showed that many employees doubted management's ability to manage costs effectively without sacrificing quality, their desire to communicate openly and honestly, and the extent to which they cared about employees. Informed by the survey findings, BA initiated a motivational programme for staff entitled *Putting People First* which was meant to train staff in customer service and to increase a sense of belonging.

In 2000, Rodd Eddington took over as the CEO of BA and faced the challenge of further cutting costs by downsizing while sustaining an acceptable level of employee morale. When he took over, Eddington said:

> It is my job to empower the organization to be able to do that [compete]. People are the lifeblood of any airline and it is the people of British Airways, both as individuals and as a team, who will deliver its future success. I look forward to meeting as many as possible over the coming weeks and months and listening to what they have to tell me about how we can further improve our products and services.

In 2001, BA laid off, 5200 employees and saved £37 million. In 2002, BA launched its *Future Size and Shape* programme, which was designed to save costs by £650 million per annum. As part of the programme, 5,800 job cuts were announced at the head office of BA. A year later, the airline introduced an electronic swiping card system in order to monitor employee absenteeism. BA wanted to reduce absenteeism from an average of 17 days per employee to 10 days within a year and save £30 million as a result. Because of these cost-cutting exercises and the ongoing pressures on staff to become more efficient in their work practices, BA recognized that it needed to look after employee morale. In late 2003, the company started the *Industrial Relations Change* programme, a joint initiative with the trade unions which was designed to develop better working relationships between BA and its trade unions. BA also announced an Employee Reward Plan, which provides employees with rewards when profit margins of the airline move towards 10 per cent.

Rodd Eddington stepped down as CEO in September 2005 and was succeeded by Willie Walsh. Walsh had attracted the nickname of 'slasher' at his previous employer Aer Lingus where he was responsible for cutting a third of the workforce. In December 2005, as a result of high fuel costs and lower ticket prices, Walsh announced plans to cut a further 600 management jobs at BA but he insisted that the airline had long-term scope to grow. The job cuts involved a 50 per cent reduction in senior managers, from 414 jobs to 207, and a 30 per cent reduction in middle managers, from 1,301 jobs to 911 jobs. Walsh rationalized the job cuts as follows: 'We are restructuring the airline to remove duplication, simplify our core business and provide clearer accountability. Managers will have greater accountability for making decisions, delivering results and leading the business.' On top of the cuts in management jobs, Walsh warned staff in March 2006 to brace themselves for a fresh wave of further job losses as BA attempted to cut £450m of costs. 'We're going to target every single aspect of the cost base', Walsh explained, 'Employee costs are an element of that but they're not the only part. We will continue to introduce new work practices and efficiencies, which will allow us to run the business with fewer people.' BA's cost-cutting target in 2006 was for £225m of savings and the same in 2007. The airline has put a squeeze on suppliers and has told every internal department to produce monthly reports on progress towards cuts. It is also anticipated that the opening of Heathrow's fifth terminal in March 2008 is also likely to bring further efficiencies with more self-service check-in kiosks and automated baggage handling. However, the Transport & General Workers' Union's (TGWU) National Secretary for Civil Aviation, Brendan Gold, expressed concern at BA's constant focus on job cuts: 'I'd be very concerned about any more jobs going, particularly from front-line areas. There have already been substantial job cuts over the last couple of years and you've got to remember that in August two years ago [2005], the whole operation collapsed at Heathrow due to understaffing.'

Questions for reflection

1. Discuss the effectiveness of employee communication within BA in the light of upward and downward communication, employee voice and participation.
2. Identify the change communication strategy that BA used to communicate the cost reductions and job cuts. Was this the right strategy for the company or should another strategy have been used?

Note: *This case study is based on Clark, A. (2006), 'British Airways warns staff of further job cuts', *The Guardian,* 10 March 2006 and INSEAD (2002), *Flying into a Storm: British Airways (1996–2000).*

9.6 Chapter summary

The chapter started by defining the importance of internal communication in terms of its impact on employee commitment, moral and organizational identification. One important message in the chapter has been the importance of combining downward and upward communication between management and employees in such a way that employees feel valued, feel that they are listened to and feel that they can speak out about organizational decisions, practices and relationships with their colleagues. Combining upward and downward communication is especially important during processes of organizational change in order to get employees to commit to the change and to make the change happen.

KEY TERMS

Communication climate	Need to know strategy
Corporate information and	Organizational change
communication systems	Organizational identification
Employee participation	Organizational silence
Employee voice	Prestige
Equal dissemination strategy	Quid pro quo strategy
Equal participation strategy	Tell and sell strategy
Identify and reply strategy	Underscore and explore strategy
Management communication	Withhold and uphold strategy

Notes

1   *The Economist* (2005), 'Robert Scoble, Microsoft's celebrity blogger', 10 February.
2   See, for example, Hales, C.P. (1986), 'What do managers do? A critical examination of the evidence', *Journal of Management Studies*, 23: 88–115; Tengblad, S. (2006), 'Is there a "new managerial work"? A comparison with Henry Mintzberg's classic study 30 years later', *Journal of Management Studies*, 43: 1437–1461.
3   Andrews, P.H. and Herschel, R.T. (1996), *Organizational Communication: Empowerment in a Technological Society*. Boston: Houghton Mifflin Company.
4   See, for example, Dutton, J.E., Dukerich, J.M. and Harquail, C.V. (1994), 'Organizational images and member identification', *Administrative Science Quarterly*, 39: 239–263.
5   Mael, F.A. and Ashforth, B.E. (1992), 'Alumni and their alma mater: a partial test of the reformulated model of organizational identification', *Journal of Organizational Behavior*, 13: 103–123, quote on p. 104.
6   Dutton, et al. (1994); Smidts, A., Pruyn, A.T.H. and Van Riel, C.B.M. (2001), 'The impact of employee communication and perceived external prestige on organizational identification', *Academy of Management Journal*, 44: 1051–1062.

7   Smidts et al. (2001); Bartels, J. (2006), 'Organizational identification and communication: employees' evaluations of internal communication and its effect on identification at different organizational levels', PhD dissertation, University of Twente.

8   Christensen, L.T., Cornelissen, J.P. and Morsing, M. (2007), 'Corporate communications and its reception: a comment on Llewellyn and Harrison', *Human Relations*, 60: 653–661.

9   De Vita, E. (2007), 'John Lewis: partners on board', *Management Team*, August: 44–47.

10   Morrison, E.W. and Milliken, F.J. (2000), 'Organizational silence: a barrier to change and development a pluralistic world', *Academy of Management Review*, 25: 706–725.

11   See, for example, Conrad, C. and Scott Poole, M. (2002), *Strategic Organizational Communication in a Global Economy*. Fort Worth, TX: Harcourt.

12   Lewin, K. (1947), 'Frontiers in group dynamics 1', *Human Relations*, 1: 5–41.

13   Greenwood, R. and Hinings, C. (1996), 'Understanding radical organizational change: bringing together the old and the new institutionalism', *Academy of Management Review*, 21: 1022–1054.

14   Clampitt, P., DeKoch, R. and Cashman, T. (2000), 'A strategy for communicating about uncertainty', *Academy of Management Executive*, 14: 41–57.

15   Timmerman, C.E. (2003), 'Media selection during the implementation of planned organizational change', *Management Communication Quarterly*, 16: 301–340.

16   Larkin, T.J. and Larkin, S. (1994), *Communicating Change: Winning Employee Support for New Business Goals*. New York: McGraw-Hill.

17   See also Llewellyn, N. and Harrison, A. (2006), 'Resisting corporate communications: insights into folk linguistics', *Human Relations*, 59: 567–596.

18   See, for example, Poole, M.S. and McPhee, R.D. (1983), 'A structurational analysis of organizational climate', in Putnam, L.L. and Pacanowksy, M.E. (eds), *Communication and Organization: An Interpretive Approach*. Beverly Hills, CA: Sage; Smidts et al. (2001).

19   Heracleous, L. (2002), 'The contribution of discourse in understanding and managing organizational change', *Strategic Change*, 11: 253–261.

20   Lewis, L.K., Hamel, S.A. and Richardson, B.K. (2001), 'Communicating change to nonprofit stakeholders', *Management Communication Quarterly*, 15: 5–41.

21   Dent, E.B. and Goldberg, S.G. (1999), 'Challenging a "resistance to change"', *Journal of Applied Behavioral Science,* 35: 25–41.

22   Schweiger, D. and Denisi, A. (1991), 'Communication with employees following a merger: a longitudinal experiment', *Academy of Management Journal,* 34: 110–135.

10

Issue and Crisis Management

CHAPTER OVERVIEW

Issues and crises have the potential to damage an organization's reputation and the relationships with its stakeholders. It is therefore important that organizations understand how certain issues and crises may affect them and know how best to respond to them through different communication strategies. Drawing on frameworks and principles from theory and practice, the chapter discusses how organizations can effectively manage issues and crises by being prepared and by identifying communication strategies that match stakeholder perceptions of the organization's responsibility for the issue or crisis.

10.1 Introduction

Issue and crisis management is a rapidly growing field in corporate communication practice. It has grown partly as a result of many high-profile issues and crises (e.g., Enron, Worldcom, Parmalat) that have damaged corporate reputations and the image of business in general. In extreme circumstances, an issue or crisis may even threaten the existence of an organization. The American airline Pan Am, for example, failed to survive the aftermath of the Lockerbie disaster. The Belgian airline Sabena equally went bankrupt in the aftermath of 9/11 and Enron stopped trading after a well-known fraud scandal in 2001. While many issues and crises may not have such dramatic consequences for organizations, these examples do signal the importance of having protocols and communication strategies in place to 'manage' issues and crises when they emerge. Issues and crisis management involves identifying and analysing issues and crisis and developing an appropriate communication response so that damage to the organization's reputation and relationships with its stakeholders is minimized.

This chapter defines the nature of issue and crisis management and presents a number of principles for effective issue and crisis communication (Sections 10.3

and 10.4). Before these principles are outlined in greater detail and illustrated with case examples, the chapter starts with a brief introduction to what issues and crises are (Section 10.2).

10.2 Defining issues and crises

Both issues and crises can negatively affect the reputation of the organization. For example, an issue of a fraud allegation may damage a company's reputation as a financially solid and reliable investment target. Similarly, a product recall may lead to questioning of the safety of a company's products and the reliability of its production and supply chain operations. While issues and crises often overlap in practice, they can be distinguished analytically.

An *issue* can be defined as: (1) a concern about the organization's decision and operations; that may or may not also involve (2) a point of conflict in opinions and judgements regarding a company's decisions and operations. For example, when Mattel recalled millions of toys in 2007 because of dangerously high levels of chemicals and toxins, the recall became an issue of public concern about the safety of the company's supply chain and manufacturing in China. Mattell, however, acknowledged the problems and hence there was no difference of opinion with customers and members of the general public about the severity of the issue and about the necessity of a product recall. In contrast, the petroleum company Exxon Mobil has been at loggerheads with scientists and environmental groups about the issue of global warming and its own role in reducing its carbon emissions.

In many cases, before issues become connected to an organization and before activists, the public or stakeholders campaign for a specific organization to change, such issues often already exist as a matter of concern in public debates within society. For example, in many contemporary societies, healthy eating and obesity were already issues of public concern before they became connected to organizations such as Coca-Cola and McDonald's. Similarly, there has been an ongoing concern about executive pay and remuneration in many Western societies which has often led to direct action against large corporations. When in 2003 shareholders of GlaxoSmithKline, a pharmaceutical firm, voted against an excessive pay package for the company's CEO Jean-Pierre Garnier, they acted upon a 'mood' against 'fat cat pay' that was already present in investment circles in the UK.

Howard Chase, a well-known expert on issues management defines an issue as 'an unsettled matter which is ready for a decision'.[1] Chase emphasizes that an issue often involves a point or matter in contention between an organization and another party and often requires decisive action of the organization in order to protect its reputation. He also suggests that issues and crises are closely related as an issue may develop into a crisis.

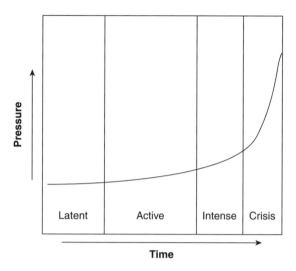

Figure 10.1 The development of an issue into a crisis

A *crisis* is defined as an issue that requires not just decisive but also immediate action from the organization. The necessity of immediate action may be triggered by, for example, mounting public pressures, intense media attention or because of the direct danger (in case of an accident, product tampering or faulty products) to employees, customers or members of the general public. The organization theorist Karl Weick defines a crisis as a critical and intense issue that threatens the very existence of an organization in terms of its basic assumptions, values and ways of operating.[2] For example, when Shell attempted to dispose of the Brent Spar oil rig in the North Sea, its actions led to a public boycott and to legislation that not only damaged its reputation but also challenged the company to change its basic assumptions and values regarding the environmental impact of its business (see Case Study 10.1).

A useful way of thinking about the distinction between issues and crises is to consider the process of how issues develop over time. Figure 10.1 displays how issues emerge and how over time they may become more salient and potent as a result of media attention and greater public concern. As indicated on the left in the figure, there are many 'latent' issues that may become 'active' because of media attention or because of a coalition of stakeholders mobilizing themselves in relation to the issue. At this stage, it is important for organizations to monitor and scan the environment for shifts in public opinion on latent issues that stakeholders may connect with the organization and its industry. AstraZeneca, for example, continuously monitors opinions around the world towards animal testing for medical purposes. This issue of animal testing is seen as 'latent' or dormant because of the generally positive attitude towards responsible animal testing in the developed world and because of the condemnation by the media and governments of extreme acts of aggression by some animal rights activist groups. However, there is always the potential for the 'latent' issue to evolve into an 'active' issue when opinions towards animal testing change. When that happens, the issue becomes salient in the public domain. The media often play a crucial role in this process of making issues 'active'. The media may magnify interest in the issue through news coverage or may be the party that brought the issue up in the first place. Early in 2007, for example, *The Guardian* newspaper reported that a lobby group funded by Exxon Mobil had offered payments to scientists for articles that emphasized the shortcomings of the UN's Intergovernmental Panel on Climate Change (IPCC) in an attempt to undermine the panel's scientific evidence on climate change.[3]

After an issue has become 'active', it may develop into an 'intense' issue that increases the pressure on an organization to do something about it. An 'intense' issue is very closely related to a 'crisis' that dominates the organization's agenda and requires immediate action. An example may illustrate the distinction between 'intense' issues and 'crises'. In March 2005, a leak of nuclear material was detected in one of the plants of British Nuclear Fuels (BNFL) in the North of England. The leak involved highly radioactive nuclear fuel dissolved in concentrated nitric acid and about 20 tons of uranium and plutonium fuel. As the leak was contained within the plant, it was not of any direct danger to the public. The company therefore decided that the leak had very little news-worthiness to the general public. BNFL had started an investigation into the cause(s) of the leak and only informed local residents and local media of the leak. As far as the company was concerned, it was a 'latent' issue of little concern to the general public. However, the issue became 'active' when *The Guardian* newspaper published a front-page article in April 2005 on the leak and questioned the company's ability to process nuclear fuel in a safe and secure way. The issue subsequently intensified when it transpired that BNFL had already been warned by the European Commission (EC) that it was in breach of EU rules and was urged to tighten controls to ensure that nuclear materials 'are not diverted from the peaceful uses for which they have been declared'. The warning had followed EC inspections of the plant, which had led inspectors to conclude that 'accounting and reporting procedures presently in place do not fully meet Euratom (EU) standards'.[4] The already 'intense' issue became a 'crisis' of legitimacy for BNFL when the media broke the news on the 'culture' in the plant which had led to staff ignoring more than 100 warnings over six months that the plant had sprung a catastrophic leak. The crisis consisted of a direct challenge from the media and the government to the company's very existence as a safe and reliable operator of nuclear energy. BNFL came under direct and intense pressure to respond to the challenge by putting new safety procedures in place, by recovering the leaked material and by retraining staff in the nuclear plant.

10.3 Managing issues

The aim of this section is to present guidelines for the management of issues so that 'latent' and 'active' issues do not morph into 'intense' issues or a crisis. Although it may not be always possible to completely 'manage' issues, as communication practitioners cannot always foresee or control how an issue evolves, it is important that practitioners are prepared and have communication strategies in place. The starting point of issues management involves scanning and monitoring the environment and detecting potential and actual issues. Environmental scanning and an analysis of the issue form the basis for deciding on an appropriate issue response strategy. The entire process of managing issues consists of the following stages: (1) environmental scanning; (2) issue identification and analysis; (3) issue-specific response strategies; and (4) evaluation.

Environmental scanning

All organizations exist in the context of a complex commercial, economic, political, technological, social and cultural world. This environment changes and is more complex for some organizations than for others: how this affects the organization could include an understanding of historical and environmental effects, as well as expected or potential changes in environmental variables. This is a major task for communication practitioners because the range of variables is so great. Many of those variables will give rise to *opportunities* and others will exert *threats* on the organization. Whether environmental forces have such an impact on the organization, depends furthermore on how the organization itself, in terms of the *strengths* and *weaknesses* in its values, resources, and competences, can respond to them. A problem that has to be faced is that the range of variables is likely to be so great that it may not be possible or realistic to identify and analyze each one. Thus, there is a need to distill out a view of the main or overarching environmental impacts on the organization. Two analytical tools can be used for this: DESTEP analysis and SWOT analysis.

A DESTEP analysis is a broad analysis of the various *d*emographic, *e*conomic, *s*ocial, *t*echnological, *e*cological and *p*olitical developments and factors that are expected to have an impact upon the organization and its operations. This includes a summation of factors such as government regulations (political) that affect the industry in which the organization operates, changing societal attitudes towards certain industries and increasing demand for 'corporate citizenship' (social), and the effects of an economic slump and recession for the organization's supply and pricing strategies (economic). The DESTEP analysis provides a framework for summarizing and prioritizing all these factors. Through such a guided analysis of the environment, practitioners are able to describe the most important current environmental changes and to predict future ones.

A SWOT analysis stands for an investigation of the Strengths, Weaknesses, Opportunities and Threats. The first half of this analysis – strengths and weaknesses – examines the company's position, its capabilities, operations and products vis-à-vis stakeholders, competitor activities, environmental trends and company resources. The second half of the SWOT takes this review further to examine the opportunities and threats identified within the environment, including, for instance, market opportunities, political regulation, and shareholder activism. The result of the SWOT analysis should be a thorough understanding of the organization's status, of its standing with important groups in its environment and of the factors in the environment that may impinge upon it. A SWOT analysis should be carried out in an objective and detailed manner, with evidence provided to support the points cited.

Together, these two analytical tools can help practitioners identify trends and detect potential issues in relation to the organization's operations and in relation to important stakeholder groups.

Issue identification and analysis

Through environmental scanning, communication practitioners will identify potential and emerging issues that they need to keep an eye on. A number of these emerging issues may become active. Once they become active, they will have to be further analysed. The aim of issue analysis is to determine the present intensity of the issue in the public domain; how likely it is to trigger government action or impact on public opinion; the likelihood of the issue continuing; the ability of the organization to influence its resolution; and the key stakeholder groups and publics that are involved with the issue. 'Active' issues may concern stakeholders of the organization (Chapter 3) but also publics (e.g., activist groups) that the organization would not count as legitimate stakeholders but who nonetheless have mobilized themselves in relation to the issue and against the organization.

A useful device to analyse stakeholder and public opinions on a particular issue is the position–importance matrix. The position–importance matrix is very similar to the power–interest matrix (Figure 3.4) but is less concerned with the general salience or interests of stakeholders and is specifically concerned with the position of a stakeholder or public in relation to a particular issue. Stakeholders and publics are categorized in the matrix according to their position on a particular issue and according to their importance to the organization. Relevant stakeholders and publics are identified and assessed in terms of whether they oppose the organization on the issue or support it on the vertical axis. A numerical value of 0 to −5 is assigned to those stakeholders and

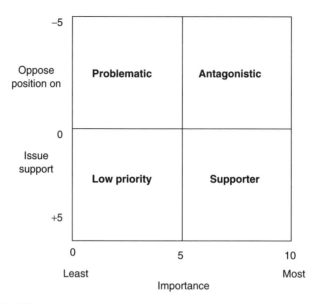

Figure 10.2   The position-importance matrix

publics opposing the issue and a value of 0 to +5 to those supporting it. The importance of stakeholders and publics to the organization and towards an effective resolution of the issue is measured on a horizontal axis and varies from a value of zero (least important) to a value of 10 (most important). After stakeholders and publics are positioned on the two values, the location of the stakeholders and publics in the matrix is plotted. As displayed in Figure 10.2, four categories of stakeholders and publics result from this analysis:[5]

1. *Problematic stakeholders/publics*: those stakeholders or publics who are likely to oppose or be hostile to the organization's course of action, but are relatively unimportant to the organization because they are not normally recognized as important stakeholders or publics and have little power to exert strong pressure on the organization.
2. *Antagonistic stakeholders/publics*: those stakeholders or publics who are likely to oppose or be hostile to the organization's course of action and hold power or influence over the organization.
3. *Low priority stakeholders/publics*: those stakeholders or publics who are likely to support the organization's course of action but are relatively unimportant in terms of their power or influence on the organization.
4. *Supporter stakeholders/publics*: those stakeholders or publics who are likely to support the organization's course of action, and are important to the organization in terms of their power or influence.

After the analysis and categorization are completed, the idea is that communication practitioners can work out communication strategies to most appropriately deal with each stakeholder or public. For example, practitioners may use educational programmes with 'problematic' stakeholders and publics to change their opinions on an issue and may prepare defensive statements or crisis plans in case problematic stakeholders and publics form a coalition and together voice their discontent about the organization. Strategies for 'antagonistic' stakeholders or publics typically involve anticipating the nature of their objections and developing and communicating counter-arguments as well as bargaining with selected stakeholders or publics to win their support. Finally, strategies for 'low priority' stakeholders or publics often consist of educational programmes and promoting the company's involvement with these supporting stakeholders while strategies for 'supporter' stakeholders or publics often only involve a case of providing information to reinforce their position and possibly asking them to influence indifferent stakeholders.[6]

Besides analysing the opinions of stakeholders and publics on a particular issue, it is also important for communication practitioners to identify the current 'stage' of an issue. For example, it will be useful to know whether an issue can be classified as 'active' or 'intense' based on the amount of public debate about the issue and the pressure upon an organization to do something about it. The issues expert Healey provides a useful framework of the 'lifecycle' of an issue (Figure 10.3) which consists of four stages: (1) emergence; (2) debate; (3) codification; and (4) enforcement.[7] The basic idea behind the framework is that it is important for organizations to detect issues when they first 'emerge' and to engage publicly in the 'debate' on the issue. In doing so, organizations may be able to influence opinions in a favourable direction before the issue becomes 'codified' or defined within the public domain and 'enforced' through government legislation, industrial action or consumer boycotts. For example, when Greenpeace first tabled the issue of Shell's disposal of the Brent Spar oil rig in the North Sea, Shell ignored the *emerging* issue and defended the disposal decision as 'business as usual' and as the 'best option with the least environmental

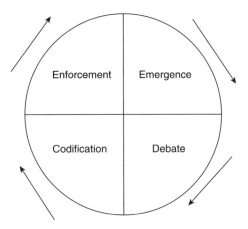

Figure 10.3   The 'life-cycle' of an issue

damage'. The scientific evidence behind the decision convinced Shell that the company did not need to engage in any *debate* about the issue and explain its decision to the general public. The result was that Greenpeace's framing of the issue as an 'ecological disaster' and 'toxic dump' came to define how the general public viewed the issue (*codification*); a view that was subsequently enforced through consumer boycotts and political action by many European governments (*enforcement*). The general principle that arises from the framework and the Brent Spar example is that organizations need to detect issues early on because only in the early stages of 'emergence' and 'debate' can stakeholder or public opinions on an issue be influenced.

Issue-specific response strategies

The analysis of an issue provides the basis for identifying an appropriate response. The repertoire of issue-response strategies involves the following three options: (1) a buffering strategy; (2) a bridging strategy; and (3) an advocacy strategy. The choice of any one of these three options is based upon the 'intensity' of the issue, the importance of the issue to the organization's stakeholder groups, values and beliefs of managers in an organization, and costs.

A buffering strategy is essentially an attempt to 'stonewall the issue' and delay its development. This strategy is one in which organizations attempt to continue with their existing behaviour by postponing decisions or by remaining silent. Buffering involves trying to keep claims from stakeholders or publics in the environment from interfering with internal operations. A good example of buffering involves Exxon Mobil's initial attempt to remain silent on the issue of climate change and avoid organizational ownership of the issue.

A bridging strategy, on the other hand, involves organizations being open to change and recognizing the issue and its inevitability. Bridging occurs when organizations seek to adapt organizational activities so that they conform with external expectations and claims of important stakeholders and publics. In response to those expectations and claims, organizations attempt to find a way to accommodate them within the organization's plans and operations. For example, both BP and Shell have started to reduce their carbon emissions to respond to stakeholder expectations. Both organizations are also trying to be more transparent in reporting progress on their environmental performance and actively engage in a dialogue with their stakeholders about environmental issues and expectations.

An advocacy strategy, finally, is an attempt to try to change stakeholder expectations and public opinions on an issue through issue campaigns and lobbying. Within this strategy, organizations do not directly 'stonewall' an issue (buffering) or adapt to external expectations (bridging) but use campaign and lobbying to alter the opinions and stakeholder expectations on an issue so that these conform to the organization's present practices, output and values.[8] The aim is to persuade external stakeholders and publics that the organization's position on an otherwise controversial issue is both rationally acceptable and morally legitimate. For example, Exxon Mobil has lobbied governments on climate change and has sponsored 124 think-thanks and campaign organizations that have directly or indirectly taken money from the company. These 124 organizations take a consistent line on climate change: that the science is contradictory, that scientists are split and that if governments took action to prevent global warming they would be endangering the global economy for no good reason. In other words, Exxon Mobil has lobbied and campaigned to sow doubt about whether serious action needs to be taken on climate change.[9] In doing so, the company attempts to change public opinion on climate change and on the necessity of the company having to take direct action to curb carbon emissions.

Broadly speaking, organizations can choose between these three strategy options. Organizations can deny the existence of an issue and remain silent (buffering); they can recognize the issue, adapt their operations and actively communicate and engage with stakeholders (bridging); or they can try to change stakeholder expectations and public opinions on an issue so that these expectations and opinions conform to current practices and values (advocacy). The choice of one of these strategies often depends on the 'intensity' of the issue and its importance to the organization's stakeholder groups, as well as on the values and beliefs of managers in an organization. BP and Shell both 'bridged' on the issue of climate change and their own environmental impact because of mounting public pressure and because of their own stakeholders calling for change. Exxon Mobil, on the other hand, has not bridged on this particular issue, because the company's dominant coalition of senior managers and shareholders dispute the evidence on climate change and feel that an environmental stance would be in conflict with the company's economic principles. To choose any of these strategies determines how the organization communicates about the issue. For example, with a buffering strategy, organizations often communicate very little publicly on the issue but may issue defensive statements to the media that defend the company's policy or stance on a particular issue. A bridging strategy often involves extensive communication in the form of a corporate advertising campaign on the issue, dialogue forums with stakeholders and the publication of progress on the issue. An advocacy strategy, finally, will typically consist of lobbying and campaigning on the issue. This may involve sponsorship of campaigning organizations or NGOs, a mass media corporate issue campaign and face-to-face presentations to key opinion leaders on the issue.

Evaluation

The final stage of the issues management process involves an evaluation of how the issue has developed and how stakeholder expectations and public opinions have changed. First of all, it is important for organizations to know what the 'stage' of the issue is and whether there is still an opportunity to influence public debate on the issue in question. In addition, depending on the strategy chosen by an organization, communication practitioners need to evaluate the success of their buffering, bridging or advocacy strategy. They need to find out whether and how stakeholder expectations and public opinions have changed, whether their activities contributed to a change in public opinion on the issue and whether the organization's response strategy has been appreciated by stake-holders and the general public.

10.4 Responding to crises

When organizations do not deal with issues in a timely or responsible manner or when stakeholders or the general public feel that an organization has not adequately responded to an issue, a crisis situation may emerge. However, not all crises are self-inflicted by organizations or emerge from widely debated public issues. Crisis expert Timothy Coombs defines four types of crises based on two dimensions: internal–external and intentional–unintentional.[10] The internal–external dimension refers to whether the crisis resulted from something done by the organization itself (e.g., the actions of managers) or instead was caused by some person or group outside of the organization. The intentional–unintentional dimension relates to the controllability of the crisis. Intentional means that the crisis event was committed deliberately by some actor. Unintentional means that the crisis event was not committed deliberately by some actor. The two dimensions together give four mutually exclusive crisis types as illustrated in Figure 10.4.

	Unintentional	Intentional
External	*Faux pas*	**Terrorism**
Internal	**Accidents**	**Transgressions**

Figure 10.4   Crisis type matrix

A *faux pas* is an unintentional action that an external agent (e.g., NGO) unintentionally transforms into a crisis. A *faux pas* often begins as an issue between an organization and a particular external agent who challenges the appropriateness of the organization's actions. When an organization does not engage in debate with this external agent or when public opinion and stakeholder expectations move against the organization, the issue may turn into a crisis. Social responsibility tends to be the focal point of most *faux pas*. The term *faux pas* comes from French and literally means 'false step'. It generally refers to a violation of accepted, although unwritten, social rules and expectations.

Accidents are unintentional and happen during the course of normal organizational operations. Product defects, employee injuries and natural disasters are all examples of accidents. The unintentional and generally random nature of accidents often leads to attributions of minimal organizational responsibility, unless of course the organization was directly responsible for the accident. Accidents can be further divided into acts of nature (e.g., hurricanes, earthquakes, epidemics, etc.) and human-induced errors (e.g., industrial accidents). The rationale for this division is that stakeholders and publics are less likely to attribute blame and react negatively to acts of nature than to human-induced error.[11]

Transgressions are intentional acts taken by an organization that knowingly place stakeholders or publics at risk or harm. Knowingly selling defective or dangerous products, witholding safety information from authorities, violating laws, or 'creative' bookkeeping are all examples of transgressions.

Terrorism refers to intentional acts taken by external agents. These intentional actions are designed to harm the organization directly (e.g., hurt customers through product tampering) or indirectly (e.g., reduce sales or disrupt production). Product tampering, hostage taking, sabotage and workplace violence are all examples of terrorism.

Classifying crises into these four types is useful because it provides a basis for identifying the most appropriate crisis communication strategy. The principle for choosing an appopriate communication strategy (Table 10.1) is the degree to which the organization is perceived by stakeholders and the general public to be reponsible or culpable for the crisis. When the perception is that the organization is not directly responsible or culpable the organization may attempt to distance itself from the crisis or deny that the crisis exists or is as serious as external actors make it out to be. On the other hand, when the organization is seen as directly responsible or culpable for the crisis, the organization will have to defend its position or may simply have to apologise for the crisis and change its behaviour.

The unintentional nature and external challenge of a *faux pas* may lead to an attribution of minimal organizational responsibility. However, an organization can often change in response to the challenge which means that the possibility of a perception of organizational responsibility for the crisis does exist. When the perception of organizational responsibility is low or weak, the organization may use a distance strategy to further weaken the linkage between the crisis and the organization (Table 10.1). For example, an organization may excuse itself by scapegoating a third party as responsible for the crisis or may downplay the

Table 10.1   Crisis communication strategies

	Perception of low level of responsibility
Nonexistence strategies	**Claim of denying the crisis**
1. denial	A simple statement denying that a crisis exists
2. clarification	An extension of the denial tactic with attempts to explain why there is no crisis
3. attack and intimidation	A tactic of confronting the person or group who claims that a crisis exists; may include a threat to use "force" (e.g., a lawsuit) against the accuser
Distance strategies	**Claim of distancing the organization from direct responsibility for the crisis**
1. excuse	A tactic of denying intention or volition by scapegoating others for the crisis
2. downplay	A tactic of convincing stakeholders or the general public that the situation is not that bad in itself or compared to other crises
Association strategies	**Claim of connecting the organization to things positively valued by stakeholders and publics**
1. bolstering	A tactic of reminding stakeholders and the general public of existing positive aspects of the organization (e.g., reminders of past charitable donations or a history of fair worker treatment) in order to offset the negatives the crisis brings to the organization
2. transcendence	A tactic of associating the negatives and loss arising from a crisis with a desirable, higher order goal (e.g., animal testing to develop life-saving drugs)
Suffering strategy	**Claim that the organization suffers from the crisis**
1. victimization	A tactic of portraying the organization as a victim of the crisis in order to win public sympathy
	Perception of high level of responsibility
Acceptance strategy	**Claim accepting responsibility or culpability for the crisis**
1. full apology	A tactic of simply apologising for the crisis and accepting the blame
2. remediation	A tactic of announcing some form of compensation or help to victims (money, goods, aid, etc.)
3. repentance	A tactic of asking for forgiveness. The organization apologises for the crisis and asks stakeholders and the general public to forgive its misdeeds
Accommodative strategy	**Claim promising to prevent the crisis from recurring again**
1. rectification	A tactic of taking corrective action to prevent a recurrence of the crisis in the future

actual seriousness and scale of the crisis. Exxon Mobil's denial of climate change is a good example of a strategy of downplaying the crisis. Alternatively, an organization may follow an association strategy to remind stakeholders and the general public of past good behaviour that may offset the negatives that the crisis brings to the organization. For example, an organization may associate an unfair dismissal with its past track record of fair worker treatment to put the incident in a wider context. However, when the perception of organizational responsibility for a *faux pas* is high or strong, an organization will have to follow an acceptance or accommodative strategy (Table 10.1). Besides apologizing for the crisis and openly accepting the blame, this may consist of remediation (giving compensation to victims) or rectification (taking corrective action to prevent the crisis from happening again).

Natural accidents are unintentional and outwith the control of organizations. Such accidents can therefore be easily responded to with a distancing strategy which serves to reinforce the organization's lack of responsibility for the crisis. For example, an organization may legitimately claim that it was not directly responsible for the crisis. *Human-error accidents* are more difficult to justify and will require an apology from the organization and an admission that it will take action to prevent a recurrence of the crisis in the future. BNFL's admission of a nuclear leak in one of its plant and its actions regarding new safety procedures is an example of a full apology and rectification tactic (Table 10.1).

Transgressions are intentional actions taken by organizations which make organizations directly responsible for their impact. A strategy of distancing the organization from the crisis or a non-existence strategy that denies the existence of the crisis is thus futile. Organizations instead need to follow an acceptance strategy where they admit their responsibility but work to atone for the crisis in some fashion. For example, an organization may remediate by willingly offering some form of compensation or help to victims, may repent by publicly asking for forgiveness, or may follow a rectification tactic of ensuring that the crisis will not recur in the future. Ahold, the Dutch retailer found guilty of fraudulent bookkeeping, apologized for the fraud crisis and has since made extensive changes to its corporate governance and accounting. Anders Moberg who took over as CEO in 2003 explained the rectification strategy: 'We learned that as a company you can lose your reputation overnight, but it takes some time to rebuild it and restore trust.' He felt that in order to meet stakeholder expectations, 'we knew we needed to be at the forefront of implementing corporate-governance reforms'.[12]

Terrorist attacks are directed at the organization by external agents and often there is very little direct organizational responsibility or culpability. An organization may therefore adopt a suffering strategy which portrays the organization as an unfair victim of some malicious, outside actor. Johnson & Johnson's famous portrayal of itself as wounded by product tampering during the 1982 Tylenol crisis is a good example of the suffering strategy.

In short, depending on the degree to which organizations are seen as responsible or culpable for a crisis in the eyes of stakeholders, organizations can employ different communication strategies (Table 10.1). It is important to stress at this point that the *perception* of whether an organization is responsible or culpable matters as much as whether the organization is *factually* responsible or culpable. For example, in August 2005, British Airways (BA) had to cancel flights affecting 17,000 passengers as a result of a wildcat strike of BA baggage handlers who walked out in sympathy with workers sacked by Gate Gourmet, the firm which provides BA's in-flight meals. The crisis cancellation of flights which left many passengers stranded at Heathrow airport was effectively outside of BA's control; the strike of the baggage handlers was illegal and unannounced and was the result of the unfair dismissal of workers in another firm (Gate Gourmet). Nonetheless, BA was held responsible for the knock-on effect of having to cancel flights and was pressured to apologize for the crisis situation. BA's CEO at the time Rod Eddington said: 'I apologize unreservedly to our customers for the disruption to their travel plans and cancellation of our flights.' BA, however, did not choose to remediate the crisis by giving compensation to the 70,000 stranded passengers but choose to offer the option that passengers' tickets would be rebooked or refunded. This decision was rationalized by a BA spokesperson as 'We are so, so sorry about all this. We are doing all we can. We have become embroiled in a dispute not of our making'.[13]

Stakeholder and public perceptions of a crisis are thus of central concern. As perceptions of crisis responsibility strengthen, the threat of image damage becomes greater, which means that communication practitioners need to utilize acceptance and accommodative strategies. Acceptance and accommodative strategies emphasize image repair, which is what is needed as image damage worsens. Defensive strategies, such as denial or downplaying, logically become less effective as organizations are viewed as more responsible for the crisis.[14]

Once a strategy has been identified, the key to effective crisis management is to maintain effective control of the release of information and to ensure that no unauthorized information or potentially damaging rumours are allowed to circulate. Failure to respond effectively to the media's enquiries about a crisis will invariably lead to journalists seeking information from whatever sources they can (perhaps with only limited regard for the accuracy of information obtained). It is therefore important to develop contingency plans for crises and establish key responsibilities for communication practitioners before a crisis actually happens. This includes:

- the identification of the organization's key spokespersons;
- media training of the CEO, executive directors and key spokespersons;
- establishing a communication team and in major crises a press office to field media enquiries and to handle the release of information;
- establishing safe crisis locations where the media can meet and be briefed in the event of hazardous situations;
- identification of contacts at relevant external agencies (e.g., police, fire services) who may need to be contacted in case of a crisis.

Critical differences exist between how extensively organizations prepare themselves for crises including natural disasters and human-error related accidents. Crisis experts Mitroff and Pearson highlight five different stages of planning and preparing for a crisis.[15] Stage 1 involves minimal planning around a few contingency plans drawn up for an emergency response. This may involve a limited set of plans such as evacuating a building during fire or giving first aid to employees who suffer injury or sudden illness. Stage 2 involves more extensive planning but is limited to natural disasters and potential human errors. Planning at this stage involves measures for damage containment and business recovery. Stage 3 involves extensive contingency plans with crisis procedures for typical natural disasters and human errors and with training of personnel so that employees can implement these crisis procedures. Stage 4 is similar to stage 3 but involves an organization-wide consultation of potential crises and their impact on stakeholders. The scope of stage 4 is wider than typical natural disasters and human errors to products defects, tampering and social issues regarding the company's supply chain, operations and contributions towards society. Stage 5, finally, involves all of the previous stages but also incorporates environmental scanning and early warning systems to identify crises as early as possible.

CASE STUDY 10.1

ISSUES AND CRISIS MANAGEMENT IN SHELL*

Shell is one of the first truly international corporations and has been one of the ten largest companies in the world for nearly a century. Historically, its regional operating units were the dominant elements in a decentralized management structure. The company is now more centrally controlled through a committee of managing directors and is organized globally into five lines of business: exploration and production, chemicals, gas and coal, international renewables, and oil products. Shell historically had a strong technical and engineering orientation in all its strategies and operations, and placed strong emphasis on long-range planning based on the construction of competing 'scenarios' of major long-term market trends that would affect its economic status and market operations.

In the 1990s, Shell executives came to believe that its corporate identity and reputation were at stake in both the marketplace and the policy arena. One reason for this, executives believed, was Shell's weak organizational structure, which was clearly inadequate for effective control of a global enterprise and hindered them in their desire to build a strong reputation in the marketplace. In March 1995, the CEO of the Dutch parent company, partly for this reason, announced that the group wished to drastically change its organizational structure. The old matrix structure, with regions, sectors and functional responsibilities, would disappear. The proposed new structure consisted of separate business organizations, each led by a business committee with world-wide responsibility. And a newly created strategy and business

(Continued)

(Continued)

services unit would control strategy, finance, personnel and corporate communication ('public affairs') at the group level. Corporate communication activities would thus become more centralized after these changes, with the aim of controlling communications better and channelling messages more effectively to Shell's audiences.

At the height of this restructuring exercise, of which one of the aims was thus to strengthen its corporate communications, Shell, ironically, got entangled in two communication crises. In June 1995, Royal Dutch Shell found itself in heated debates with a whole range of critics (including The Movement for the Survival of the Ogoni People, Greenpeace, the Sierra Club, Amnesty International, and the media) over the environment and associated human rights that were played out in a variety of public forums. These crises resulted from the public dismay over Shell UK's proposed action to dispose of Brent Spar, an enormous oil storage and loading platform, in the waters of the North Sea, and Shell's failure to take a high-profile public stance against the Nigerian government, Shell's local business partner in Nigeria, when it executed nine Ogoni environmentalists including Ken Saro-Wiwa, an internationally acclaimed journalist and writer who had spearheaded protest against Shell.

Brent Spar and Greenpeace

Shell's first crisis arose in May 1995 when Greenpeace occupied the Brent Spar, an offshore oil storage installation in order to mobilize resistance to Shell UK's plan to sink the installation in the North Sea. The Brent Spar had already been decommissioned in 1991 because there was no longer any use for the installation platform. Shell had already investigated the various options for disposing of the platform and had negotatiated a deal with the British Government to legally approve disposal of the Brent Spar in the North Sea. Shell spent over £1 million on environmental studies which had concluded that deep-sea disposal was the 'best practical environmental option' with less potential harm to the environment than any other options such as disposal on land. In October 1994, the British Government approved the plan for deep-sea disposal. Greenpeace, however, opposed Shell's plans for a number of reasons. They disputed the environmental studies and argued that deep-sea sinking would release heavy metal, oils and radioactive material into the sea and importantly would set a precedent for other petroleum companies to do the same. To voice its concerns, Greenpeace then decided to occupy the Brent Spar before the platform was dismantled and sunk into the North Sea.

Shell's strategic planners and communication personnel had contemplated a number of worst-case scenarios, including challenges from environmental groups, but no response plans had been formulated before 30 April 1995. Shell wanted to ensure that the process of dismantling would continue and decided to respond first with a series of civil court cases for trespassing. Shell got a court order to forcibly remove the people occupying the Brent Spar. But while Shell won the battle to evict Greenpeace off the platform, it was losing ground in public opinion on the issue. Shell had decided to lie low and did not want to appear too defensive in the media. The company also felt that it had sound legal, economic and environmental support for its actions. The company had done all the necessary planning and research before the decision was taken. Greenpeace, however, argued that harmful chemical residues and radioactive wastes remained in the Brent Spar's storage tanks. Greenpeace called it a 'toxic time bomb' and a platform 'laden with toxic cocktails'. Greenpeace accused Shell of 'contempt for public concern about its operations, fishermen's livelihoods and for the health of the North Sea' and said that the company was hiding behind a 'veil of secrecy'. In response, John Wybrew, Director of Public Affairs and Planning at Shell UK, defended the company's plan and actions arguing that the 'case' for deepwater disposal had been 'sound'. From the company's perspective, ocean dumping represented tbe 'best practicable environmental option'. Using cost-benefit analysis, Shell had concluded that sinking the Brent Spar would have 'negligible impacts on the marine environment, but the safety and occupational health risks of injury during onshore disposal would be six times higher'. Wybrew said that 'painstaking analysis and over 30 studies' supported this assessment, and it had been 'endorsed by independent experts and oceanographers, and supported by environmentalists, conservationists, and fishermen during extensive consultations'. He criticized Greenpeace for relying on "single-issue" campaigning which freely exploited dramatic visual stunts; and accused them of being 'adept at packaging misinformation in ready-to-use word snips'.

However, Greenpeace succeeded in turning the Brent Spar into a symhol of man's misuse of the oceans, *irrespective of the reality*. They aroused powerful emotions connected with 'litter-louting' on a grand scale and of David versus Goliath. The arousal of such powerful emotions brought in its wake escalating violence (e.g., three violent attacks on Shell service stations in Germany and physical damage to others) and a widespread consumer boycott of Shell across Europe. Major media coverage and public protest, especially in continental Europe, eventually led several European heads of government to criticize Shell and the British Government, which had approved the Shell proposal. Although at first rejecting criticism, by the end of June 1995 Shell agreed to change its plan. The Brent Spar was towed to Norway, where it was dismantled while stationed in a deep-sea fjord.

Nigeria and the Ogoni

The second major crisis for Shell emerged in relation to its operations in Nigeria. Shell has been operating in the Niger Delta since the 1930s and is by far the largest operator with an output of more than 1m barrels a day. But the company's 90 oil and gas fields have suffered spills and sabotage, damaging the livelihood of farmers and fishermen and threatening the half-million

(Continued)

(Continued)

Ogoni people who live in the Niger delta in which the bulk of Shell's production is located. The ethnic minority communities, such as the Ogoni, people who live in the Niger Delta have seen almost no return of Shell's revenues. Moreover, because of weak environmental regulation, these indigenous peoples who live traditionally by fishing and farming have suffered severe ecological and health impacts from oil spills. In Nigeria much of the gas by-products from oil drilling was flared (i.e., burned off in the open air) which caused some of the worst local environmental pollution. Flaring is held responsible for acid rain in the Niger Delta which is said to corrode roofs, pollute lakes and damage vegetation. Together oil spills and gas flaring threaten the Niger Delta; which is one of the largest and most ecologically sensitive wetlands in the world. In 1993, a massive nonviolent protest organized by the Movement for the Survival of the Ogoni People (MOSOP) against Shell and other oil companies led Shell to withdraw its staff and close operations in the part of the Niger Delta where the Ogoni lived. The Nigerian government, as Shell's business partner, blamed the MOSOP leadership for local resistance, which not only affected Shell's most valuable production sites in the Niger Delta but also set an unsettling precedent for other Delta tribes. The government then tried Saro-Wiwa and others by a kangaroo court of the military tribunal. Nine Ogonis, including Saro-Wiwa, were executed on 10 November 1995.

Since the early 1990s, Ogoni environmental activists and Delta tribal chiefs had documented the environmental degradation stemming from oil company activity. Their accounts were taken up in the African media and in media around the world. Saro-Wiwa's high public profile with environmental movements worldwide forced a communication response from Shell, which had to deal with the executions as well as its corporate environmental record and history in Ogoni. Shell expressed 'shock' and 'sadness' over Saro-Wiwa's death. However, in the first instance, Shell also tried to minimize and displace blame for both the political and ecological problems in Nigeria.

Shell Nigeria released a briefing statement which was mainly argumentative and defensive in nature. Overall, Shell characterized itself as a victim, positing that the company had been 'unfairly used to raise the international profile' of the MOSOP campaign against the Nigerian government. While the company acknowledged there had been environmental problems, it downplayed them. For instance, Shell admitted that its facilities needed upgrading, but blamed sabotage rather than the corrosion of ageing pipes for the oil spills. It said that Ogoni claims of environmental 'devastation' were grossly exaggerated, citing conclusions of journalists who said that Shell's limited presence in the Delta area meant that the damage was only a tiny 'fraction' of that 'routinely claimed by campaigners'. In addition. Shell cited a 1995 World Bank study that characterized the problem of 'oil pollution . . . only of moderate priority' in comparison to other poverty-related factors that contributed to environmental deterioration (i.e., population growth, deforestation, erosion, and over-farming). It further relied on the World Bank study and a report by the World Health Organization to dispute the connection between gas flaring and health. Thus, it claimed lack of 'evidence' that such problems as asthma and skin rashes were due to its activities. Shell Nigeria also claimed that it had 'some influence' with the government but that 'force' was impossible: 'What force could we apply – leaving aside the question of whether it would be right for us to do so?' This mirrored the position of Shell Group Chairman at the time, Cor Herkstroter, who defined Shell's role as strictly economic and commercial and said that the company lacked 'licence' to interfere in politics or the sovereign mandate of government.

Since the crisis in 1995, Shell has continued to remain under fire over its environmental record in Nigeria. In January 2007, advertisements calling on Shell to 'clean up its mess' appeared in *The Guardian* and the Dutch newspaper *De Volkskrant*. The adverts were signed and financially supported by more than 7,000 people worldwide in an effort to encourage Shell to live up to the aims of its corporate social responsibility (CSR) policies. Nnimmo Bassey, from Environmental Rights Action in Nigeria, said:

> Despite Shell's public commitment to CSR and specific promise it has made to communities, life on the fence line can too often be likened to hell. From Nigeria to Ireland, the Philippines to South Africa, Shell still too often fails to respect the environment or the needs of local communities.

Shell's poor environmental record in Nigeria is given prominence in the adverts, which demand the company pay $10bn to clean up oil spills and compensate communities in the Niger Delta. Environmental Rights Action, Friends of the Earth and others estimate that as much as 13m barrels of oil have been spilled into the Niger Delta ecosystem over the past 50 years by Shell and its partners, an amount they say is 50 times more than that associated with the infamous *Exxon Valdez* tanker grounding off Alaska. 'The spills pollute the land and water of the communities. Drinking water is affected, people get sick, fish populations die and farmers lose their income because the soil of the land is destroyed.'

Shell has since responded to the adverts and has stated that the adverts 'neither reflect the realities of the situation and the very real progress made, nor represent the views of the wider communities around these locations. Shell is committed to being a good neighbour and maintains productive relationships with many local communities and their representatives.'

Both the Brent Spar and Ogoni crises led Shell to reflect upon its mission and identity and effectively challenged the company's modernist, technical and rational way of approaching its operations. In one sense, these crises have moved the company from a taken-for-granted discourse of economic development towards a cautious adoption of the language of sustainable development, with attempts to balance interests of economic development with environmental well-being. Shell has since adopted a stakeholder orientation in its business principles and has set up platforms for stakeholder engagement and dialogue. The company also publishes an annual report documenting its

(Continued)

(Continued)

environmental and social progress and announced its focus on sustainable development in the recent Profits and Principles campaign. Shell claims to 'listen' to all its stakeholders, who have explicitly told the company that 'a commitment to sustainable development is key to a company's reputation.'

Questions for reflection

1. Describe how and why the two issues developed into crises for Shell.
2. Discuss the communication tactics that Shell used to manage both crises. Should Shell have used different tactics?

Notes: ★This case study is based upon Macalister, T. (2007), 'Campaigners urge Shell to put profits into clean-up', *The Guardian,* 31 January 2007, and Livesey, S.M. (2001), 'Eco-identity as discursive struggle: Royal Dutch/Shell, Brent Spar and Nigeria', *Journal of Business Communication,* 38, 58–91.

10.5 Chapter summary

Issues and crisis management is an increasingly important specialist discipline within corporate communication. Managing issues and crises effectively starts with scanning the environment and with identifying latent and emerging issues before they become salient in public debates. Communication practitioners are better prepared for issues and crises when they know whether stakeholders and publics hold the organization responsible or culpable for them. Based on the perception of organizational responsibility, they can choose between different communication strategies ranging from accommodative strategies to advocacy and defensive strategies.

KEY TERMS

Acceptance strategy	DESTEP
Accommodative strategy	Distance strategy
Active issue	Environmental scanning
Advocacy	Intense issue
Association strategy	Issue
Bridging	Latent issue
Buffering	Nonexistence strategy
Crisis	Suffering strategy
Crisis preparedness	SWOT

Notes

1   Chase, W.H. (1984), *Issue Management: Origins of the Future*. Stamford, CT: Issue Action Publishers.

2   Weick, K.E. (1988), 'Enacted sensemaking in crisis situations', *Journal of Management Studies*, 25: 305–317.

3   Sample, I. (2007). 'Scientists offered cash to dispute climate study', *The Guardian*, 2 February.

4   European Commission, 'European Commission issues nuclear safeguard obligations warning to British Nuclear Group Sellafield', Brussels, 15 February 2006. (http://europa.eu/rapid/pressReleasesAction.do?reference=IP/06/171&format=HTML&aged=0&language=EN&guiLanguage=en)

5   Nutt, P.C. and Backoff, R.W. (1992), *Strategic Management of Public and Third Sector Organizations: A Handbook for Leaders*. San Francisco: Jossey-Bass Publishers, p. 191; J.M. Bryson (1995), *Strategic Planning for Public and Nonprofit Organizations: A Guide to Strengthening and Sustaining Organizational Achievement,* revised edition. San Francisco: Jossey-Bass Publishers, p. 284.

6   Nutt and Backoff (1992), pp. 196–198; Bryson (1995), pp. 285–286.

7   Healey, M.C. (1978), 'The dynamics of exploited lake trout populations and implications for management', *Journal of Wildlife Management*, 42: 307–328.

8   Dowling, J. and Pfeffer, J. (1975), 'Organizational legitimacy: social values and organizational behavior', *Pacific Sociological Review*, 18: 122–136; Heugens, P.M.A.R., Van Riel, C.B.M. and Van den Bosch, F.A.J. (2004), 'Reputation management capabilities as decision rules', *Journal of Management Studies*, 41: 1349–1377.

9   Monbiot, G. (2006), 'The denial industry', *The Guardian*, 19 September.

10 Coombs, W.T. (1995), 'Choosing the right words: the development of guidelines for the selection of the "appropriate" crisis-response strategies', *Management Communication Quarterly*, 8: 447–476.

11 Mitroff, I.I. and Pearson, C.M. (1993), *Crisis Management*. San Francisco: Jossey-Bass.

12 *Business Week* (2004), 'Royal Ahold: from Europe's Enron to model citizen?', 17 May.

13 *The Guardian* (2005), 'Compensation "unlikely" for stranded BA passengers', 12 August.

14 Benoit, W.L. (1995), *Accounts, Excuses and Apologies: A Theory of Image Restoration Discourse*. Albany: State University of New York Press.

15 Mitroff and Pearson (1993).

Appendix

INTEGRATED CASE STUDY

The concepts, principles, models, tools and techniques of corporate communication have been outlined in detail in this book. Although quite wide in scope, all the theories and practices presented in the book share a focus on how organizations can manage communication in such a way that the company's reputation with important stakeholder groups is enhanced and protected. This central focus is illustrated in the full-length case study of Toyota. The case study integrates many of the concepts, principles, models, tools and techniques discussed in Parts 2, 3 and 4.

The Toyota case study invites the reader to identify and recognize corporate communication situations and problems and to apply the themes and learnings from the previous chapters of the book.

Corporate Communication in Toyota

Introduction: Toyota Motor Corporation

Toyota Motor Corporation (TMC) is the world's largest vehicle manufacturer offering a full range of models from mini-vehicles to large trucks. Toyota and its luxury line, Lexus, have been among the top automotive brands in terms of reliability, quality and long-term durability. Toyota is also the most profitable carmaker: in the financial year that ended in March 2007, the company made a profit of $13.7 billion while General Motors (GM) and Ford reported losses of $1.97 billion and $12.61 billion respectively. Global sales of the Toyota and Lexus car brands, combined with those of the Daihatsu and Hino brands, totalled 8.81 million units in 2006. Besides its own 12 plants and a number of manufacturing subsidiaries and affiliates in Japan, Toyota has 52 manufacturing companies in 26 countries and regions, which produce Lexus- and Toyota-brand vehicles and components. As of March 2007, Toyota employs approximately 299,400 people worldwide, and markets vehicles in more than 170 countries.

In April 2002, Toyota adopted a new strategic direction articulated in its 2010 Global Vision programme. The programme describes long-term policies for Toyota's strategic direction and operations (see Box 1). In it, Toyota describes how by 2010, the company expects society to encourage a pro-environmental stance and, specifically, to encourage the reuse and recycling of goods. In addition, the Global Vision suggests that nationalism will have declined by 2010 and given way to a mature society that respects all people regardless of nationalities and ethnic backgrounds – global corporations therefore need to respect their working environments and the different people and communities that they serve and interact with. The Global Vision also articulates new marketing opportunities, including China, India and other emerging markets, that have yet to become fully car-oriented, and sets the ambitious marketing aim of capturing around 15 per cent (Toyota's global market share was 10 per cent on 2 April 2002) of the global vehicle market by tapping these emerging markets.

A vision for the corporation

The 2010 Global Vision also sets out the corporate image (i.e. 'how each stakeholder views the organization') that Toyota should strive for, in line with the mentioned changes in society and societal expectations. The corporate identity that Toyota has been seeking to project among its stakeholders is that of a leader in global regeneration and in the application of IT in automobiles for better and safer motoring. The company also wants to be seen as one that is expanding the appeal of automobiles across the world, creating more 'fans' and achieving a global market share of around 15 per cent in the early 2010s. Moreover, the company wants to be considered a truly global enterprise that transcends nationalities and ethnicities and is respected by all peoples around the world.

BOX 1

**EXCERPTS FROM THE GLOBAL VISION 2010
DOCUMENT (SEE TOYOTA.CO.JP)**

Innovation into the future—a passion to create a better society

Since its founding, our company has been aiming to enrich society through car making. Our goal is to be a 'good corporate citizen,' constantly winning the trust and respect of the international community. Continuing in the 21st century, we aim for stable long-term growth, while striving for harmony with people, society and the environment. From this perspective, centred on the theme 'Innovation into the Future,' the Toyota Global Vision 2010 proposes the corporate image for which all of Toyota should strive and the paradigm change Toyota should undergo. Under Toyota's Basic Principles, we practice openness and fairness in our corporate activities, strive for cleaner and safer car making, and work to make the earth a better place to live. Through 'Monozukuri—manufacturing of value—added products' and 'technological innovation,' Toyota is aiming to help create a more prosperous society. To realize this, we aim for the following:

1. To be a driving force in global regeneration by implementing the most advanced environmental technologies.
2. To create automobiles and a motorized society in which people can live safely, securely and comfortably.
3. To promote the appeal of cars throughout the world and realize a large increase in the number of Toyota fans.
4. To be a truly global company that is trusted and respected by all peoples around the world.

Effectively, Toyota's environmental responsibilities go back to 1992. In 1992, the company adopted a set of Guiding Principles (see Box 2), which among other things, urge Toyota to 'respect the culture and customs of every nation and contribute to economic and social development through corporate activities in local communities'. These Principles also appeal to employees to dedicate themselves to 'providing clean and safe products and towards enhancing the quality of life everywhere through our activities'. In the same year (1992), the company adopted the Toyota Earth Charter. Based on this charter, the company began to produce cars that were friendlier to both people and the environment. In January 1998, Toyota created an Environmental Affairs Division under the direct supervision of its President. Toyota also received the US Environmental Protection Agency's Global Climate Protection Award 1998 for developing Prius (the world's first passenger vehicle in mass production planned to be powered by a hybrid power train system). The introduction of Prius in 1997 allowed the company to make a clear statement on its commitment to environmental protection. Since 1998, Toyota has been disclosing information on its environment-related activities through an Environmental Report. On 25 June 1999, Toyota became the first vehicle manufacturer to be awarded the United Nations Environmental Programme (UNEP) Global 500 award for the leadership it demonstrated 'in the development of environmental technologies and measures'. On 11 September 2003, it was reported that Toyota had earned the leading position on the 'Dow Jones Sustainability Index (DJSI)' in the automobile sector. DSJI analysts maintained that 'while VW [Volkswagen] scored significantly higher in the social dimension (i.e. standards for suppliers, human right issues in the value chain) than Toyota, Toyota seems to execute more systematically its strategies regarding environmental issues, including recycling, efficiency and technology'.

BOX 2

GUIDING PRINCIPLES AT TOYOTA
(SEE TOYOTA.CO.JP)

1. Honour the language and spirit of the law of every nation and undertake open and fair corporate activities to be a good corporate citizen of the world.
2. Respect the culture and customs of every nation and contribute to economic and social development through corporate activities in the communities.
3. Dedicate ourselves to providing clean and safe products and to enhancing the quality of life everywhere through all our activities.

(Continued)

(Continued)

4. Create and develop advanced technologies and provide outstanding products and services that fulfil the needs of customers worldwide.
5. Foster a corporate culture that enhances individual creativity and team-work value, while honouring mutual trust and respect between labour and management.
6. Pursue growth in harmony with the global community through innov-ative management.
7. Work with business partners in research and creation to achieve stable, long-term growth and mutual benefits, while keeping ourselves open to new partnerships.

Since 2000, Toyota has worked steadily on improving employee awareness of its environmental credo through in-company bulletins, environmental pocket books supplied to employees, seminars, and events held during the Environment Month. The company also encourages employees by giving them awards. For instance, Toyota employees who involve themselves in volunteer activities such as the cleaning up of river banks and tree-planting, are considered for the 'Award for Good Conduct' instituted by the company. In January 2002, Toyota initiated a new internal communication exercise: screening movies (such as *Erin Brokovich*) on the environment for the benefit of its employees.

The environment and corporate social responsibility

According to Toyota, cars have often been seen in a negative light because of air pollution, oil exhaustion and global warming. With more than 30 per cent of people worldwide using automobiles, Toyota felt that environmental issues would increasingly become a central issue for the car industry. Toyota therefore has given high priority to manufacturing cars that are safe and environmentally friendly. Viewing it as a strategic opportunity, Toyota has taken many initiatives to earn an environmentally friendly image. Fujio Cho, a former president of Toyota, said 'Environmentally friendly cars will soon cease to be an option, they will become a necessity.'

Toyota came out in 2005 with its Fourth Environmental Action Plan. Acting as a blueprint for Toyota's contribution to the environment, the plan outlines the activities that Toyota needs to undertake to sustain an environment-friendly corporate image. It includes enhancements in fuel efficiency and reduction in the CO_2 emission from vehicles. Through the adoption of superior environ-mental technologies, Toyota plans to reduce CO_2 emission from its own vehicles by 15 per cent.

Toyota launched Prius, the world's first mass-produced gasoline/electric hybrid vehicle, in 1997. The company believes that the introduction of the Prius has given it a 'green reputation'. Fujio Cho, commented: 'Hybrids like the Prius are a starting point to address long-term environmental issues. Automakers that deliver practical, greener products will command the market in the 21st century.'

Toyota's stance with regards to technological development is to 'zeronize' and 'maximize'. 'Zeronize' symbolizes the company's efforts in minimizing the negative aspects of cars, such as environmental impact, traffic congestion and traffic accidents. 'Maximize' refers to efforts in maximizing the positive aspects of cars such as comfort and convenience. Toyota is striving to combine the two by creating ecologically superior and safe cars.

In 2007, Katsuaki Watanabe, Toyota's president articulated the challenge to the car industry in terms of 'the increasing demand for corporate social responsibility [and] to take on global environmental problems such as global warming, depletion of natural resources and air pollution'. Watanabe also articulated the leadership position that Toyota has taken on environmental issues in the car industry. He specifically referred to hybrid technologies as an example of Toyota's environmental leadership: 'Toyota has positioned hybrid technologies as core technologies and will develop them with a commitment to leading the way in that field'.

Stakeholder management

Toyota has formally identified five general categories of stakeholder which the company feels need to be communicated with on an ongoing basis. These are customers, employees, business partners, shareholders, and the global society and local communities.

Toyota has been trying to give something and contribute to the communities in which it operates and conducts business with. This contribution has taken the form of financial grants and the volunteer time of Toyota associates. Toyota has been engaging local communities in the areas of education, the environment, culture and the arts, international exchanges etc. In 2001, for instance, Toyota initiated a reforestation project in China's Hebei Province, where the environment had undergone considerable degradation over the years. Toyota employees volunteered to plant 500 ha of land with poplar, pine and wild apricot trees. The 'Toyota Teach Primary School Project' has been serving 140 schools in the areas of Umlazi and Umbumbulu in South Africa. Toyota South Africa Manufacturing, based in Prospecton, has been sourcing most of its employees from these areas. The project has been aiming to swell the number of students with maths and science competencies who may later pursue technology-related careers. In Thailand and Cambodia, Toyota, in association with the Japan Alliance for Humanitarian De-mining Support (JAHDS), has been providing landmine detection technologies and back-up systems to international NGOs. In Britain, Toyota has joined with the British Red Cross to hold interactive road shows to raise awareness levels regarding road accidents among children. In 1987, the Toyota Equal Access for Minorities (TEAM) programme was started to increase meaningful opportunities available for minorities and women in all areas of business. The percentage of ethnic minority dealers of the Toyota and Lexus brands rose by 37 per cent by 1988. A Corporate Diversity Department was established in April 1998 to develop enterprise-wide awareness of diversity issues.

Communication strategy

As a monolithic corporate brand, Toyota has been using both product-led communications around specific cars as well as corporate-led communications around themes identified in its Global Vision document. In March 2003, for example, Toyota ran advertorials in the *Japan Times* enlightening the readers about the company's 'green' or environmentally friendlier cars. In addition, the vehicle manufacturer has been intending via its leaf car logo to convey its 'commitment to reduce the environmental impact of products, plants and processes'.

The 'Leaf Car' Logo has featured in corporate advertising to symbolize the company-wide drive toward environmental awareness. The company's green credentials are in such adverts backed up by reference to the launch of Prius and the Lexus LS Hybrid, the company's global earth charter and guiding principles promoting environmental responsibility throughout the company and the reduction of carbon emissions at manufacturing plants.

In 1990, because of its contributions to motor sport in previous decades, Toyota had been given the green flag to join the ranks of the Formula One (F1) World Championship Racing as a full constructor. This, in other words, meant that Toyota would be developing an entire racing car. Toyota announced its participation in F1 in January 1999. Having made the announcement, Toyota made preparations on several fronts – it prepared its 'Toyota Panasonic Racing Team' for the F1 event, the F1 car was being developed, and on March 23, 2001, Toyota unveiled its first ever F1 race car. Toyota's performance in the 2003 British Grand Prix has so far been the most memorable one in the company's brief F1 history. Toyota's Cristiano da Matta and Olivier Panis led the race for some time before Barrichello scooped victory.

Although the team's performance at F1 events has been patchy at best, Toyota's participation in the F1 World Championships is seen as 'the company's most successful communication tool yet. Internally and externally, the F1 programme has had a significant impact' (Times Inc., 2003). Toyota's own communications to its employees suggests the same:

It [the F1 project] helped to motivate Toyota's 260,000-strong workforce around the world. All the employees take great pride in the Toyota TF103, the racing car that competes in the F1 Grand Prix, which was built using the same technological basis as the production cars they build and sell.

Externally, the F1 participation enabled Toyota to invite stakeholders such as dealers, suppliers and sales personnel to the events, to watch the F1 spectacle and to talk business.

Issue and crisis management

Notwithstanding its community outreach, communication and stakeholder engagement programmes, two promotional materials issued by Toyota – a print ad carried by *Jet* magazine in 1998 and another a postcard for the youth market distributed by the company in May 2001 – were at the centre of controversies. On 23 May 2001, Reverend Jesse Jackson threatened a boycott against Toyota accusing the company of using racist advertising while excluding blacks among its dealers and board of directors. Jackson also demanded that the company fire its advertising agency, Saatchi and Saatchi (Los Angeles), for its racism and cultural insensitivity. The postcards, which were dispensed at bars and restaurants in six cities, involve a close-up shot of an African American smiling, with a gold version of the Toyota model adorning one tooth. 'This ad depicts a male, African American mouth, exaggerated lips, white, pearly teeth and a gold Toyota emboldened on the tooth. All that is missing is the watermelon', said the Reverend Jesse Jackson at the time on behalf of his Rainbow/PUSH Coalition. A spokesperson for Toyota Motor Sales explained that the postcard was meant to 'communicate RAV4 styling to a youthful, fashion-conscious audience'. Jackson, however, asserted that the image caused 'widespread outrage and indignation' within the African American community.

Don Esmond, senior vice-president and general manager for the Toyota division of Toyota Motor Sales USA, apologized in May 2001 for the postcards. The statement from Toyota said 'Toyota offers its sincere apologies to anyone who was offended by the postcard. Toyota is a good company that made a mistake in this instance and is determined to improve.' As the controversy over this postcard raged, sections of the media alluded to Toyota's 'controversial' print ad for Corolla released in 1998. This ad had highlighted the car's legendary reliability with the line 'unlike the boyfriend, Toyota gets up in the morning'. Intended for general magazine media, the ad played upon classic conflicts in young male–female relationships. The ad, however, had been mistakenly issued for insertion in *Jet* Magazine, an African-American publication. At that time, the publisher of Jet shared responsibility for the error and with Toyota, printed a joint apology to Jet's readers. Toyota also came out with the following statement in 2001:

> Some discussion of this issue [involving the controversial postcard] has referred to a 1998
> print ad for Corolla that highlighted the car's legendary reliability. Intended for general
> magazine media, it played upon classic conflicts in young male–female relationships. The
> ad featured a picture of the Corolla and does not depict an African American couple or
> any people, as has been reported.

Thereafter, Toyota has been working with its advertising agency in the US, Saatchi & Saatchi, to explore possibilities of affiliating with an African American agency. The company has been hoping to face the criticism and expand its multi-cultural marketing abilities this way. The company now has an affiliation of this kind with an Hispanic agency, Conill Advertising. Toyota also established a 'Diversity Awareness Review Panel' comprising a cross-section of employees who screen all promotional materials before they are used and distributed. The company also held a series of meetings with Reverend Jesse Jackson with the intent of discussing and reviewing its diversity programmes. Reverend Jackson described these meetings as productive and observed; 'this company has something to offer – outstanding products, money, infrastructure and know-how'.

In September 2001, Toyota announced a $7.8 billion long-term diversity commitment for the next decade. In January 2002, as part of the organizational changes Toshiaka Taguchi, President and CEO, Toyota Motor North America Inc. – whose direct responsibilities involve corporate communications including corporate advertising, investor relations and overseeing the Toyota US Foundation – announced that Veronica Pollard, an African American, was being promoted as Group Vice President in charge of corporate communications. In this capacity, Pollard oversees investor relations, corporate advertising, corporate media relations, philanthropy and community relations, direct mail, internet etc. Pollard also became Vice-President in charge of diversity programmes of Toyota reporting directly to President Taguchi.

Another issue for Toyota emerged in January 2006 when Toyota's Indian joint-venture company (Toyota Kirloskar Motor Private Limited) reported a dispute with employees at the plant in Bidadi (Karnataki) who had decided to go on strike in sympathy with the unfair dismissal of three co-workers. The strike was the outcome of an incident that occurred in 2004 when management of the plant suspended 15 employees on the grounds of disrupting work and for unruly behaviour. In 2006, the Indian company dismissed three of these 15 employees after a year-long investigation and appraisal of their performance.

The company responded to the strike by closing down operations and sending employees home until normal work conditions would return. The strike in 2006, however, was not the first time that relations between management and workers were disturbed at this plant. The plant had already experienced three other strikes: two in 2001 and one in 2002. The reason for these earlier strikes was the view of workers that the working conditions at the plant were unfavourable with a too heavy workload. Management of the Indian subsidiary responded that the plant had established health and safety guidelines and employee protocols which meant that the company would deal fairly with all workers and considered them as an important stakeholder. However, the company said that it acted firmly on issues of indiscipline. When the workers went on strike in 2006, management declared the strike as 'illegal' and 'destructive'. The company, however, resumed operations in January 2006. Workers who reported for duty were asked to sign an undertaking to maintain good conduct. Operations in the plant are now again towards full capacity. Nonetheless, the intensity of the labour dispute may have led to doubts for Toyota in relation to its supply chain and specifically in relation to investments in the Karnataka region in India.

Organizing corporate communication

In July 2003, Toyota revamped its corporate communication efforts. According to the Toronto-based *Globe and Mail* newspaper (24 July, 2003) Toyota combined its advertising and public relations departments into one integrated group. In the words of Peter Renz (National Manager PR and advertising, Toyota Canada).

> We combined all the departments to ensure that we were speaking with a consistent voice and sending out a consistent message all the time. It's given us an opportunity to think more 'out of the box' in terms of ideas. When we get together we think of unique ways of communicating. Our agencies are thinking that way too and you get all three elements – Internet, PR and advertising – working together, you find tremendous efficiencies.

Effectively, communications within the Toyota corporation is to a large extent decentralized to its of the geographically separated subsidiaries in Argentina, Australia, Belgium, Brazil, Canada, China, France, Germany, India, Indonesia, Korea, New Zealand, Philippines, Poland, Singapore, South Africa, Taiwan, Thailand, USA, Venezuela, and Vietnam. Each of these subsidiaries has its own communications staff, including marketing communications and product brand managers, internal communications staff and a number of specialists in media relations, public affairs and, in some cases, investor relations. Within both smaller and larger subsidiaries like the USA and Canada, staff has been consolidated into one single communications department, to have a point of call with the central communications department at Toyota HQ and to ease coordination and control of communications. Both the large departments in the USA and central headquarters issue communication staff around the world with themed messages around Toyota's focus on the environment, communities and safer motorizing. Toyota also uses a house-style manual which depicts the use of logotypes in communications as well as council meetings where representatives of the various subsidiaries meet with communication staff from Toyota HQ to discuss communication problems and issues within the corporation.

Questions for reflection

1. Consider the vision articulated by Toyota and its alignment with the company's image with external stakeholders and the internal culture. Is there sufficient alignment between vision, culture and image? Is there potential for any gaps to emerge between them?
2. Consider the stakeholders identified by Toyota for its stakeholder engagement and communication programmes. On what basis were these stakeholders identified do you think? Is Toyota sufficiently responsive to the needs and expectations of these stakeholders through its programmes and communications?
3. Identify the themed messages and message styles in Toyota's communications. Do you think that these message styles were wise choices? What other message styles would have been possible?
4. Reflect upon the organization of communication in Toyota. What vertical and horizontal structures exist to coordinate communication?
5. Evaluate the handling of the Jesse Jackson/cultural diversity incident and the strike at the plant in India from the perspective of issues and crisis management. Would you define these incidents as issues or crises for Toyota? How would you characterize the response strategy of Toyota towards both incidents? Should the company have handled these incidents in a different way?

Glossary

4 Ps	Product, Price, Promotion (marketing communications) and Place (distribution)
Above the line	All media that remunerate agencies on the basis of commission (e.g. advertising)
Acceptance strategy	Organizational claim accepting responsibility or culpability for a crisis
Accommodative strategy	Organizational claim accepting responsibility for a crisis and preventing it from happening again
Account management	The process by which a communications (PR, advertising) or marketing agency or supplier manages the needs of a client (corporation)
Accountability	An evaluation of the contribution of functions or activities against their costs
Added value	The increase in worth of an organization's product or services as a result of a particular activity – in the context of communications, the activity might be effective stakeholder dialogue
Advertisement	A paid-for dedicated space or time in which only the advertiser is represented
Advertising	The process of gaining the public's attention through paid media announcements
Advertising agency	An agency specializing in advertising and other marketing communications on behalf of a client organization
Advertising campaign	A planned use and scheduling of advertising over a defined period of time
Advertising media	Paid-for communications channels such as newspaper (print) or television
Advertising value equivalent (AVE)	A measure of evaluating press publicity by counting the column inches of press publicity and seconds of air time gained and then multiplying the total by the advertising rate of the media in which the coverage appeared
Advertorial	An editorial feature paid for or sponsored by an advertiser

Advocacy   An attempt to try to change stakeholder expectations and public opinions on an issue through issue campaigns and lobbying

Advocacy advertising   Advocacy advertising expresses a viewpoint on a given issue, often on behalf of an institution or organization

Agenda setting   Media reporting on organizations that primes awareness of an organization and certain content about that organization

Ambient media   Originally known as 'fringe media', ambient media are communications platforms that surround us in everyday life – from petrol pump advertising to advertising projected onto buildings to advertising on theatre tickets, cricket pitches or even pay slips

Ansoff matrix   Model relating marketing strategy to general strategic direction. It maps product-market strategies – e.g. market penetration, product development, market development and diversification – on a matrix showing new versus existing products along one axis and new versus existing markets along the other

Association strategy   Claim of connecting the organization to things positively valued by stakeholders and publics

Attitude   A learned predisposition towards an object (e.g. organization, product), person or idea

Audience fragmentation   The process or trend whereby audience segments become more heterogeneous and divided (and therefore more difficult to reach in one shot)

Audit   See *Communication audit*

Awareness   Measure of a proportion of target audience who have heard of the organization, product or service.

BCG matrix   Boston Consulting Group matrix based on market share and market growth rate

Below the line   Non-media advertising or promotion when no commission has been paid to the advertising agency. Includes direct mail, point of sale displays and giveaways

Boundary spanning   The role of corporate communication to act as an intermediary between the organization and external stakeholder groups

Brand   The set of physical attributes of a product or service, together with the beliefs and expectations surrounding it – a unique combination which the name or logo of the product or service should evoke in the mind of the audience

Brand acceptance	The condition wherein an individual, usually a customer, is well disposed towards a brand and will accept credible messages
Brand awareness	The condition wherein an individual, usually a customer, is aware of the brand
Brand equity	The notion that a respected brand name adds to the value of a product (and therefore generates returns to an organization upon customer purchase)
Brand image	The perception of a brand in the eyes of an individual, usually a customer
Brand loyalty	Extent to which individuals, usually customers, repurchase (or utilize) a particular branded product or service
Brand management	The process by which marketers attempt to optimize the 'marketing mix' for a specific brand
Brand positioning	The way in which a brand is communicated to its target market, describing the attributes and values of the brand and its added value/appeal relative to its customers and the competition
Branded identity	A structure whereby businesses and product brands of an organization each carry their own name (without endorsement by the parent company) and are seemingly unrelated to each other
Bridging	Organizations adapting their activities so that they conform with external expectations and claims of important stakeholder groups
Budgeting	The costing of communication activities against a specified amount of money
Buffering	Organizations trying to ignore the claims and interests from stakeholders or stop them from interfering with internal operations
Business communication	The (vocational) discipline of writing, presenting and communicating in a professional context
Business plan	A strategic document showing cash flow, forecasts and direction of a company
Business strategy	The means by which a business works towards achieving its stated aims
Business-to-business	Relating to the sale of a product for any use other than personal consumption. The buyer

may be a manufacturer, a reseller, a government body, a non-profit-making institution, or any organization other than an ultimate consumer

Business-to-consumer   Relating to the sale of a product for personal consumption. The buyer may be an individual, family or other group, buying to use the product themselves, or for end use by another individual

Buzz   Media and public attention given to a company, its products or services

Centralization   Bringing tasks and/or activities together as the responsibility of one person or department in an organization

Change communication   Communication activities to support the formulation, implementation and routinization of a change (e.g., restructuring) within an organization

Channel noise   Confusion caused by too many messages trying to be delivered at one time

Channels   The methods and media used by a company to communicate and interact with its stakeholders

Clutter   The total number of message competing for attention of the audience; usually mentioned in the context of excessive amounts of communications

Cobweb method   A technique whereby individuals rate an organization on a number of selected attributes, which is then visually represented in the form of a wheel or web with eight or more scaled dimensions

Communication audit   A systematic survey of members of a target audience (often members of the media or potential customers) to determine awareness of or reaction to a message about a product, service or company

Communication climate   The ease with which information flows freely between managers and employees through an organization's formal and informal networks

Communication effects   The impact of communication programs or campaigns on the awareness, opinions, reputations and behaviours of stakeholder groups

Communication efficiency   The accomplishment of communication with a minimum expenditure of time, effort and resources

Communication facilitator   Role in which practitioners act as liaisons, interpreters, information brokers and mediators between the organization and its stakeholders

Communication strategy	The general set of communication objectives and related communication programs or tactics chosen by an organization in order to support the corporate strategy of the organization
Competence	Knowledge of a certain (professional) area that is difficult to emulate/a domain of knowledge or specific expertise that an individual needs to properly perform a specific job
Competitive advantage	The product, proposition or benefit that puts a company ahead of its competitors
Competitors	Companies that sell products or services in the same market place as one another
Consumer	Individual who buys and uses a product or service
Consumer behaviour	The buying habits and patterns of consumers in the acquisition and usage of goods and services
Consumer research	Research into the characteristics, changes, usage and attitudes of consumers
Continuous research	Research conducted constantly to pick up trends, issues, market fluctuations, etc.
Copy	The written words (storyline, formatting, etc.) to appear in a communications medium (press release, commercial, etc.)
Copy date	The date by which a publication or medium requires copy
Copy testing	Research into reactions and responses to written copy
Copywriting	Creative process by which written content is prepared for communication material
Corporate advertising	Advertising by a firm where the corporate entity, rather than solely its products or services, is emphasized
Corporate brand	See *monolithic identity*
Corporate citizenship	Expressions of involvement of an organization in matters concerning society as a whole
Corporate communication	The function and process of managing communications between an organization and important stakeholder groups (including markets and publics) in its environment
Corporate identity	The profile and values communicated by an organization. The character a company seeks to establish for itself in the mind of its stakeholders, reinforced by consistent use of logos, colours, typefaces, and so on

Corporate image	The way a company is perceived, based on a certain message and at a certain point in time. The immediate set of meanings inferred by an individual in confrontation or response to one or more signals from or about a particular organization at a single point in time
Corporate information and communication systems	Technologies (e.g., intranet) used to disseminate information about the organization to employees across all ranks and functions within the organization in order to keep them informed on corporate matters
Corporate personality	The core values of an organization as shared by its members (see also *organizational identity*)
Corporate public relations	Public relations activities towards 'corporate' stakeholders, which excludes customers and prospects in a market; includes issues management, community relations, investor relations, media relations, internal communication and public affairs
Corporate reputation	An individual's collective representation of past images of an organization (induced through either communication or past experiences) established over time
Corporate social responsibility (CSR)	Actions which do not have purely financial implications and which are demanded or expected of an organization by the society at large, often concerning ecological and social issues
Corporate strategy	The general direction taken by a company with regard to its choice of businesses and markets and approach of its stakeholder groups
Coverage	Percentage of target audience who have the opportunity to be confronted with the communications message at least once
Crisis	A point of great difficulty or danger to the organization, possibly threatening its existence and continuity, and that requires decisive change
Crisis management	The reactive response to a crisis in order to preempt or limit damage to the organization's reputation
Culture	The general values and beliefs held and shared by members of an organization
Customer	A person or company who purchases goods or services (not necessarily the end consumer)

DAGMAR	Defining Advertising Goals for Measured Advertising Response – a model for planning advertising in such a way that its success can be quantitatively monitored
Database	A collection of information about relevant data, e.g. information about past, current and potential customers
Database marketing	Whereby customer information, stored in an electronic database, is utilized for targeting marketing activities. Information can be a mixture of what is gleaned from previous interactions with the customer and what is available from outside sources
Decoding	Process where receiver converts the symbolic forms transmitted by the sender
Demographics	Information describing and segmenting a population in terms of age, sex, income, and so on, which can be used to target communication campaigns
Departmental arrangement	The administrative act of grouping or arranging disciplines, activities and people into departments
Depth interview	An interview, usually one-to-one, exploring deeper motivations and beliefs
Desk research	Using publicly available and previous data (e.g. on certain issues, markets)
DESTEP	Demographic, Economic, Social, Technological, Ecological, and Political analysis. A broad analysis of macro factors that may impinge upon an organization's business and operations
Dialogue strategy	A process of communication in which both parties (organizations and stakeholders) mutually engage in an exchange of ideas and opinions
Differentiation (competitive strategy)	A competitive strategy whereby the unique and added value of a product or service is emphasized (which then warrants a premium price)
Direct mail	Delivery of an advertising or promotional message to customers or potential customers by mail
Direct marketing	All activities which make it possible to offer goods or services or to transmit other messages to a segment of the population by post, telephone, e-mail or other direct means
Direct response	Communications (e.g. advertising) incorporating a contact method such as a phone number,

	address and enquiry form, web site identifier or e-mail address, with the intention of encouraging the recipient to respond directly to the advertiser by requesting more information, placing an order, and so on
Distance strategy	Claim of distancing the organization from direct responsibility for the crisis
Distribution channels	The process and ways of getting the goods from the manufacturer or supplier to the user
Dominant coalition	The group of people, usually the executive or senior management team, within an organization making the important decisions (concerning the direction and focus of the firm, etc.)
Downward communication	Electronic and verbal methods of informing employees about their organization, its performance, and their own performance in terms they can comprehend
Emotional message style	Attempts to provoke involvement and positive reactions through a reference to positive (or negative) emotions
Employee voice	A state in which employees are able to speak up, express opinions and are listened to by managers
Encoding	The process of putting information into a symbolic form of words, pictures or images
Endorsed identity	A structure whereby businesses and product brands of an organization are endorsed or badged in communications with the parent company name
Environmental scanning	The process whereby the environment of an organization is continuously scanned for issues and trends, usually in relation to important stakeholder groups
Equal dissemination strategy	A process of communication in which managers disseminate information to all stakeholders early, often and, most importantly, on an equal basis
Equal participation strategy	Two-way communication (i.e., both disseminating information and soliciting input) between managers and stakeholders
Evaluation	An assessment of the effects of a communication program or campaign
Exchange	The process by which two or more parties give up a desired resource to one another
Execution	The act of carrying something out (usually a set of planned for communications programs)

Executive team	The senior management team of an organization, typically led by the Chief Executive Officer, responsible for the overall management and strategic direction of the firm
Expert prescriber	A role in which a communication practitioner acts as a specialist on communication problems but largely independently of senior management
External analysis	Study of the external environment of an organization, including factors such as customers, competition, and social change
Faux pas	A claim made by an external agent (e.g., NGO) that the organization violates accepted, although unwritten, social rules and expectations
FMCG	Fast Moving Consumer Goods – such as packaged food, beverages, toiletries, and tobacco
Focus groups	A tool for market, communications and opinion research where small groups of people are invited to participate in guided discussions on the topic being researched
Forecasting	Calculation of future events and performance
Frame alignment	A situation where an organization's explanation of a decision, issue or event coincides with the way in which journalists think about the same decision, issue or event
Frame contest	The negotiation between communication practitioners and journalists about the preferred angle to a story about an organization
Framing	Presenting a story about an organization from a particular angle
Frequency	Average number of times the target audience will have the opportunity to be confronted with (see) a certain communications message
Full service agency	An agency that specializes in a whole range of communications disciplines and can assist the client in the full process of communications planning and execution
Gatekeeping research	An analysis of the characteristics of a press release or video news release that allow them to "pass through the gate" and appear in a news medium
Generic message style	Straight claim about industry or cause with no assertion of superiority
Geodemographics	A method of analysis combining geographic and demographic variables

Global brand	A brand which has world-wide recognition (e.g., Coca-Cola)
Goal	The primary and direct result a company is attempting to achieve through its communications efforts
Image	An individual's perceptions of an organization, product or service at a certain point in time
Industrial goods	Products/resources required by industrial companies
Informational strategy	A process of making information available about the organization to its stakeholders
Informercials	An advertising commercial that provides extensive information
Integration (integrated communication)	The act of coordinating all communications so that the corporate identity is effectively and consistently communicated to internal and external groups
Intentional communications	Message that an organization intends to convey
Intermediary	Any individual/company in the distribution channel between the supplier and final consumer
Internal analysis	The study of a company's internal resources in order to assess opportunities, strengths or weaknesses
Internal communication	All methods (internal news letter, intranet) used by a firm to communicate with its employees
Issue	An unsettled matter (which is ready for a decision) or a point of conflict between an organization and one or more publics
Issues management	The pro-active attempt to identify and control issues in order to preempt or limit damage to the organization's reputation
Kelly grids	See *Repertory grids*
Laddering	A research technique whereby people's opinions are represented as means-end chain; used to infer the basic values and motivations that drive people
Legitimacy	The assessment of an organization against the norms, values and expectations of its stakeholders in terms of what those stakeholders deem acceptable and favoured of the organization
Licensing	The act of formally accrediting an agency or professional, often done by a professional association or legal body

Lifecycle	Stages through which a product or brand develops (see *PLC*)
Lifestyle	Research classification based on shared values, attitude and personality
Likert scale	Research scale which uses statements to indicate agreement or disagreement
Line extension	Extending existing brands to other products in the same product category
Line function	An organizational function that is directly involved in the core and operational business process (i.e. the 'line') of producing products and bringing them to market (e.g. marketing)
Logo	A graphic, usually consisting of a symbol and/or group of letters, that identifies a company or brand
Low-cost (competitive strategy)	Competitive strategy where the lower cost of a product or service is emphasized
Macro environment	The external factors which affect a company's planning and performance, and are beyond its control, for example, socio-economic, legal and technological change.
Management communication	Communication between managers and employees restricted to dyads and small groups
Manager (communications manager)	Practitioner who makes strategy or program decisions concerning communications, and is held accountable for program success or failure; engages in research, strategic planning and management of communications
Market	A defined group for whom a product is or may be in demand (and for whom an organization creates and maintains products and service offerings)
Market development	The process of growing sales by offering existing products (or new versions of them) to new customer groups (as opposed to simply attempting to increase the company's share of current markets)
Market orientation	Steadfast adherence to the marketing concept: an approach in which customer needs and wants are the underlying determinants of an organization's direction and its marketing programs
Market penetration	The attempt to grow one's business by obtaining a larger market share in an existing market
Market research	The gathering and analysis of data relating to market places or customers; any research which

	leads to more market knowledge and better-informed decision-making
Market segmentation	The division of the market place into distinct sub-groups or segments, each characterized by particular tastes and requiring a specific marketing mix
Market share	A company's sales of a given product or set of products to a given set of customers, expressed as a percentage of total sales of all such products to such customers
Market structure	The character of an industry, based on the number of firms, barriers to entry, extent of product differentiation, control over price, and the importance of non-price competition
Marketing	Marketing is the management process responsible for identifying, anticipating and satisfying customer requirements profitably
Marketing audit	A comprehensive and systematic review and appraisal of every aspect of a firm's marketing program, its organization, activities, strategies and people
Marketing communications	All methods (advertising, direct marketing, sales promotion, personal selling, and marketing public relations) used by a firm to communicate with its customers and prospective customers
Marketing concept	The process by which the marketer responds to the needs and wants of the consumer
Marketing mix	The combination of marketing inputs that affect customer motivation and behaviour. These inputs traditionally encompass four controllable variables 'the 4 Ps': product, price, promotion and place
Marketing objective	A market target to be achieved reflecting corporate strategy
Marketing public relations	The use of what are traditionally seen as public relations tools (media, free publicity) within marketing programs; used to reach marketing objectives
Marketing strategy	The set of objectives which an organization allocates to its marketing function in order to support the overall corporate strategy, together with the broad methods chosen to achieve these objectives
Matrix structure	A structure where a professional has a dual reporting relationship; this structure aims to

	foster both functional expertise and coordination at the same time
Media	1. Members or tools for disseminating the news; unbiased third parties (press representatives) 2. Communication channels for a certain campaign
Media coverage	Mention in the media of a company, its products or services
Media favourability	Positive news coverage of an organization in which the organization is praised for its actions or is associated with activities that should raise its reputation
Media plan	Recommendation for a media schedule including dates, publications, TV regions, etc.
Media relations	The function or process of gaining positive media attention and coverage
Media richness	The ability of a medium to allow for immediate feedback between the two parties and for expressing and articulating the message in different ways
Media schedule	Records of campaign bookings made or a proposal (with dates, costs, etc.) for a campaign
Merchandising	Traditionally in-store promotion and displays
Message style	The way in which a message is given form and delivered to a target audience
Micro environment	The immediate context of a company's operations, including such elements as suppliers, customers and competitors
MIIS	Management Intelligence and Information System – system of collecting and examining environmental and/or market data
Mission	A company's overriding purpose in line with the values or expectations of stakeholders
Mission statement	A company's summary of its business philosophy and direction
Monolithic identity	A structure whereby businesses and product brands of an organization all carry the same corporate name
Multinational	A corporation whose operational and marketing activities cover multiple countries over the world
Need to know strategy	A process of communication in which managers keep quiet about decisions or changes except to those stakeholders who really need to know or who explicitly express a desire for the information

News routines	The way in which news is produced in a particular media organization starting with the journalist consulting sources and ending with the editor making the final decisions about an article or feature
Niche marketing	The marketing of a product to a small and well-defined segment of the market place
Noise	See *Channel noise*
Non-existence strategy	Claim made by an organization denying an issue or crisis
Non-verbal communications	Transmission of a message without the use of words or language
Objective	A company's defined and measurable aims for a given period
Organizational identification	The perception of oneness with or belonging to an organization, where the individual defines him or herself in terms of the organization(s) of which he or she is a member
Organizational identity	The set of values shared by members of an organization (see also *corporate personality*)
Organizational silence	A state in which employees refrain from speaking up and withhold information about potential problems or issues
OTH	Opportunities to Hear – number of opportunities a target consumer has of hearing advertisement
OTS	Opportunities to See – number of opportunities a target consumer has of seeing advertisement
Output analysis	A measurement of the amount of exposure or attention that the organization receives in the media; often done by collecting press clippings (copies of stories or articles in the press) and by recording the degree of exposure in terms of column inches in print media, the number of minutes of air time in the electronic media or the number of cites on the web
Partnership promotion	Joint promotions aiming to achieve additional exposure
Perception	The way a corporation/product/event/stimulus is received and evaluated by an individual
Personal selling	One-to-one communication between seller and prospective purchaser
Persuasion	A means by which a person or organization tries to influence and convince another person to

	believe something or do something, using reasoning and coaxing in a compelling and convincing way
Persuasive strategy	A process of communication in which an organization through campaigns, meetings and discussions with stakeholders tries to change and tune the knowledge, attitude, and behaviours of stakeholders in a way that is favourable to the organization
Pitch	Prepared sales presentation by an agency to a client organization, usually one-on-one
Planning	Setting communication activities and campaigns on the basis of communication objectives and against a time-line
PLC	Product lifecycle. Supposed stages of a product, e.g. birth, growth, maturity and decline
POS	Point-of-Sale – The location, usually within a retail outlet, where the customer decides whether to make a purchase
Porter's five forces	An analytic model developed by Michael E. Porter. The five forces in terms of which the model analyses businesses and industries are: Buyers, Suppliers, Substitutes, New Entrants and Rivals
Portfolio (and portfolio analysis)	The set of products or services which a company decides to develop and market. Portfolio analysis is the process of comparing the contents of the portfolio to see which products or services are the most promising and deserving of further investment, and which should be discontinued
Position–importance matrix	A tool to categorize stakeholders and publics according to their position on a particular issue and according to their importance to the organization
Positioning	The creation of an image for a company, product or service in the minds of stakeholders, both specifically to that entity and in relation to competitive organizations and offerings
Power–interest matrix	A tool to categorize stakeholders on the basis of the power that they have and the extent to which they are likely to have or show an interest in the organization's activities
PR	See *Public relations*

Preemptive message style	Generic claim about an organization with a suggestion of superiority
Press agentry	The use of press agents, promoters and publicists to promote and publicize an organization and its products or services through the media; often used to describe communications during the early decades of the twentieth century
Press conference	An organized gathering or event where an organization announces decisions or fiscal results to journalists
Press kit	Several press deliverables combined in one package (usually a folder)
Press release	A paper or electronic document submitted to the media with the intent of gaining media coverage
Problem-solving process facilitator	Role in which communication practitioners collaborate with other managers to define and solve organizational problems
Process effects	Evaluation of the cost-effective manner in which a communication program or campaign has been planned and executed
Projective technique	Qualitative research technique by which an individual is asked to respond to ambiguous stimuli such as vague statements or objects; designed to measure feelings, opinions, attitudes and motivations
Proposition	The message that the advertiser wants the customer to focus upon
Psychographics	A base for segmentation derived from attitude and behavioural variables
Public	People who mobilize themselves against the organization on the basis of some common issue or concern to them
Public affairs	The public policy aspect of corporate communication
Public information	The use of writers and publicists to inform and reassure the general public of corporate practices; often used to describe communications before the Second World War
Public relations	The function or activity that aims to establish and protect the reputation of a company or brand, and to create mutual understanding between the organization and the segments of the public with whom it needs to communicate

Publicity	Media coverage
Pull strategy	Pull communications, in contrast to push communications, addresses the customer directly with a view to getting them to demand the product, and hence 'pull' it down through the distribution chain. It focuses on advertising and above the line activities
Push strategy	Push communications relies on the next link in the distribution chain – e.g. a wholesaler or retailer – to 'push' out products to the customer. It revolves around sales promotions – such as price reductions and point of sale displays – and other below the line activities
Qualitative research	Research that does not use numerical data but relies on interviews, 'focus groups', 'repertory grid', and the like, usually resulting in findings which are more detailed but also more subjective than those of 'quantitative research'
Quantitative research	Research that concentrates on statistics and other numerical data, gathered through opinion polls, customer satisfaction surveys, and so on
Quid pro quo strategy	A process of communication in which managers give more communicative attention to those stakeholders who have something valuable (e.g., expertise, approval power, resources) for a decision or change process
Rational message style	A superiority claim based upon actual accomplishments or delivered benefits by the organization
Reach	The percentage or number of people exposed to a media vehicle at least once
Recall	Used by researchers to establish how memorable a certain communications message was
Receiver	In communications theory the party receiving the message
Repertory grid	A technique for representing the attitudes and perceptions of individuals; also called Personal Construct Technique. The technique can be useful in developing market research (and other) questionnaires
Reputation	See *Corporate reputation*
Return on investment (ROI)	The value that an organization derives from investing in a project

Sales promotion	A range of techniques used to engage the purchaser. These may include discounting, coupons, guarantees, free gifts, competitions, vouchers, demonstrations, bonus commission and sponsorship
Sampling	The use of a statistically representative subset as a proxy for an entire population, for example, in order to facilitate quantitative market research
Secondary research	See *Desk research*
Segmentation	See *Market segmentation*
Selective attention	Where receivers only notice some of the message presented
Selective distortion	To see and hear differently from the message presented
Selective exposure	Idea that individuals only expose themselves to certain messages
Selective perception	The process of screening out of information that is not of interest, and retaining information of use
Sender	In communications theory the party sending the message
Share of voice	Calculation of a brand's share of media expenditure in a particular category
Shareholder value	The worth of a company from the point of view of its shareholders
Skill (communication skills)	The ability to produce or craft something (e.g. a written document by way of writing skills) or perform a certain task
Slogan	Frequently repeated phrases that provide continuity in messages and campaigns of a certain corporation, its products or services
SMART objectives	Objectives which are Specific, Measurable, Achievable, Realistic and Timely
SME	Small to Medium Enterprise. Variously defined: according one EU definition, it must employ under 250 people, have either a turnover of less than EUR 40 million or net balance sheet assets of less than EUR 27 million, and not be more than 25% owned by a larger company
Spin	The attempt to manipulate the depiction of news or events in the media through artful public relations – often used with derogatory connotations

Spokesblogger	Official spokesperson for an organization who, while publishing an independent blog, often does not speak only for himself, but also on behalf of their employer or the organization that he represents
Spokesperson	Official representative of the organization who deal with journalists and the media
Sponsorship	Specialized form of sales promotion where a company will help fund an event or support a business venture in return for publicity
Staff function	An organizational function (e.g. communications) carrying no direct executive power over the primary operational process or responsibility for it, but fulfils an advisory role to other functions within the organization
Stakeholder	Any group or individual who can affect or is affected by the achievement of the organization's objectives
Stakeholder audit	A systematic survey of stakeholders to determine the nature of the relationship, issues and possible reactions to corporate actions
Stakeholder collaboration	A situation where an organization builds long-term relationships through working together with stakeholders on issues of common concern
Stakeholder mapping	An analytical tool whereby stakeholder groups are identified and their relationship to the organization becomes visually represented in a map
Stakeholder salience	The visibility or importance of a stakeholder based on their possession of one or more of three attributes: power, legitimacy, and urgency
Strategic intent	The general direction of an organization, often articulated in objectives, together the general patterns of actions that will be taken to achieve these objectives
Strategy	General broad patterns of actions to accomplish corporate, market and/or communications objectives
Suffering strategy	Claim that the organization suffers from crisis or a public policy decision
SWOT	A method of analysis which examines a company's Strengths, Weaknesses, Opportunities and Threats. Often used as part of the development process for a corporate or marketing plan

Symbolic association message style	Claim of associating the organization with general (culturally shared and recognized) moral values, symbols and sentiments
Tactics	Specific action items to support strategies and objectives
Target audience	The key groups or individuals that a company wants to receive with its communications messages
Target market	The segment of a market at which marketing efforts are directed
Targeting	The use of market segmentation to select and address a key group of potential purchasers
Technician (communication technician)	A practitioner who in his/her day-to-day work focuses primarily on programmatic and tactical communication activities such as writing, editing, producing brochures, etc.; a technician thus tactically implements decisions made by others
Telemarketing	The marketing of a product or service over the telephone
Themed message	Messages that are identified as central to the organization's reputation and that are designed to change or reinforce perceptions in line with the vision of how the organization wants to be known
Through the line	Mixture of below and above the line communications
Tracking	Surveying attitudes and perceptions (images and reputations) of individuals to an organization, products or services on a continuous basis
Trademark	Sign or device, often with distinctive lettering, that symbolizes a brand
Transgression	An intentional act taken by an organization that knowingly places stakeholders or publics at risk or harm
Transparency	The state where the image or reputation of an organization held by stakeholder groups is similar to the actual and/or projected identity of an organization
Triple bottom-line	The idea that organizations have social ('people') and ecological ('planet') responsibilities besides their economic imperative of generating of profits and healthy financial accounts
Unintentional communication	Message that an organization does not intend to convey

Upward communication	Information from employees that is cast upwards towards managers within the organization; involves information about the employee him/herself, information about co-workers, information about organizational practices and policies, and information about what needs to be done and how it can be done
USP	Unique Selling Proposition (USP) – the benefit that a product or service can deliver to customers that is not offered by any competitor: one of the fundamentals of effective marketing and business
Vision	The long-term aims and aspirations of the company for itself
Word-of-mouth	The spreading of information through human interaction alone
Zero-based planning	A review of media options during communications planning based on research, analysis and insight, not habit and preference

Index

Page numbers in *italics* refer to figures and tables, those in **bold** indicate case studies.